World Class Worldwide

World Class Worldwide

Transforming Research Universities in Asia and Latin America

Edited by

Philip G. Altbach & Jorge Balán

THE JOHNS HOPKINS UNIVERSITY PRESS
Baltimore

Printed in the United States of America on acid-free paper
2 4 6 8 9 7 5 3 2 1

The Johns Hopkins University Press
2715 North Charles Street
Baltimore, Maryland 21218-4363
www.press.jhu.edu

Library of Congress Cataloging-in-Publication Data

World class worldwide : transforming research universities in Asia and Latin America /
edited by Philip G. Altbach and Jorge Balán.
p. cm.
Includes bibliographical references and index.
ISBN-13: 978-0-8018-8661-4 (hardcover : alk. paper)
ISBN-13: 978-0-8018-8662-1 (pbk. : alk. paper)
ISBN-10: 0-8018-8661-9 (hardcover : alk. paper)
ISBN-10: 0-8018-8662-7 (pbk. : alk. paper)
1. Education, Higher—Asia. 2. Education, Higher—Latin America. 3. Education,
Higher—Aims and objectives—Asia. 4. Education, Higher—Aims and objectives—Latin
America. I. Altbach, Philip G. II. Balán, Jorge, 1940–
LA1058.W67 2007
378.5—dc22 2006100960

A catalog record for this book is available from the British Library.

Contents

PART II Latin America

Preface

This book is dedicated to the idea that research universities are central to almost all the world's academic systems. Often ignored in the analysis of research universities are developing and middle-income countries. Our concern is how these countries can successfully support research universities. In the knowledge-based world of the 21st century, research universities are of great importance. Not all countries can afford "world-class" universities, but most can—and must—have universities that fully participate in the world of research and development.

We are convinced that a comparative and international perspective can yield insights on this theme. Although it is seldom possible to copy from one country to another, a comparative framework highlights common problems and accomplishments and suggests new ways of thinking.

We brought together a team of outstanding researchers to think deeply and write thoughtfully about this topic from seven countries. We focus on Latin America and Asia. The countries included are all committed to research universities. To provide a range of perspectives on our main themes, we commissioned two essays for each of four key countries that are part of this analysis: Brazil, China, India, and Mexico. These multiple perspectives provide added depth to the analysis. Our other case study countries, Argentina, Chile, and South Korea, are represented by one chapter each. Africa is not represented among the case studies in this volume. We believe that Africa's academic challenges are sufficiently different from those of the nations represented here that comparison would not be appropriate. We have also not included any of the smaller and less academically developed nations of Asia and Latin America.

We asked our research group to write country-based case studies, and we discussed these case studies at a conference at Boston College in June 2005. Authors then revised their work based on our discussions, and this volume reflects their thoughtful work.

This project was supported by the Ford Foundation and organized by the Center for International Higher Education at Boston College. Staff support was provided by Leslie Bozeman and Salina Kopellas. Edith Hoshino wrote a useful summary of the conference and edited the final chapters. Without her assistance, this book would not have been possible.

World Class Worldwide

1

Empires of Knowledge and Development

Philip G. Altbach

The research university is a central institution of the 21st century. It is essential to the creation and dissemination of knowledge. As one of the key elements in the globalization of science, the research university is at the nexus of science, scholarship, and the new knowledge economies. The research university educates the new generation of personnel needed for technological and intellectual leadership, develops new knowledge so necessary for modern science and scholarship, and, just as important, serves as an element of worldwide communication and collaboration.

All but a few research universities are located in the developed economies of the industrialized world. Any of the recent world rankings of top universities show that the main research-oriented universities are found in a few countries. This chapter, however, looks at the realities and prospects for research universities in developing and middle-income countries—a small but growing subset of research universities worldwide. If knowledge production and dissemination are not to remain a monopoly of the rich countries, research universities must become successful outside of the main cosmopolitan centers. In establishing and fostering research universities, developing countries face problems that are to some extent unique.

Research universities are defined here as academic institutions committed to the creation and dissemination of knowledge in a range of disciplines and fields and featuring the appropriate laboratories, libraries, and other infrastructures that permit teaching and research at the highest possible level. While typically large and multifaceted, some research universities may be smaller institutions concentrating on a narrower range of subjects. Research universities educate students, usually at all degree levels—an indication the focus extends beyond research. Indeed, this synergy of research and teaching is a hallmark of these institutions, which employ mainly full-time academics who hold doctoral degrees (Kerr 2001).

Motivating this discussion is a conviction that knowledge production and dissemination must spread internationally and that all regions of the world need a role in the knowledge network (Altbach 1987). While there will always be centers and peripheries—the centers mainly concentrated in the major industrialized countries for the foreseeable future—there is room, indeed a necessity, for a wider dissemination of research capacity throughout the world. It may not be possible for each country to have a research university, but many developing and middle-income countries can develop universities with research capacity and the ability to participate in the world knowledge system. Smaller countries can form regional academic alliances to build enough strength in selected fields to promote participation in global science.

The argument can be made that all countries need academic institutions linked to the global academic system of science and scholarship so that they can understand advanced scientific developments and participate selectively in them. Academic institutions in small or poor countries cannot compete with the Oxfords or Harvards of the industrialized nations. But most countries can support at least one university of sufficient quality to participate in international discussions of science and scholarship and undertake research in one or more fields relevant to national development.

Research universities generate growing enthusiasm worldwide. Countries come to the conclusion that such institutions are the key to gaining entry into the knowledge economy of the 21st century. Not only do these institutions train key personnel, but they form windows to scientific information worldwide by providing opportunities for top-level scientific communication. Faculty members and students at these institutions connect with colleagues everywhere and participate in global science and scholarship. Even in the United States and the United Kingdom, concern is rising about maintaining the standards of existing research universities (Rosenzweig 1998). Germany worries about the international competitiveness of its top universities and has allocated resources to some key institutions, while the Japanese government has funded competitive grants to create "centers of excellence." China has placed emphasis on creating "world-class" research universities, and India is finally beginning to think about the quality of its mainstream institutions. Similar programs to enhance standards exist in South Korea, Chile, Taiwan, and elsewhere. Several of Africa's traditionally strong universities are seeking to improve their quality in an effort to achieve research university status, with assistance from external funders, although it is, in general, behind levels of academic development on the other continents.

All of these trends show a considerable shift from the 1980s, when developing countries concentrated on providing basic schooling rather than higher education. In much of the world, especially in developing countries, policymakers engaged almost exclusively with meeting mass higher education demand, largely ignoring the research role of universities. Circumstances in several of the world's regions also created crises for higher education and slowed the development of research universities. In Latin America, the military dictatorships of the 1960s and later were unfriendly toward higher education, and many of the prominent scholars went into exile. China suffered under the Cultural Revolution, which closed all of the universities for a period of time and severely damaged the system. The advent of mass higher education and the demands for access that ensued, combined with the inability of the state to support both quantity and quality financially, retarded the development of research universities. India is a good case regarding this phenomenon. Political and economic instability, combined with policies that favored basic schooling, largely destroyed the quality of sub-Saharan Africa's few academic institutions. In short, in the late 20th century few research-oriented universities existed in developing countries—even in countries that had made some earlier progress in this area.

In keeping with the rising profile of research universities in developing countries, many national policymakers, analysts of higher education, and even the international aid agencies and the World Bank, previously convinced that only basic education was worth supporting, now understand that research universities are important for national development. Research universities have emerged on the policy agenda in many developing countries, especially larger nations that seek to compete in the global knowledge economy. In Africa, the region of the world with the most severe structural, economic, and political challenges, an initiative by a partnership of donor foundations and African universities aims to build the research capacity of key African academic institutions in Kenya, Mozambique, Ghana, and several other countries. China has been particularly active in transforming a number of its major universities into research universities; the government has invested significant funding in this effort and has merged many universities to provide better economies of scale. India has created a Knowledge Commission to develop strategies for promoting academic excellence. Taiwan and South Korea have been engaged for a decade or more in building up their key institutions.

HISTORY AND PERSPECTIVES

Universities, since their origins in medieval Europe, have always been concerned with the transmission, preservation, and interpretation of knowledge, although not primarily with the creation of new knowledge (Perkin 2006). While they have served as cultural and intellectual institutions in their societies, universities have not traditionally been research oriented. Science was conducted elsewhere for the most part. Wilhelm von Humboldt largely invented the modern research university when the University of Berlin was established in 1818. Von Humboldt's idea was that the university should directly enhance German national and scientific development. This revolutionary idea harnessed science and scholarship—produced, with state support, in universities—to national development. The Humboldtian concept proved to be highly successful, and the new German universities (and others that were reformed to conform to the new model) contributed to the emergence of Germany as a modern nation by producing research and educating scientists. A significant additional contribution of the Humboldtian model that affected both science and the organization of higher education was the idea of the "chair" system—the appointment of discipline-based professors. This innovation helped to define the emerging scientific fields and also shaped the organization of the university.

Two countries focused on modernization and development. After 1862 the United States and, several decades later, Japan quickly adopted the German model. The American "land grant" model proved to be particularly successful. It combined the Humboldtian emphasis on research and science and the key role of the state in supporting higher education based on the idea of public service and applied technology (Altbach 2001b). The great American public university, as exemplified by the University of Wisconsin and the University of California in the latter 19th century, opened the door to direct public service and applied technology. It also "democratized" science by replacing the hierarchical German chair system with the more participative departmental structure. Variations of the German, American, and Japanese research university concepts largely characterize today's research universities.

Almost all contemporary universities, regardless of location, are European in structure, organization, and concept. Academic institutions from Tokyo to Tashkent and from Cairo (although the Islamic Al-Azhar survives with a different structure) to Cape Town are based on the Western model. This trend means, for most developing countries, that higher education institutions are not integrally linked to indigenous cultures and in many cases were imposed by colonial rulers. Even in such countries as China, Thailand, and Ethiopia, which were never colonized, Western academic models were chosen (Altbach and Umakoshi 2004). For developing countries subjected to colonialism, higher education growth was generally slow paced. Colonizers cared little about the research function of the universities, being more interested in providing midlevel training for civil servants. In much of Africa and some other parts of the developing world, universities were not established until the 20th century.

RESEARCH UNIVERSITIES AND ACADEMIC SYSTEMS

Research universities generally constitute part of a differentiated academic system—an arrangement of postsecondary institutions with varied roles in society and different funding patterns. Countries without such differentiated systems find it difficult to support research universities, which are always expensive to maintain and require recognition of their specialized and complex academic role. Germany, for example, considers all of its universities as research institutions, and as a result is unable to provide adequate funding to any of them. There are plans under way to recognize a few German universities as "world class" and provide enhanced resources to them, although implementing the changes are proving to be difficult. Research universities are inevitably expensive to operate and require more funds than other academic institutions. They are also generally more selective in terms of student admissions and faculty hiring and typically stand at the pinnacle of an academic system.

The creation of a differentiated academic system is thus a prerequisite for research universities and is a necessity for developing countries (Task Force on Higher Education and Society 2000). A differentiated system has academic institutions with diverse missions, structures, and patterns of funding. In the United States—the first country to design academic systems as a way to organize its expanding and multidimensional postsecondary institutions in the early 20th century—the "California" model is generally seen as the most successful approach. California's public system has three kinds of academic institutions, each with quite different purposes (Douglass 2000). This tiered model—with vocationally oriented "open-door" community colleges, multipurpose state universities, and selective research-oriented universities—has specific patterns of funding and support for each of the tiers as well as quite different missions (Geiger 2004). Britain has recently moved in a similar direction. One of the purposes of

Prime Minister Margaret Thatcher's higher education policy in the 1970s was to create a tiered system in which institutions that emerged at the top of the system as a result of quality assessment—Oxford, Cambridge, and a modest number of others—could be funded more generously than other universities.

Academic systems often evolve during the massification of higher education. As Martin Trow has pointed out, most countries have inevitably moved from an elite higher education system toward mass access, with half or more of the age cohort attending postsecondary institutions (Trow 2006). Ever-larger numbers of students, with varying levels of academic ability and different goals for study, require a range of institutions to serve multiple needs. Just as important, no country can afford to educate large numbers of students in expensive research universities.

Research universities are a small part of most academic systems. In the United States, perhaps 150 out of a total of more than 3,000 academic institutions are research universities. Yet these universities are the most prestigious and are awarded 80 percent of competitive government research funds. Academic salaries tend to be higher, teaching responsibilities for the faculty members lower, and library and laboratory facilities better than the national average. In many countries, there may just one or 2 research universities because of their cost and the resources available. Even in fairly large countries, the number of research universities is often small—in the United Kingdom, perhaps 20 institutions and a similar number in Japan. China is aiming to establish somewhat more than 20, and Brazil has fewer than 6. Some countries may have more research universities than they can afford—Sweden and the Netherlands may be examples.

To allow research universities to flourish requires a way to differentiate them from other types of postsecondary institutions, provide funding at a higher level, and legitimize the idea that these institutions are indeed special and serve a crucial role in society.

RESEARCH, WORLD CLASS, FLAGSHIP, AND STATE-BUILDING: A CONFUSION OF DEFINITIONS

A fairly simple definition of the research university was provided earlier: it is an academic institution focusing intensely on the production of research as part of its mission; offering instruction up to the doctoral level; possessing the necessary infrastructures for research, including libraries, information technology, and laboratories; employing high-quality and carefully selected academic staff (usually with doctoral degrees); maintaining working conditions that permit research activity; and selecting the best quality students available. One can quibble with this definition, as well as whether particular universities fulfill the minimal requirements. What is important is to define research universities clearly and to differentiate them from the rest of the higher education system.

This chapter is not primarily concerned with world-class universities, since there has been a mania to identify these institutions—universities at the top of a prestige and quality hierarchy. Two new international rankings, both started after 2000, have contributed to this effort—one introduced by the *Times Higher Education Supplement* in the United Kingdom and the other by Shanghai Jiao Tong University in China (see Chapter 3). Other national and international rankings are also available—the influential *US News and World Report* annual ranking of American colleges and universities and similar efforts by *McLean's* magazine in Canada, *Der Spiegel* in Germany, and other publications, as well as more academic analyses such as the one prepared by the University of Florida in the United States. In general, *world class* is a shorthand term indicating that a university is among the most prestigious and renowned academic institutions internationally (Altbach 2003a). Almost all of today's world-class universities are in the major English-speaking countries or a few large industrialized nations. All world-class universities are research universities, without exception. But not all research universities are world class, nor should they be.

There are few recognized world-class universities in developing or middle-income countries, and it is unlikely that many will emerge in the future. Relatively few new institutions settle into the ranks of world-class universities anywhere—high costs and competition from other postsecondary sectors are among the reasons. There will be some exceptions to this generalization. China today has several universities that are, or are close to, becoming ranked as world class, and the government is investing in them. South Korea and Taiwan have the same goal and the resources to join the world-class club. India would have the capacity to build such universities, although it has not as yet moved in that direction. Several of Latin America's great public universities—in Brazil, Mexico, and Argentina—also have world-class potential.

Flagship is also a frequently used term in discussions of research universities, generally referring to a leading university in a country or an academic system. These universities are the institutions looked to for influence and emulation. The flagship is typically the most prestigious university, almost always public, and often among the largest in the system or country. Systems and countries look to these institutions for leadership in higher education.

In developing countries, the leading universities have often played a central role in political and social development. These institutions have been called "state-building" universities. The National Autonomous University of Mexico (UNAM) has been used as an example (see Chapter 9). UNAM has educated Mexico's political and intellectual leaders, has served as a center of political activism, houses the national library, and is the largest and most research-oriented institution in the country. Many other countries, especially in Latin America, have similar universities that typically remain the leading academic institutions and to some extent continue to play a central role, educationally, intellectually, and often politically, for the nations. They are always among the leading research universities in the countries.

Worldwide, there is considerable confusion concerning these definitions and concepts. Policymakers may refer to world-class universities when they really mean research institutions. Academic leaders may try to "sell" their universities as world class even when the achievement of this status is impossible. A national flagship institution may seek to portray itself in a regional or international context as world class. It is useful to define terms carefully in order to aim at realistic goals.

RESEARCH UNIVERSITIES AND RESEARCH SYSTEMS

Research universities are not the only institutions in which research is conducted. Specialized research institutes, government laboratories, corporate research centers, and other agencies carry out research, and many participate in the international scientific community. In large countries, research universities form part of a more complex research system that includes other kinds of institutions. Universities, however, serve as the most effective institutions for carrying out research. In addition, they provide formal training and credentials for the future generation of researchers, scholars, and teachers. Using advanced students, typically at the doctoral level, to assist with research reduces the cost of research, provides valuable training for students, and employs the insights of the new generation of talented researchers.

Research institutes, usually publicly funded, remain common establishments in many countries. The Academy of Science system of the former Soviet Union is one of the most influential patterns (Vucinich 1984). Top researchers are appointed at discipline-based (or occasionally interdisciplinary) academies that are usually attached to a research institute. These key scientists in some cases have affiliations with universities, but their main appointments and work are based in the research institutes. The hard sciences and engineering dominate the academy system, the humanities and social sciences are underrepresented. In the case of the former Soviet Union (and contemporary Russia to some extent) and some other countries like those in Eastern Europe and China, these academies are the main providers of research. In these countries, universities have a lower research profile and little direct funding for research. Taiwan, through its Academia Sinica, operates in much the same way. The French CNRS (Centre National de la Recherche Scientifique) and the German Max Planck Institutes have similar functions. In the United States, the National Institutes of Health (NIH) resemble the European examples although in general the NIH are more focused on applied research. Many countries are moving away from the research institute model and toward embedding research laboratories in universities.

There is a growing trend, especially in the United States, of university-based research facilities that are sponsored by corporations and engaged in advanced research involving products or research themes of interest to the sponsoring company. Most focus on applied research that results in marketable products for the sponsoring corporation. American and Japanese companies have been especially active in sponsoring university-related research centers. Companies have set up research facilities near universities to take advantage of academic expertise—the relationship between biotechnology corporations and the Massachusetts Institute of Technology (MIT) is well known. In other examples, corporate laboratories have been set up at universities or agreements have been made with academic units to provide funds for research in return for access to knowledge products (Slaughter and Leslie 1997). China has been active in university-industry linkages, and there has been mixed success. Some observers have noted that not all efforts have been successful and have argued that traditional academic values are being weakened, while others have praised innovative programs (see Chapters 2 and 3).

Universities assemble in one place researchers, teachers, and students who create an effective community for knowledge, discovery, and innovation. Advanced doctoral-level students can provide highly motivated scientific personnel who at the same time can benefit from direct involvement in sophisticated research. Universities have a wide range of disciplines and scientific specializations, and research can benefit from interdisciplinary insights, which is especially significant in frontier areas such as biotechnology and environmental science. Universities can also combine basic research with applied applications in ways that other institutions cannot.

The academic environment is enriched by the unique combination of the academic norm of scientific discovery and interpretation, the link between teaching and research, and the presence of scientists and scholars from a range of disciplines. Universities also exemplify the "public good"—the idea that scientific discovery may have wider social benefits—and their focus on basic research is unique. While science can take place in other venues, universities are a particularly effective environment for discovery.

COMMON CHARACTERISTICS OF THE RESEARCH UNIVERSITY

Despite variations among research universities worldwide, common characteristics exist that are worth noting precisely because they are so nearly universal.

Research universities, with few exceptions, are government-funded public institutions. Only in the United States and to some extent Japan do private research universities exist, although with the current worldwide growth of private higher education it is possible that a small number of these institutions will aspire to the top ranks. This is the case for a number of reasons. Tuition-dependent private institutions can seldom fund expensive research universities. Research universities are typically large in terms of student enrollments and numbers of departments and faculties. The research function, the most expensive part of the university, requires public support because it typically does not produce direct income, especially basic research. The facilities necessary to produce top-quality research, especially in the sciences, are beyond the capacity of private universities to provide. Even in the United States, the research mission of some private universities is supported by the government through research grants given to individual scientists. In most of the world there is no academic tradition of private research universities. Tax laws generally do not reward philanthropic assistance to private universities. As a result, few institutions except in the United States and Japan have endowment funds that permit the support of research. The growing trend internationally toward for-profit private institutions will further weaken private interest in research universities, although it is possible that a few private institutions trying to reach a competitive place at the top of the academic system may seek to become research universities.

Research universities are generally complex institutions with a range of departments and faculties. Often, but not always, they are among the largest academic institutions in their countries. Research universities frequently have professional schools and faculties (e.g., medicine, management, arts and sciences specializations). The large size and range of disciplines permit research universities to take advantage of "economies of scale" regarding laboratories, libraries, and other infrastructures. There are some exceptions to this rule—for example, the California Institute of Technology and the campuses of the Indian Institutes of Technology are small and specialized institutions. These institutions are considered research intensive.

Most research universities are, as Clark Kerr pointed out, "multiversities" (Kerr 2001)—institutions with a multiplicity of missions among which research is only one, but where research and graduate study tend to dominate. Kerr was writing about the University of California, Berkeley, but this generalization could apply to most of the world's research universities. The mission of these universities encompasses undergraduate education on a large scale to reach out to and serve local and national communities, along with offering a range of vocational and professional credentials to students. Some universities, such as UNAM in Mexico and the University of Buenos Aires in Argentina, sponsor secondary schools as well. But in all cases, the research mission is at the top of the prestige hierarchy of the institution. This emphasis on research tends to have a negative impact on the quality of undergraduate instruction and typically has the major influence on the direction of the university (Lewis 2006; Hutchins 1995). Many, however, argue that research-active faculty members bring a vitality to their teaching that benefits students, even at the undergraduate level.

Research universities are always resource intensive. They are considerably more expensive to build and maintain than other academic institutions. Because of increasingly expensive scientific equipment; rapidly expanding, costly information technology and access to worldwide scientific knowledge; and the need to pay their professors more than the norm for the rest of the academic system, research universities are considerably more expensive to operate than other academic institutions. The cost per student is always higher than for the rest of the system. Funding must be available on a sustained basis—fluctuating budgets can damage these institutions.

Finally, research universities attract the "best and the brightest" students in the nation and, in some instances, from around the world. Because of their prestige and facilities, these universities generally attract the most able students, and the admissions process is highly competitive. Similarly, research universities generally employ the most talented professors—scientists and scholars who are attracted by the research orientation, by the facilities, and often by the more favorable working conditions at these institutions. Research university faculty generally hold doctoral degrees, even in many countries where the doctorate is not required for postsecondary teaching.

CHALLENGES

Research universities face severe challenges at a time when they are recognized as the pinnacle of the academic system and as central to the new globalized economy. The following factors are among the problems faced by research universities in all countries. While the scope and depth of the issues discussed here may vary, they are universally applicable.

Funding

As noted earlier, the basic cost of operating a research university has increased, placing more stress on traditional funding sources, mainly governmental, and forcing institutions and systems to seek new revenues. At the same time, the basic concepts underpinning public funding for higher education are being questioned. The traditional idea views higher education as a public good, serving society by means of improved human capital as well as research and service. Thus the society has the responsibility of paying for much of the cost of higher education. Since the 1980s, spurred by thinking from the World Bank and international policy organizations that have shaped the "neoliberal economic consensus," higher education is increasingly seen as a private good that mainly benefits individual graduates. From this perspective, the individual and his or her family should pay the main costs of higher education through tuition and other fees. This change in thinking occurred at the same time that massification became a key factor in many countries—dramatically increased enrollments were impossible for traditional government funding levels. Leaving aside the broader economic arguments, this combination of financial factors has been particularly difficult for research universities, which are quintessential "public good" institutions. Their costs are high and their products—educating the top echelons of society, providing research, and serving as repositories of knowledge and sources of social analysis—may not yield practical results in the short run. Student tuition alone cannot support research universities. Further, basic research cannot be expected to fund itself. For these and other reasons, research universities face severe financial strain.

Research universities are subject to the pressures of privatization (Lyall and Sell 2006). The privatization of public universities has become a common phenomenon since public funding is inadequate to support these institutions. In the United States, for example, many of the "flagship" public research universities receive as little as 15 percent of their basic funding from their primary sponsors, the state governments. The rest of the budget comes from student tuition, research grants, income from intellectual property and ancillary services, and donations from individuals and foundations, as well as endowments. To produce sufficient income, Chinese universities have increased tuition, earned income from consulting and other work by faculty members, and established profit-making companies. In some countries, such as Russia and Uganda, among others, research universities have admitted "private" students who are charged high tuitions, in contrast to the publicly supported enrollments, in order to earn extra funds. Many of these activities significantly undermine the core role of the university.

Research

A culture of research, inquiry, and quality is an essential part of a research university. Because of the financial pressures described here, there is a trend toward applied and often profit-oriented research, which can be more easily funded than basic research and may yield profits for the university. The commercialization of research has significant implications for research universities. It changes the orientation of the research community to some extent by emphasizing commercial values rather than basic research. Universities have entered into agreements with corporations to produce specific research products or provide access to university facilities. The controversial links between the University of California, Berkeley and the multinational pharmaceutical company Novartis exemplify the possible conflicts between traditional academic norms and commercial interests. The ownership of knowledge, the use of academic facilities, and the ultimate openness of scientific research are all issues raised by these new commercial linkages.

With the rising costs of university research due to expensive laboratories and equipment, large interdisciplinary scientific research teams, and other factors, raising funds to support research in the sciences grows more difficult. Even large and well-funded universities in the industrialized countries struggle to support cutting-edge research. In some fields, only the richest institutions can support frontier scientific research.

Research universities in developing countries will need to select fields of research that are affordable and linked to national needs and priorities. Appropriate links with private-sector companies, including multinational corporations, may be necessary, and a balance between applied and basic research will need to be worked out. Work in the sciences is only one part of the research agenda of a university. The social sciences and humanities are often neglected because the hard sciences are seen to be more profitable and prestigious. Yet the social sciences and humanities are important for the understanding of society and culture. They are also considerably less expensive than the hard sciences but are sometimes ignored.

The details of allocating funding for research are also central policy issues. While basic resources, from the university budget, for laboratories, libraries, and other research infrastructures are necessary, funding for specific research projects can come from a variety of sources and be allocated in different ways. A system of competitive awards encourages innovative ideas and granting funds for the best projects. Such funds can come from government ministries and granting agencies, private and foreign foundations, or business firms. An appropriate mix of funding sources and allocation mechanisms encourages competition for research funds and the best quality and most innovative research ideas.

Commercialism and the Market

The intrusion of market forces and commercial interests into higher education is one of the greatest challenges to universities everywhere. The threat to research universities is particularly great because they are quintessentially "public good" institutions. Market forces have the potential for intruding into almost every aspect of academe (Kirp 2003). Roger Geiger has written about "the paradox of the marketplace for American universities":

> Hence the marketplace has, on balance, brought universities greater resources, better students, a far larger capacity for advancing knowledge, and a more productive role in the U.S. economy. At the same time, it has diminished the sovereignty of universities over their own activities, weakened their mission of serving the public, and created through growing commercial entanglements at least the potential for undermining their privileged role as disinterested arbiters of knowledge. (Geiger 2004, 265)

For developing countries, the challenge of the market is particularly serious because there is less basic financial stability and a weaker tradition of academic autonomy. External market pressures can quickly affect the entire institution. For research universities, market forces may significantly shift the direction of research, the focus of the academic profession, and the financial balance of the institution. It is clear, however, that if research universities are forced to rely increasingly on their own resources for survival, market forces will determine institutional directions and priorities.

Autonomy and Accountability

The tension between autonomy and accountability is a perennial concern for academic institutions. Universities' tradition of academic autonomy involves the ability to make their own decisions about essential academic matters and to shape their own destiny. At the same time, external authorities, including funders, governmental sponsors, and religious organizations, held some control over higher education. Since the origins of universities in medieval Europe, these tensions were evident. In the era of mass higher education, demands for accountability have increased given higher education's rising impact on both the economy and society. Higher education is both a significant state expenditure and of growing relevance to large numbers of people. The demand for contemporary accountability almost always comes from the state, the source of much of the funding for higher education.

Research universities have a special need for autonomy, and current demands for accountability are especially problematical for them. While academe in general needs a degree of autonomy to function effectively, research universities must be able to shape their own programs, carry out a long-term perspective, and manage their budgets and the academic community. Not only do research universities require steady funding commitments, they also need autonomy to develop and maintain their strengths. The academic community itself is the best judge of the success of programs. Basic research, especially, must have autonomy to develop, since it typically emerges from the interests and concerns of the faculty.

Accountability is, of course, an essential part of contemporary higher education. Funders of academic institutions deserve to learn about spending policies and to have the power to steer public higher education institutions and systems. Students, too, have the right to know about the quality, orientation, and focus of universities. Accountability, however, is a multifaceted concept and must operate differently for research universities than for other academic institutions. The balance between accountability and autonomy must swing more toward autonomy for these institutions than for colleges and universities that focus more on teaching and service.

The Globalization of Science and Scholarship

Science in the 21st century is truly global in scope. Research results are immediately available worldwide through the Internet. Scientific journals are circulated internationally, and academics contribute to the same publications. Methodologies and scientific norms are used worldwide more than ever before. Scientific equipment, ever more sophisticated and expensive, is available everywhere, and there is pressure for research universities to have the most modern laboratories if they wish to participate in global scientific research. Further, research is increasingly competitive, with researchers and universities rushing to present results and patent or license potentially useful discoveries or inventions. Science, in short, has become a "high-stakes" and intensely competitive international endeavor. Entry into advanced scientific research is expensive, as is maintaining a competitive edge.

The challenge consists not only of laboratories and infrastructures but also the definitions and methodologies of science and scholarship. Scientific globalization means that participants are linked to the norms of the disciplines and of scholarship that are established by the leaders of research, located in the major universities in the United States and other Western nations. The methods used in funded research and presented in the main scientific journals tend to dominate world science. Further, the themes and subject areas of interest to leading scientists and institutions may not be relevant to universities at the periphery. Involvement in world science means, in general, adherence to established research paradigms and themes.

The high cost of science creates serious problems for academic institutions without a long tradition of research and the required infrastructures and equipment. It is no longer sufficient to build an infrastructure that permits research on local or regional themes if a university wishes to join the "big leagues." Universities that wish to be considered research oriented need to participate in the international scientific network and compete with institutions and scientists worldwide. The costs of joining the league of research universities is an especially serious problem for developing countries, with funding problems and no experience of building such institutions. Small academic institutions in both larger countries and small industrialized countries seeking to transform themselves into research universities face similar challenges. The world of global science is expensive to join, and sustaining participation is also costly.

The paradox of global science is similar to globalization in general. Globalization—through information technology, better communications, the worldwide circulation of highly trained personnel, and other factors—permits everyone to participate in the global marketplace of science, scholarship, and ideas. At the same time, globalization subjects all participants to the pressures of an unequal global knowledge system dominated by the wealthy universities, and imposes the norms and values of those institutions on all (Altbach 1987, 2004).

Public and Private

As discussed earlier, almost all research universities outside the United States and Japan are public and state supported. It is likely that this trend will continue, although with some changes. The fastest-growing sector of higher education worldwide is private. Thus the expansion of the private sector will have an impact on research universities, albeit indirectly, since private higher education is not focused on research (Altbach 1999). With only a few minor exceptions, the new private institutions focus on teaching and providing credentials to students in professional and other fields, often in specialized niche areas. New private universities are not full-fledged academic institutions with a range of disciplines in most fields of science and scholarship. Specialization is particularly an aspect of the rapidly expanding for-profit sector of private higher education. The sector is never concerned with building research capacity, since research does not produce profits rapidly.

A small number of nonprofit private universities may succeed in building research capacity to raise their status and contribute broadly to education and research. The Catholic University in Santiago, Chile, and the American University in Cairo, Egypt, are two examples of high-status private institutions that are focusing on developing significant research profiles to build national and international reputations. Institutions such as these generally have a tradition of academic excellence and access to philanthropic funds to develop research programs.

The growing role of private higher education worldwide means that a smaller proportion of universities will focus on research. This might, in some ways, benefit public research universities since the state may have some of the burden of mass higher education access lifted and be able to focus on promoting the research sector. It is, however, more likely that as the private sector takes on more responsibility for higher education, the state will continue to decrease its support for the sector, as has been the trend in many countries. The rise of the private sector, with its lack of focus on research, may threaten the research role of universities in most of the world, especially in developing countries.

Research Universities as Meritocracies

In some parts of the world, universities do not adhere to strict meritocratic values. Corruption is a problem and grants and promotions may be awarded for reasons unrelated to quality and merit. For research universities, adherence to meritocratic norms and academic honesty is of special importance. Universities are, of course, part of a broader social and political system, and if the polity is rife with corruption and favoritism, academe will not be immune. The problem of academic corruption in its many facets is present in some developing countries. Systemic corruption is also evident in some of the countries of the former Soviet Union as well as elsewhere. Bribery in student admissions and the awarding of degrees, flagrant plagiarism by students and academics, widespread cheating on examinations, and other forms of clearly unacceptable behavior have become endemic. In India students have demonstrated for the right to cheat on university examinations. In China there has been a growing public concern about plagiarism at all levels of the academic system and violation of intellectual property at some research universities (Pocha 2006). In a healthy academic system, when such behavior takes place, it receives the condemnation of the academic community and is rooted out.

The situation is even more dangerous when it directly involves the academic profession. Poor academic salaries contribute to unprofessional professorial practices. Widespread illegal selling of lecture notes and other course materials in Egypt by professors is linked to the need of academic staff to earn enough money to survive (Arishie 2006). Selling academic posts is a common practice in some countries, and awarding professorships on the basis of ethnic, religious, or political factors is widespread as well.

While corrupt practices are damaging in any academic environment, they are toxic to the culture and ethos of the research university. The ideal and practice of meritocratic values are central to the research university. Excellence and intellectual quality are key criteria for student admissions, academic hiring, promotion, and reward in research universities. The underpinnings of these academic institutions depend on meritocratic values. Widespread violations will inevitably make it impossible for a research university to flourish.

Academic Freedom

Academic freedom is a core requirement for research universities (Altbach 2001a). However, a few definitions are necessary. Of primary importance is the freedom to undertake research and publication in one's area of research and to teach without any restriction in one's areas of expertise. These rights are parts of the more limited German definition of academic freedom. The right of academics to express their views in any public forum or in writing on any topic, even on subjects far from the individual's academic expertise—the broader American definition—is increasingly accepted around the world. Academic freedom is in some countries protected by specific academic legislation as well as traditional norms and values. Tenure systems in many countries and civil service status in others provide guarantees of employment security so that it is difficult, if not impossible, for governmental authorities or others to terminate a professor who is protected by these guarantees.

Research universities are particularly dependent on a strong regime of academic freedom because their faculty members are directly engaged in the discovery of new knowledge. Research university professors are also more likely than other academics to be "public intellectuals," engaged in civic discourse on topics of societal importance. History shows that academic freedom—freedom in the classroom, in the laboratory, and in publishing the results of research and scholarship—is central to building a research culture.

In some countries, the norms of academic freedom are not fully entrenched, and as a result it may be more difficult to sustain top-quality research universities. Where academic freedom is entirely missing or severely restricted, as is the case in a small number of countries, research universities with reasonable standards cannot be successful regardless of financial support or resources. More common worldwide are universities with some restrictions on academic freedom. In many countries, especially developing nations, in areas of knowledge that are considered politically or socially sensitive, research, publication, or commentary is restricted. Such fields include ethnic or religious studies, environmental research, and studies of social class or social conflict, among others. The sanctions for critical analysis in these fields may be as severe as firing from academic posts, jail, or exile. More common are less serious penalties or informal warnings.

There seems to be a delicate balance between academic freedom and a viable research university. Singapore has long placed informal restrictions on research in a few areas considered to be politically sensitive, such as ethnic relations. Social scientists face some constraints on their freedom of research and publication and have occasionally faced criticism for straying over an unstated demarcation of what is officially sanctioned research. At the same time, Singapore has been successful in building research universities and establishing collaboration with respected universities abroad. The situation in China is similar, although restrictions are reportedly greater and sanctions for violations can be more severe. In the Middle East, there are taboos on research and publication concerning politically sensitive Arab-Israeli relations or certain religious or ethnic topics. In some African countries, criticism of the ruling regime in power can result in jail terms or job loss, although in general academic freedom is respected. It seems that reasonably successful research universities can be built under conditions of incomplete academic freedom so long as the restrictions are not too severe, although broad comparisons show universities with the greatest amount of academic freedom do best as effective research institutions.

In the United States and other industrialized countries, the main threat to traditional norms of academic freedom comes from the commercialization of research and the increasing links between universities or individual researchers and corporations interested in university-based research. Under the banner of university-industry collaboration, agreements are made that sometimes restrict access to research findings, center the attention of research groups on commercially focused products, and emphasize applied research at the expense of basic work (Slaughter and Rhoades 2004; Kirp 2003). This commercialization may be financially advantageous to the university and to individual researchers but often places restrictions on the free communication of knowledge, thus violating one of the principles of academic freedom.

Academic freedom is a complex and nuanced topic, central to the success of a research university. It is a core value of higher education everywhere and for all types of academic institutions, but is of special importance for research universities. The challenges to academic freedom in the 21st century come not only from repressive external authorities but also from the new commercialism in higher education. Problems may also originate from within the academy due to the politicization of the academic community or tensions caused by religious or ethnic relations in some countries.

The Academic Profession

The professoriate is central to higher education. Research universities rely especially on the quality and focus of the academic profession, and current developments relating to the professoriate worldwide are not favorable for either the profession or for research universities (Altbach 2003b). Research universities require academic staff with the highest possible qualifications—doctoral degrees from reputable universities. This seemingly obvious statement is necessary because the majority of academic staff in developing countries do not hold a doctorate.

Research universities require full-time professors, scholars and scientists who devote their full professional attention to teaching and research at the universities. Without a large majority of full-time academic staff, it is simply impossible to build a cadre to form a committed and effective professoriate. Not only required to fulfill the core functions of the university, full-time faculty also need to participate in governance and management because research universities need a high degree of autonomy and faculty governance. The lack of full-time faculty is one central reason Latin American countries have failed to build research universities.

Along with full-time commitment, salaries must be sufficient to support a middle-class lifestyle. While they need not be paid salaries similar to those of colleagues in the most highly remunerated universities internationally, professors must be solid members of the middle class in their country. Frequently, full-time professors generate a significant part of their incomes through consulting, moonlighting at other institutions, or, at some universities, taking on extra teaching loads in fee-producing programs. These arrangements detract from the core functions of the professoriate and make full academic productivity difficult to maintain. In some disciplines, consulting work, applied research for industry, and other links with external agencies may provide useful synergies for academic work, but in many countries outside work and dependence on additional income are deleterious to the research university. Just as problematic, academic salaries, overall, have stagnated worldwide at the same time that remuneration for similarly educated professionals outside universities has increased in some countries quite dramatically. In order to attract the "best and brightest" to academe, salaries must be competitive.

Teaching responsibilities must be sufficiently limited to allow time and energy for research. In the United States, the standard teaching load in most research universities is two courses per semester or four per academic year. In some scientific fields, even less teaching is expected. Similar teaching loads are common in Europe. In many developing countries, much more teaching is required, leaving little time for research. The most active research-focused professors in the United States undertake a significant part of their teaching in graduate (postbaccalaureate) programs, which helps to link teaching with research and increases productivity. In European countries, with doctoral programs that are mainly focused on research, professors are given sufficient time for doctoral supervision and mentoring. Few developing countries have instituted these practices.

The academic profession must have a career ladder that permits talented professors to be promoted up the ranks of the profession on the basis of their performance and the quality of their work and a salary structure determined by performance. In many countries, an initial full-time appointment is tantamount to a permanent job. In some, such as Germany, it is difficult for a junior academic to obtain a post that has the possibility of promotion because of the organization of the career structure. In much of the world, promotion up the academic ranks is largely a matter of seniority and not of demonstrated performance in teaching and research. In the majority of countries, academic salaries are determined by seniority, rank, and, in some places, discipline rather than by job performance. This is especially true for countries where academics are considered civil servants—mainly in Western Europe (Enders 2001). Civil service status provides strong guarantees of permanent employment but seldom measures productivity as an element of promotion.

The challenge is to link reasonable guarantees of long-term employment, both as a means of ensuring academic freedom and as a way of providing employment security and institutional loyalty. The American tenure-track system, although much criticized within the United States, may be closest to this goal (Chait 2002). It provides initial probationary appointments with a series of rigorous evaluations that, if passed, lead to a permanent (tenured) appointment after six years. Further promotion, from the rank of associate to full professor, is also merit based and depends on a rigorous evaluation. Most American colleges and universities follow this pattern although the research universities have the most stringent evaluations. Increasingly, US universities have also instituted "post-tenure review" so that productivity is measured following the award of tenure. Typically, salary raises are given based on performance as well as seniority. Even in the United States, the academic profession is threatened—from the perspective of the research universities. The two most serious problems are the growth of a part-time academic workforce and the relatively new category of non-tenure-track, full-time appointments, similar in some ways to the

German pattern of appointments that cannot lead to permanent careers. Now, half of the new positions at US colleges and universities are in these categories, although at research universities the proportion of tenure-track positions is higher (Schuster and Finkelstein 2006).

The academic profession is central to the success of the university everywhere. A research university requires a special type of professor—highly trained, committed to research and scholarship, and motivated by intellectual curiosity. Full-time commitment and adequate remuneration constitute other necessities. A career path that requires excellence and at the same time offers both academic freedom and job security is also required. Academics at research universities need both the time to engage in creative research and the facilities and infrastructures to make this research possible.

DEVELOPING COUNTRIES: GOALS, ASPIRATIONS, AND REALITIES

Many developing and middle-income countries need research universities to participate in the expanding knowledge and service-oriented economy of the 21st century. Aspirations, however, must be tempered by realities. The goals of research universities in developing countries necessarily differ from those of the large industrialized nations. For developing countries, the goals include a number of core elements.

The Creation and Retention of a Scientific Community

Research universities employ scientists and scholars in a range of disciplines. Without these institutions, highly trained academics would leave the country—as happens in many developing countries today that lack these institutions—or would fail to be trained in the first place. Research universities provide the institutional base for top professors, scholars and scientists who comprehend what is happening at the frontiers of science in all fields and can participate in the global scientific community. The institutions retain local talent at the same time as they produce additional talent. The academic community in the local research university can communicate with scholars abroad and can participate in the global scientific community.

The Relevance of Research and Teaching to Industry and Society

Local research universities are the only institutions able to focus attention on local needs. They understand the specific problems of the country in which they are located and are able to focus attention on these themes. External institutions have neither the interest nor the knowledge to do so. Research universities can bring international scientific trends to bear on local problems and contribute to the development of domestic industry, agriculture, and society.

Cultural and Social Development and Critique

Research universities everywhere constitute centers of culture and critique. In developing countries, they are of special importance in this regard because there are few other societal institutions with relevant expertise. In many countries, there are few museums, orchestras, or other cultural institutions capable of building and interpreting indigenous culture. Research universities are often the only places with a "critical mass" of expertise and resources in a range of cultural areas. These institutions also provide social commentary, analysis, and critique. Again, they are uniquely positioned for these roles; they have academic freedom and a community of faculty and students interested in a range of disciplines. While political authorities may find criticism unwelcome, it is of central importance for the development of a civil society.

Research and Analysis in the National Language(s)

Research universities must, of course, function in the international languages of science and scholarship. Simultaneously, they have a responsibility to disseminate research and analysis in local languages. Indeed, they may provide a key source for national-language development by producing scientific and literary work in the language and building up vocabulary. The role of indigenous languages in developing country research universities is a highly complex one. In many countries, including almost all of Africa, India, and other regions, higher education takes place in nonindigenous languages (English, French, etc.) and the issues are quite complex. But it is clear that research universities play a key role in supporting and developing local languages.

Educating a New Generation of Scientists, Scholars, and Technicians

It goes without saying that the central role of the research university is education—the training of the next generation of educated personnel for the society. Society's leaders, in politics, intellectual life, industry, and, of course, education, are trained mostly in the local research university. The role of UNAM in educating generations of the Mexican elite is just one example of a common trend (see Chapter 9).

The aspirations of the research universities in developing countries must be realistic. With the exception of a few of the largest and most successful developing nations, including China and India, aspiring to compete with Harvard or Oxford or to build a top-ranking world-class university is not a reasonable goal. Rather, developing countries can seek to compete with second-rank but quite distinguished research universities in the industrialized world, such as Indiana University or the University of Nebraska in the United States, York University in the United Kingdom, or the University of Amsterdam in the Netherlands.

It is also necessary to select specific areas of science and scholarship to emphasize. Most research universities provide instruction in the main academic disciplines, and many have associated professional schools in fields such as medicine and law. A few research universities are smaller specialized institutions, such as the California Institute of Technology. Few research universities are outstanding in all fields. They make choices concerning which disciplines will be emphasized to build and maintain the highest standards of quality. In some other fields, good quality can be achieved but not necessarily at the highest international levels. These decisions may be made on the basis of available resources, an examination of national or regional needs, or a simple assessment of existing strengths.

Some smaller developing countries may lack the funds to build and sustain a research university. In such cases, it may be possible to build a regional research university. Information technology makes this more practicable. Some regions make such initiatives easier to implement than others. For example, Central America is a relatively limited area with a common language and a group of small countries with similar economic and social needs. East Africa, francophone West Africa, and the central Asian states of the former Soviet Union might also have similar potential. However, efforts to establish regional universities have not been successful in the past half century. Many discussions have yielded few results and at least one case, the University of East Africa—an institution designed to serve Kenya, Tanzania, and Uganda—did not succeed. However, the

University of the West Indies and the University of the South Pacific have succeeded in serving distinct regions. Countries often believe that they need their own national university, and thus sharing resources with neighbors may go against national policy. It may also be possible for research universities in some of the larger developing countries to partner with institutions in small nations, such as Mexico working with Central American universities.

CONCLUSION

Research universities stand at the apex of a higher education system, providing access to international scholarship and producing the research that may contribute to the growth of knowledge worldwide or in local economies. These universities are also the means of communication with the international world of science and scholarship. For developing countries, research universities play a special role because they are often the sole link to the international knowledge network. Industrialized nations possess many points of access—multinational corporations, scientific laboratories, and government agencies, among others. The best local academics are employed at research universities, which provide them with a home and with the possibility of contributing to science and scholarship without leaving the country. Research universities are, thus, centrally important for the success of any higher education system.

Maintaining research universities requires sustained funding to keep these institutions abreast of emerging fields and advances in knowledge. Research universities have special characteristics that may not be common in the academic systems of many developing countries. These aspects include a cadre of full-time faculty, academic freedom, a salary structure permitting a local middle-class lifestyle, promotion and salary enhancement based on performance rather than just seniority, reasonable guarantees of long-term appointment, absence of corruption in all sectors of academic work, and an academic culture of competition and research productivity. These elements may not be present in existing universities. They require resources as well as a cosmopolitan academic environment. Research universities constitute a kind of "flagship" for the rest of the academic system, providing examples of the best academic values and orientations. At the same time, the norms of the research university, which do not characterize the rest of the academic system, require support.

For developing countries to join the ranks of modern economies, research universities are a requirement. These institutions link the nation to the broader world of science, technology, and scholarship. Research universities provide the skills needed by 21st-century economies and societies and reflect the best academic values. Research universities are central institutions for the global economy.

REFERENCES

Altbach, P. G. 1987. *The knowledge context: Comparative perspectives on the distribution of knowledge.* Albany: State University of New York Press.

———, ed. 1999. *Private Prometheus: Private higher education and development in the 21st century.* Westport, CT: Greenwood.

———. 2001a. Academic freedom: International realities and challenges. *Higher Education* 41 (1–2): 205–19.

———. 2001b. The American academic model in comparative perspective. In *In defense of American higher education*, ed. P. G. Altbach, P. J. Gumport, and D. B. Johnstone, 11–37. Baltimore: Johns Hopkins University Press.

———. 2003a. The costs and benefits of world-class universities. *International Higher Education,* no. 33:5–9.

———, ed. 2003b. *The decline of the guru: The academic profession in developing and middle-income countries.* New York: Palgrave.

———. 2004. Globalization and the university: Myths and realities in an unequal world. *Tertiary Education and Management* 10:3–25.

Altbach, P. G., and T. Umakoshi, eds. 2004. *Asian universities: Historical perspectives and contemporary challenges.* Baltimore: Johns Hopkins University Press.

Arishie, M. 2006. Keeping the profs in funds. *Egyptian Gazette* (Cairo), March 16, 2.

Chait, R. P., ed. 2002. *The questions of tenure.* Cambridge, MA: Harvard University Press.

Douglass, J. A. 2000. *The California idea and American higher education: 1850 to the 1960 Master Plan.* Stanford, CA: Stanford University Press.

Enders, J., ed. 2001. *Academic staff in Europe: Changing contexts and conditions.* Westport, CT: Greenwood.

Geiger, R. L. 2004. *Money and knowledge: Research universities and the paradox of the marketplace.* Stanford, CA: Stanford University Press.

Hutchins, R. M. 1995. *The higher learning in America.* New Brunswick, NJ: Transaction. Originally published in 1936.

Kerr, C. 2001. *The uses of the university.* Cambridge, MA: Harvard University Press.

Kirp, David. 2003. *Shakespeare, Einstein, and the bottom line: The marketing of higher education.* Cambridge, MA: Harvard University Press.

Lewis, H. R. 2006. *Excellence without a soul: How a great university forgot education.* New York: Public Affairs.

Lyall, K. C., and K. R. Sell. 2006. *The true genius of America at risk: Are we losing our public universities to de facto privatization?* Westport, CT: Praeger.

Mollis, M. 2006. Latin American identities in transition: A diagnosis of Argentina and Brazilian universities. In *The university, state, and markets: The political economy of globalization in the Americas*, ed. R. A. Rhoads and C. A. Torres, 203–20. Stanford, CA: Stanford University Press.

Perkin, H. 2006. History of universities. In *International handbook of higher educa-*

tion., ed. J. J.F. Forest and P. G. Altbach, 159–206. Dordrecht, Netherlands: Springer.

Pocha, J. S. 2006. Internet exposes plagiarism in China, but punishment of professors rare at universities. *Boston Globe*, April 9.

Ranking and league tables of higher education institutions. 2002. *European Journal of Education* 27 (4): 361–481.

Rosenzweig, R. M. 1998. *The political university: Policy, politics, and presidential leadership in the American research university.* Baltimore: Johns Hopkins University Press.

Schuster, J. H., and M. J. Finkelstein. 2006. *The American faculty: The restructuring of academic work and careers*. Baltimore: Johns Hopkins University Press.

Slaughter, S., and L. L. Leslie. 1997. *Academic capitalism: Politics, policies, and the entrepreneurial university.* Baltimore: Johns Hopkins University Press.

Slaughter, S., and G. Rhoades. 2004. *Academic capitalism and the new economy: Markets, state, and higher education.* Baltimore: Johns Hopkins University Press.

Task Force on Higher Education and Society. 2000. *Higher education in developing countries: Peril and promise.* Washington, DC: World Bank.

Trow, M. 2006. Reflections on the transition from elite to mass to universal access: Forms and phases of higher education in modern societies. In *International handbook of higher education*, ed. J. J.F. Forest and P. G. Altbach, 243–80. Dordrecht, Netherlands: Springer.

Vucinich, A. 1984. *Empire of knowledge: The Academy of Sciences of the USSR (1917–1970).* Berkeley: University of California Press.

PART I

Asia

2

The Flagship University and China's Economic Reform

Wanhua Ma

Higher education in China has undergone unprecedented changes since the late 1970s. Economic change along with social transition, the need for knowledge and technological innovation, the growing demand for internationalization of higher education, and economic globalization are considered factors underlying the shifting missions and roles of universities in China. With respect to scientific discovery and technological innovation, universities' traditional values for developing human resources and transmitting cultural heritage have given way to more pragmatic and instrumental functions. The paradigm shift in higher education poses both challenges and opportunities to leading universities in China.

OVERVIEW OF THE FLAGSHIP UNIVERSITY IN CHINA

The success of American research universities has been recognized as a model for higher education worldwide, and in the 1980s even the Organization for Economic Cooperation and Development (OECD) countries started to discuss the model of the US scientific research system. The American model has also had a great impact on higher education in China. Since 1978, thousands of Chinese students and faculty have rushed to the United States, interested in advanced knowledge and education. Educational policymakers in China have tried to learn more about the development and governance of US research universities. Many conferences and publications have focused on American research universities: how they work and what lessons can be learned from them. American experiences have been the source for many ideas regarding higher education reform in China—including the building of research universities.

Traditionally, higher education in China was characterized by the terms of *key* and *non-key* (or ordinary) universities. In 1978, 88 universities were recognized as key universities by the State Council, while the other universities (about 500) were considered to be ordinary universities. Peking University, Tsinghua University, and Fudan University ranked as the top three key universities. A key university was recognized on the basis of several indicators: strong teaching resources, nationally well-known disciplines and programs, and basic scientific research. Regional distribution was another factor in the selection of key universities—most key universities were located in the eastern part of the country. The key university system was established to improve the quality of teaching and learning and to strengthen basic scientific research in higher education.

Key universities played an important role in the development of higher education in the 1980s. In 1980, key universities were the first to offer master's and doctoral degree programs in certain disciplines. Since the mid-1980s, key universities have given more attention to both the basic and the applied sides of scientific research. Policies and strategies have been adapted to infuse research funds into these universities.

While China's economy was growing at a fast pace in the 1980s and there was a great need for university research and scientific innovations, investment in higher education seemed to be on the decline. For example, investment in higher education was 3.04 percent of national gross domestic product (GDP) in 1990; in 1995, it dropped to 2.41 percent (Ma 2004). Subsequently, what was frequently heard was the request to reform the structure of higher education finance. The Chinese government has adopted three strategies to address the issue: restructuring the higher education system, collecting fees from students, and adjusting the university finance mechanism. These strategies were at least partly learned from the US model. Traditionally, Chinese universities were tuition free, with the government providing stipends for students covering most of the costs of accommodation, living expenses, and books. In 1994, the introduction of tuition and the establishment of loan programs with the involvement of commercial banks represented a fundamental shift for Chinese universities in generating resources.

During the same period, the restructuring of the system provided an opportunity for the growth of Chinese flagship universities. Here the term *flagship university* simply means a university that holds a leading position in a country's system of higher education. Two important projects are worth mentioning in this regard: the 211 Project and the 985 Project. The 211 Project, initiated in 1994, was created to build 100 universities in the early years of the 21st century. Before the establishment of the 211 Project, the "Outline for Education Reform and Development in China" was issued by the State Council in 1993 (Central Committee 1993). This document has been widely cited as important for higher education reform, because it clearly states that the central government will reorganize the structure of higher education, with a focus on investing in a few universities that will take a leading position in the country's economic and social development and in international competition. The 211 Project is considered a product of this policy decision. For that project, the Chinese government first allocated 400 million RMB yuan (US$50 million) to the selected universities for improvement of teaching, learning, and research. At the same time, provincial or municipal governments were also invited to provide financial support to those selected universities. For instance, the municipal government of Shanghai contributed 120 million RMB yuan (US$15 million) each to Fudan University and Shanghai Jiao Tong University in 1995 to improve teaching and research conditions at both universities. This event shows a local government's willingness to support the leading institutions located in its regions.

To further enhance public funds for higher education, at the centennial of Peking University in May 1998, the 985 Project was launched. This project initially provided Peking University and Tsinghua University, the two leading universities in China, a three-year funding package of 1,800 million RMB yuan (US$234 million) each as a special grant for building world-class universities. The project was later expanded to cover nine leading universities in the country: Peking University, Tsinghua University, Fudan University, Nanjing University, University of Science and Technology of China, Shanghai Jiao Tong University, Xi'an Jiao Tong University, Zhejiang University, and Harbin University of Technology. Funding from the central government for each university was reduced in scale, while support from different ministries and provincial or municipal governments was encouraged. For instance, between 1999 and 2001 Harbin University of Technology received 100 million RMB yuan (US$12.3 million) from the Ministry of Education, the Commission of Science, Technology and Industry for National Defense, and the Heilongjiang provincial government.

Evaluating what these nine universities achieved during the initial three years of investment has resulted in the concept of the world-class university being questioned and challenged extensively in China, in part because there does not seem to be a universal standard on which to base the definition.

Some researchers have tried to establish a classification or ranking system (see Chapter 3) to identify world-class universities and to use the ranking system to survey Chinese universities. Other researchers appear to focus on defining the characteristics of world-class universities. For instance, the case has been made that an advanced concept of a university, adequate material support and financing, strong research capacity, and a firm degree of university autonomy in governance should be viewed as more important in defining a world-class university than the number of alumni of an institution who have won Nobel Prizes and the number of articles published in highly valued journals such as *Nature* and *Science* (Ding 2004).

Some higher education decision makers and administrators have expressed impatience with the ongoing debate over world-class universities. People have began to realize that building a world-class university is a long process rather than the immediate result of goodwill or a lump-sum investment. In fact, some people even doubt that China can really create world-class universities, because the widely recognized models of world-class universities, such as Oxford and Cambridge in the United Kingdom or Harvard and Yale in the United States, have gone through centuries of development. Moreover, they evolved in different policy environments and with different forms of university governance structures.

Actually, the Chinese policy environment may not have much to do with creating standards of classification or rankings. The process may need to involve the central government's setting up priorities to develop a few leading universities in the country and to strengthen those universities' research capacity for knowledge creation and technological innovation. As stated in "The Action Plan for Education Re-vitalization between 2003–2007" by the Ministry of Education in 2004, the purpose of building world-class universities is to raise the country's competitiveness in science and education (Ministry of Education 2004).

The 985 Project has received attention from both the central government and the higher education system in China. Competition among universities to be included in the world-class ranking was thus created. In order to become part of the project, many universities added new buildings on their campuses, sought to improve teaching facilities by establishing computer laboratories, increased the hiring of faculty with foreign degrees, and adjusted their curriculum, among other actions. Some universities even requested more support from local governments, either in the form of land or money for more facilities.

Even though just a small number of universities are in the category of potential world-class institutions, the goal of developing such institutions and the efforts undertaken to do so have shown the general public a serious concern of the central government. The dynamics of economic globalization mean if one is not in a leading position it is easy to be left behind; especially in the high-technology world, the issue of the "digital divide" is not a fiction but a reality. The brain-drain issue China has experienced since the 1990s is only one aspect of the world-class problem, and the goal of building research universities in China is also seen as a central concern.

The 211 Project and the 985 Project replaced the traditional distinction of key and non-key universities in Chinese higher education with a new system. The 211 Project includes about 99 universities out of the 1,683 public colleges and universities in China. Of these 99 universities, 34 are considered as highly research-oriented universities. Of these 34 universities, 9 are in the category of institutions to be built up into world-class universities, with Peking University and Tsinghua University at the top.

THE ECONOMY'S IMPACT ON THE FLAGSHIP UNIVERSITY IN CHINA

Why has China launched so many programs or projects to promote the development of the leading universities? What has the impact been on the country's higher education system? Answering these questions, requires looking first at the country's economic structural changes and higher education paradigm shift. In the late 1970s, China adopted an open-door policy. Under this policy, foreign investors were allowed to open businesses and industries in China, although ideological, cultural, and social differences caused hesitation or even resistance both domestically and abroad. Creating an economic developmental zone, with tax exemptions, was an innovative idea for foreign investors in "Red China" at the beginning of China's economic reform. Shenzhen, which was China's first special economic zone, grew from a small town into a large city within a decade. It is a successful initiative that proves China's determination for change.

But any policy change has multiple effects. When McDonald's opened its first restaurant in Beijing, it not only offered an exotic food but also introduced many Chinese to a different way of service and living. People began to consider how such food could become so popular worldwide and realized that business strategies incorporating a certain cultural psychology could raise competitiveness, which the Chinese food service industry and business in general needed to acquire.

As more foreign companies opened branches in the country and foreign investments kept on growing, the need for talent and knowledge together with the pursuit of capital gain required a fundamental change in China's old knowledge-production system and traditional values with regard to productivity and wealth. Most notably, the phenomenon of young men and women, dressed in ties and high heels and employed in high-paying multinational companies or foreign enterprises, not only signifies higher income levels and status but also a different sense of social mobility and other changes.

No doubt the adoption of the open-door policy in China stimulated the development of the country's economy as well as reforms of its education system. For example, to increase productivity and improve the quality of products in the late 1980s and 1990s, many state-owned enterprises tried to establish international cooperative programs for technical innovation, and many of them imported technology from abroad. Due to lack of knowledge about using new equipment or machinery, many of these imports were left to rust on the factory grounds. Yet a growing number of joint-venture businesses have resulted in a great demand for skilled and qualified workers. Thousands of young students compete for limited higher education access. These factors are the internal dynamics. The influence of information technology, the speed of knowledge growth, and the need for international cooperation are the external forces behind China's higher educational change.

In such a situation, higher education in China has been under great pressure to respond to the country's need for economic reform in human resources development, new scientific discovery, knowledge production, technical innovation, and the transformation of new knowledge into productivity. Research reveals that in the past 25 years, higher education in China has undergone a series of reforms that can be seen as an active response to the country's economic needs (Min 2004; Ma 2003).

Of these reforms, the primary one involves the expansion of the higher education system. In 1978, China had only 405 higher learning institutions; by 1995, there were more than 1,300 public colleges and universities. This expansion was followed by system diversification, permitting the development of private colleges and universities. In 2004, there were more than 1,405 so-called private colleges and universities, the first of which was established in 1983 in Beijing. At the same time, building comprehensive universities through mergers was another pattern of China's higher education structural change. The rationale of merging universities has been widely discussed. One of the most important purposes of merging is to create a cross-disciplinary research environment for knowledge development as well as to help leading universities build up the capacity for high-quality education. Chinese higher education has experienced tremendous growth in student enrollments. In 1999, a policy for increasing university enrollments by 30 percent was adopted by the central government. Five years later, the student enrollment rate in China reached 18 percent, with 12 million students in colleges and universities. Through those reforms, the missions and roles of leading universities in China have been changed. The leading universities are no longer solely teaching institutions. They have taken up teaching, research, and public services as their ultimate goals for development (Ma 2003).

INDUSTRIALIZING RESEARCH THROUGH UNIVERSITY ENTERPRISES

Given their new missions and roles, the leading universities in China are not only expected to provide more undergraduate education opportunities and offer more master's and PhD degrees but also to produce new knowledge and discoveries and provide more technological innovation for the improvement of the country's industry. It is recognized that in the era of social and economic transition, knowledge and human-capacity building should be taken as the most crucial elements for development, and the best place to accomplish these two important missions should be educational institutions. Thus, at the centennial of Peking University in 1998, Chen Jia'er (1998), president of Peking University, first used the term *engine* to indicate the university's role in China's socioeconomic reform. Traditionally, university research was not judged as important because China's scientific research system had been independent from the universities since the establishment of the Chinese Academy of Sciences in 1952. Universities in China were then mainly teaching institutes; only a few basic research programs existed in key universities.

In 1986, the first national key research laboratory was established at Peking University. This marked the beginning of university research with R&D funding in nationally sponsored laboratories on university campuses and university research as part of the nation's basic scientific research system. The idea of establishing national key laboratories at universities actually came from the model of research universities in the United States. During the late 1980s and early 1990s, the US federal government's financial support of university research influenced the scientific research system reform in China. The most commonly used examples are the Lawrence Berkeley National Laboratory, the Lawrence Livermore National Laboratory, and Los Alamos National Laboratory in the University of California system. While the national key laboratories at Chinese universities are mostly discipline-based, with the goal of creating centers of excellence in related areas of study, their establishment signifies the hope that Chinese universities will eventually have laboratories like those of the University of California.

Based on information provided by the China Education and Research Network, in 2002 there were 91 national key research laboratories at the leading universities. Peking University alone now has 13 such national key laboratories whose research projects are closely linked to the country's most urgent problems in development. In 1986, a famous national scientific research project was established. Because the proposal was made by four well-known scientists in March 1986, it was called the 863 Plan. The plan was intended to pursue advanced research in such areas as information technology, automation, energy, new materials, and biotechnology, among others, by using the country's R&D fund. To administer the fund, the Chinese National Science Foundation was established in 1985 as a sponsoring organization for research in science and technology, both in universities and in the Academy of Sciences.

The establishment of national key laboratories at universities has increased university research capacity. The statistics (Z. Wang 2003) show that in 1998/99, the 9 leading universities awarded 2,465 doctoral degrees; 5,891 research papers were indexed in the Science Citation Index (SCI) in 2000; and in 2002, those 9 universities had 295 key research disciplines. In the same year, university research received 78 percent of national technology invention awards and 49 percent of national technology progress awards. Among the 6,118 patents, 32.4 percent came from the 9 leading universities (Zhao 2003).

In the 1980s, industry in China had limited resources and capacity to absorb new inventions; how to translate university research and inventions into productivity was a major concern of the central government and universities. However, low salaries and lack of funding created difficulties for faculty to continue their research. Instead of having their inventions patented by industry, some faculty members decided to put their inventions directly into production themselves. At Peking University, the Founder Group was started up by Wang Xuan and his colleagues in the Department of Computer Science. With the university's investment, in 1986 they started a company that produced a Chinese computer typesetting system by integrating research findings from mathematics, physics, the Chinese language, and computer science. In two years, the company's product succeeded in entering the market as a high-technology commodity. The company has established a national key laboratory, an engineering research center, a market sales and training program, and a maintenance service center. Its business has extended to Southeast Asia, North America, and Europe. Following Wang's success, many other faculty members in different departments and schools at Peking University have established companies in biomedicine, computer software, and the service industry. By 2005, Peking University had 10 large companies.

Tsinghua University also started university-run high-technology enterprises in the 1980s, the most famous ones being the Tsinghua Unisplendor Group and the Tsinghua Tongfang Co. Ltd. The stories of the high-technology enterprises founded at Tsinghua University are similar to those at Peking University. With some startup funds from the university, a few faculty members in the Computer Science Department established companies that have turned out well. Between 1993 and 1998, the output and profit of the Tsinghua Unisplendor Group and Tsinghua Tongfang Co. Ltd. grew by 290 and 230 percent, respectively (D. Wang 1998).

Why are there are so many university-run enterprises in China and how do they operate? Actually, it is not a new thing for universities in China to run factories or enterprises. In the late 1950s and early 1960s, universities and colleges were asked to open factories as student internship or training bases. Most of the university-run factories were closed during the Cultural Revolution (1966–1976), but the tradition remained. In the late 1980s, it became a common practice for faculty members to use university facilities and research funds to open small enterprises, intending to collect further research funding by transferring their inventions to production directly and also to get some subsidies for their salaries.

At the time, the purpose of such companies was to create a base for scientific research and teaching. Universities were also allowed to collect some money from university enterprises for institutional development. This was stated in a related document jointly issued by the Ministry of Education and the Ministry of Finance. In the 1990s, the central government recognized that establishing university enterprises was the most effective way for universities to transfer their research findings. In order to promote the development of such enterprises, a policy was adopted in 1994 to provide partial tax exemption to university enterprises.

After 20 years of practice and with policy support, China's university enterprises not only helped convert some university inventions into products for the consumer market but also played an important function in advancing China's high-technology industry. The annual profits of the leading university enterprises have kept on growing at a pace of 30 percent. More important, these university enterprises served as extensions of university research and teaching by providing students with internship opportunities. Statistics show that in 1997, about 520,000 students worked or carried out their research in university enterprises. Among them, 1,419 students earned their doctoral degrees and 2,817 students their master's degrees (Ma 2004).

In 2001, the Ministry of Education carried out a project to undertake a full evaluation of the efficiency and effectiveness of university enterprises. The report based on that research, "A Statistical Report of the Country's University Enterprises in 2001," shows that 575 regular higher learning institutions in the country own 5,039 enterprises, among which 993 are high-technology enterprises (40 percent of the total university enterprises). Of the 5,039 enterprises, 4,059 are independently funded by the universities, 718 jointly by the university and the state, and 94 jointly by foreign companies and Chinese universities (Ministry of Education 2001). The sales revenues of these 5,039 enterprises were 60.748 billion RMB yuan (US$7.5 billion)—74.45 percent from high-technology companies. This shows that though the number of high-technology university enterprises is not high, sales revenues are much higher compared with profits of service and other university enterprises.

The report states that in 2001, the total profit of those university enterprises was 4.851 billion RMB yuan (US$600 million). The return of those university enterprises to the university totaled about 1.842 billion RMB yuan (US$230 million), which included salary and administration fees paid to the university administration, faculty, and students. From these figures, one can see that university enterprises, especially those at the leading universities, have already become an important part of the country's economy in promoting the transfer to the market of university research, shortening the time from research to market, and providing some profit to universities.

However, not all university enterprises in China are successful or profitable. Some have become burdens on the universities and some are even on the verge of bankruptcy. Even apparently successful ones like Peking University's Founder Group and Tsinghua University's Unisplendor Group and Tongfang Co. Ltd sometimes have problems with internal management, refinancing, and their relationships with the sponsoring university. Because managing a university differs from managing a business, one cannot expect a good university president to be a good CEO—an increasingly difficult job since running university enterprises becomes more complicated as their businesses keep on expanding and China's market economy diversifies in response to information technology and international competition. Criticism of the commercialization of universities might also have some connection with university enterprises.

LINKAGES WITH INDUSTRY AND THE REGIONAL ECONOMY

Through the activities of university enterprises, some university research findings and innovations have been successfully transferred to production. However, university enterprises do not have the ability to absorb all new inventions and innovations. In response to the urgent need for promotion of knowledge transfer in the 1990s, a new strategy was adopted for universities to develop linkages with both local industry and regional governments.

In the 1990s, the central government and general public focused intently on the role of universities as the primary source for new skills, knowledge, and ideas to boost China's economy. Calls were made for better interaction between universities and industry and integration of university research with economic activities. For example, on March 19, 1998, at the press conference for the first session of the Ninth National People's Congress, Premier Zhu Rongji highlighted the rejuvenation of China through science and education as the major task to be fulfilled by the government. He also announced that the State Science and Technology and Education Directorate would be set up by the central government to promote the link between the two sectors.

On May 4 of the same year, at the centennial of Peking University, President Jiang Zemin proclaimed the policy of building world-class universities, emphasizing the importance of science and education in the country's economic development and of knowledge innovation and talent cultivation to press ahead with economic and social progress at a time featuring a knowledge-based world economy.

The leading universities in China had already begun to link science and education and to connect knowledge with industry and local government. Universities like Tsinghua and Peking had already started developing relationships with industry and regional government for cooperation in technology innovation and knowledge transfer. In 1997, 1,020 colleges and universities spent 7.05 billion RMB yuan (US$0.87 billion) on research (Zhang 1998). Of this 7.05 billion, 75 percent came from industry. In the same year, universities and state-owned industries together organized 2,000 R&D institutes and economic entities. Up to that year, 50,000 university research findings and innovations had been successfully transferred to industry. Universities signed 4,514 contracts with industry and received 618 million RMB yuan (US$75 million) in payment from these contracts.

In order to speed up knowledge transfers, leading universities used different forms to cooperate with industry and local government. Zhang (1998) provided some models of universities' partnerships with industry and local government. The models can be summarized as follows:

> First, the university and the enterprise jointly apply national R&D funding to carry out relevant research. In such cases, inventions and technical innovation go directly to the partner enterprise. Second, the university disseminates research findings by establishing a professional extension center on campus. Such a center should be approved and supervised by related governmental organizations. According to Zhang's research, in 1996, there were a total of 30 professional extension centers in the country, 15 of them were at universities. Third, the university and the enterprise develop a joint research center on campus. In this model, it is the industrial enterprise that provides the research funding and the university provides the facilities. This model of industry and university cooperation is very popular both for universities and enterprises, because what the enterprises need the most are inventions and what universities need is money. Fourth, human resources training for regional development, some provincial or municipal governments create joint R&D funds for universities. In this case, the university provides services, research, and training based on regional need, and the local government provides funds. Fifth, the university invites industry to participate in the university scientific research management—thus the university can better understand industry's needs involving research. Sixth, regional or local governments organize various kinds of trade exhibitions and innovation fairs to exhibit university research findings and to help the university find local contractors from industry and enterprises. (Ma 2004, 187)

These linkages with industry and local government enable university research to become more focused and relevant with regard to industry and local needs. For example, in 1999, Peking University first established the Shenzhen-Hong Kong Institute with the government of Shenzhen and the University of Science and Technology in Hong Kong. The major focus of the institute is to carry out research in such areas as information technology, coastal environment research, and protein and plant genetic engineering, among others. Since then, Peking University has signed contracts with eight provincial and autonomous regional governments in scientific research and education. To better coordinate those joint research and training activities, Peking University opened an office with special focus on knowledge transfer, production, and learning. Similarly, Tsinghua University had established partnerships with 98 well-known national and international enterprises up to 1998. To coordinate those partnership activities, Tsinghua University established a special committee for university and entrepreneurial cooperation. It is unclear how successful the universities' activities are with local government and industries. These developments need further investigation.

UNIVERSITY RESEARCH AND UNIVERSITY SCIENCE PARKS

China's economic growth in the past 25 years was fueled mostly by labor-intensive industries and agricultural produce. Heavy reliance on raw materials for export has become a problem, given the country's limited natural resources. According to the 2000 United Nations Conference on Trade and Development *World Investment Report*, China's high-technology products comprised 0.4 percent of exports in 1985 (United Nations Conference on Trade and Development 2003); in 2000 the proportion rose to 6 percent. From a developmental perspective, this rate of growth may look good; however, compared with the United States and other developed countries, China remains far behind and still has a long way to go. In 1997, a new project, the 973 Plan, was initiated by the Ministry of Science and Technology to focus on basic research in material science, energy, natural resources, agriculture, and other fields. Professors from leading universities were invited to work together with scientists from the Academy of Sciences, with the intention of making a joint effort to solve the most urgent scientific problems.

To establish links in research between universities and the Academy of Sciences, reforms have been undertaken regarding the academy. Some basic research institutes in the academy were transferred to related universities. Indicating the government's ongoing interest in promoting university research and the links between the Academy of Sciences and universities, in the late 1990s most leading university presidents were either nominated by the academy or were academicians from the academy. Xu Zhihong, the current president of Peking University, is an academician of the Academy of Sciences and still holds a position of vice president at the academy.

To combine basic research at universities with the applied side of new knowledge, in 1999 the Chinese government announced a special decision to establish more university science and technology parks, an idea borrowed from the United States. The success of Silicon Valley with high-technology industries was attractive to China, and the direct result was the establishment of Zhongguancun Science Park in Beijing, which is located near the Academy of Sciences, Peking University, and Tsinghua University.

The regulations regarding Zhongguancun Science Park, which were adopted on December 8, 2000, at the 23rd session of the standing committee of the 11th People's Congress of the Beijing municipality, declared that the science park was to serve as an experimental area for comprehensive reforms intended to push ahead with the strategy of developing the country, through science and education, and the market economy. The park is considered to be a national model of scientific and technological innovation and a base for the incubation and dissemination of scientific and technological achievements, the industrialization of new and high technologies, and the training of innovative talents. The regulations also confirm that in this park colleges, universities, and scientific research institutes can jointly set up enterprises and organizations engaged in technological innovations or can jointly undertake research and development activities related to technological innovation projects.

Zhongguancun has been labeled as China's Silicon Valley. By 2001, there were almost 10,000 high-technology enterprises in the park. These enterprises realized a total revenue of 201.42 billion RMB yuan (US$25 billion) from transfer of technology, industry, and trade, with an added value of 45.57 billion RMB yuan (US$5.63 billion). Sales taxes paid to the government amounted to 8.94 billion RMB yuan (US $1.1 billion) (Liu 2002). These figures provide some perspective on the performance of the science park.

Though there are different opinions about the development of Zhongguancun, it has clearly served as a model for other science parks in China. Leading universities in China started to develop science parks as incubators for scientific research, technical innovations, and knowledge transfer. In 1990, the first university science park was established at Northeast University, in Liaoning Province, followed by parks at Tsinghua University, Peking University, Fudan University, Shanghai Jiao Tong University, Wuhan University of Science and Technology, Yanshan University, and Xi'an Jiao Tong University. In 2000, the Chinese government made a decision to confirm the contribution of university science parks to the development of the country's economy and to include university science parks in the national scientific research system. In the same year, the Ministry of Science and

Technology and the Ministry of Education jointly decided to build more national university science parks.

According to information provided by China's University Technology Transfers Web site, by 2004 there were 44 university science parks affiliated with 104 universities. By October 2002, university science parks, with 1,200 R&D institutes and 5,500 enterprises, had already attracted 29.7 billion RMB yuan (US$3.4 billion) in investments. In the parks, 920 enterprises had been incubated, and 29 of them were already on the stock market; 4,116 new products had been invented. Currently, 1,300 overseas enterprises have started operating in university science parks, and 2,300 enterprises are under incubation. So far, university science parks have created 100,000 job opportunities.

These figures offer some impressions about what has been achieved by the university science parks. But since the parks are a relatively new phenomenon at Chinese universities and many are still under development, it is hard to evaluate whether they are fully successful. Furthermore, an official report tends to present only successful examples and things that have been achieved. Actually, in this developmental stage, universities might face many challenges, which will require further research.

While most university science parks consist of elegant buildings with highly commercialized businesses adjacent to university campuses, one really has to think carefully where these leading universities are heading and how education on campuses will be affected.

STRATEGIES FOR FACULTY RETENTION AND RECRUITMENT

This chapter has focused thus far on policies and strategies of the leading universities on scientific research and knowledge transfer. Of course, there is an urgent need for scientists and highly qualified professors to carry out the activities. As mentioned earlier, since the late 1980s, the leading universities in China suffered most from the "tide of overseas study" because young faculty and students from the top universities were more likely to get scholarships and financial awards abroad. For example, in the 1990s, Peking University was described as a "preparatory school" for overseas study because one-third of its graduates went on to study in the United States or other developed countries. After their graduation from foreign institutions, these overseas students, especially those who majored in science and engineering, were more likely to find jobs in the countries where they got their final degrees rather than returning to China. From 1978 to 2004, a total of 815,000 Chinese students studied overseas, but only

198,000 of them returned; thus, the return rate is about one-quarter.

To help retain and recruit qualified faculty, in 1992 a policy for overseas students was adopted to support study abroad, encourage students to return, and guarantee freedom for those who might want to leave again. In 1993, the Ministry of Education established a project called the Plan for Cross-Century Talent with Extraordinary Ability. This project targeted the retention of faculty members who were more likely to leave their current posts for better pay in other sectors. Faculty selected in this plan would receive special subsidies from the government and be promoted as full professors. Overseas students were thus shown they would enjoy the same advantages if they chose to return, but the return rate remained low. While there are many reasons students and faculty want to stay abroad, the more important ones include uncertainty about the country's political stability, lack of knowledge about career development opportunities, the change in lifestyle after several years of living abroad, and concern about their children's education.

In the late 1990s, leading universities in China faced serious problems with faculty retention and recruitment. The shortage of qualified scientists and professors had resulted in overloading faculty with teaching and research responsibility. Cases of overburdened faculty who died at the peak of their academic careers caught the attention of the general public as well as that of policymakers and university administrators. It was then recognized that there was an urgent need to improve faculty economic as well as social status in general instead of the status of a privileged few. So with the help of the 985 Project, the leading universities could use some funds to increase faculty salaries.

In conjunction with the 985 Project, the Changjiang Scholar Award Plan was initiated in 1998. The Changjiang Scholar professors will receive an annual bonus of 100,000 RMB yuan (US$12,500), other bonuses from the universities and schools, and allowances from their research funds. The plan was largely oriented toward professors who studied abroad in fields of science and engineering. For instance, as of 2005 China University of Science and Technology had invited 14 Chinese scholars in the field of science back to work over the previous three years with the support of the plan. Similarly, in 2003, there were 57 Changjiang Scholars at Peking University—all of them in science and engineering. While since 2004 the social sciences and humanities are included in the plan, only a few professors have been selected—for example, two professors in the social sciences and humanities at Peking University.

The program is selective and only well-established scholars and recognized professors are likely to be invited. It shows the Chinese government's determination to get the best scientists abroad back for scientific research. Besides the Changjiang Scholar Award Plan, there are many other programs that enable overseas Chinese scholars to teach or carry out research at leading universities in China. One of them is the Chunhui Plan, also established in the late 1990s, for overseas Chinese scientists who may not choose to come back permanently but only for short-term visits. Interested scholars can use summers or sabbatical leaves to teach or carry out research on Chinese campuses either independently or cooperatively with faculty at Chinese universities. Changjiang Scholars are also given the flexibility or freedom to go back and forth in connection with their work abroad, increasing their involvement with the most advanced knowledge in the developed countries.

In addition to the efforts made to invite overseas Chinese scholars to return, there are also some programs for foreign scientists to conduct research or teach at the leading universities in China. These universities have been permitted to invite foreign scientists or experts to teach and carry out research with the provision of funds from the National Foreign Expert Bureau. This policy has been working so effectively that every year at Peking University around 600 scholars are invited to carry out research or teach on campus.

With all of these efforts, most leading professors at top universities either hold foreign degrees or have had some foreign educational experience; some of them have already become internationally recognized scientists. But the trends raise fundamental questions regarding the intellectual and academic development of the leading universities in China. Will the universities remain focused on science or seek a balanced development of science, social sciences, and the humanities? Thus far, most of the professors recruited are in scientific fields.

Faculty salaries are differentiated by the overall priorities and strategies. There are major variations in salaries and income in applied science, professional schools, the humanities, and social sciences. Faculty in the humanities and social sciences obtain fewer research grants, are paid less, and have less chance for promotions as well. These disparities indicate that the leading universities in China need to create a more balanced faculty development, recruit famous social scientists and natural scientists worldwide, and provide social scientists equal benefits and chances for promotion. Failing to address these issues will hurt the overall development of leading universities in the long run.

BRIDGING THE WORLD WITH EDUCATION AND RESEARCH

After nearly 30 years of isolation from the rest of the world, since the 1980s, China has invested great efforts to join the World Trade Organization (WTO) and to become part of the world economy. Though ordinary people did not seem to pay much attention at the start and during the long process of negotiations, right after China joined the WTO in November 2001 concerns rose over how WTO membership would affect the country and people's lives. What is the government's obligation once foreign investors want to open a university in China? What will be the effect on China's higher education system since most of the foreign investors would be much more competitive than their Chinese counterparts financially and technologically? The discussion has been so overwhelming that some scholars have even warned that "the wolves are coming."

The wolves are not only coming but are also actually taking part in the process. Just about a year after China joined the WTO, many foreign banks, supermarkets, construction firms, and other businesses opened branches in China. While profit seeking is the nature of business, there are many positive effects of foreign investments, such as bringing in some advanced technology, offering more job opportunities, and diversifying the domestic consumer markets. In education, there have been many exhibitions organized by foreign embassies and international education collaborations in different parts of the country. Many intermediary organizations were established to introduce students to study abroad while charging high fees.

At the same time, China's fast-growing economy has become attractive to foreign higher education institutions. According to the statistics provided by the Ministry of Education, by the end of 2002 there were already 712 foreign-related educational institutions in China. Many other foreign institutions are now seeking to develop joint training programs, establish research centers, and build campus extensions with related organizations in China. These developments are the direct results of China's economic globalization.

Yet globalization does not mean equalization. Countries participating in the process of globalization do not have the same economic, cultural, and social backgrounds. In the world of increased competition the have-nots would be greatly restricted from even participating in the process. Between the haves and have-nots, there is going to be an imbalance in development. Recently, two terms are frequently used in the public media and other publications to express the attitude and feelings of the Chinese people toward economic globalization: *jie-gui*, which means "to be in line with" or "to be connected with," and *shuang-ying*, which means "to be mutually beneficial" or "to create a win-win situation." However, keeping in line with the rest of the world and creating a win-win situation without sacrificing China's economic growth are real challenges to decision makers in China, as illustrated by current trade negotiations with the European Union and the United States on China's textile products.

In this context, it was announced that by 2005 universities would be required to offer 15 percent of their undergraduate courses in English. This policy choice was not undertaken for the sake of language itself but to prepare future leaders who would think with a global perspective and be able to work internationally without language and culture barriers. For leading universities, this decision meant much more than just teaching a course in English. The range of responsibility included creating a new curriculum, providing highly advanced knowledge to students, developing joint teaching and research programs with foreign universities, disseminating information on the achievements of China's economic reforms through academic exchange, and meeting the global need for education in China. In other words, the leading universities are expected to bridge the world with knowledge in scientific research, culture exchange, and communication.

Peking University has established a joint program with the University of California (UC), in which students from Peking University will have classes with UC students on the Peking campus. In September 2004, Stanford University opened a branch at Peking University. Other programs, such as the Peking-Waseda Joint Teaching Center and London Summer School, are already in place. Some of the programs are funded with outside resources, and some require students to pay fees. Peking University has established research and teaching relationships with more than 200 universities in 49 countries—57 universities in Asia, 69 universities in Europe, 46 universities in America, 4 universities in Africa, and 8 universities in Oceania. Besides the relationships with foreign universities, Peking University has established links with international organizations, such as the World Bank, OECD, and United Nations Educational, Scientific and Cultural Organization (UNESCO), to carry out and develop training programs. Similarly, Tsinghua University has established research and teaching relationship with 150 universities worldwide. It also has developed cooperative research agreements with some well-known foreign enterprises worldwide. Through those relationships and agreements, faculty are encouraged to engage in the process: to teach, offer lectures, and organize seminars worldwide.

All of these programs and activities are transnational in nature. These transnational activities take four different forms: (1) expanding foreign student enrollments and research exchange programs; (2) increasing faculty visits and exchange activities with foreign universities; (3) establishing joint R&D centers or joint research projects with foreign enterprises and universities; and (4) working with international organizations to address common issues, such as environmental protection and energy shortages (Ma 2005).

In order to become integrated with the rest of the world in higher education, leading universities in China have been actively participating in regional and international university associations. In the past decade, Peking University has become a member of university associations in Asia, the Pacific Rim, and other regions. All of these developments represent important measures taken by leading universities to link China and the world in terms of knowledge and education.

CONCLUSION

In the process of China's economic reform, the leading universities have been instrumental in meeting the country's need to adjust and readjust the economy. The driving forces for the adjustment and readjustment are multiple, but the key elements in stimulating the changes are national educational and scientific policies. For further development of the leading universities, policy consistency and ongoing financial support from the central government are crucial factors. People have gradually realized that building research universities, especially world-class ones, is expensive. Whether China's economy is able to support the development of such universities has been questioned, and the recent change in the financing of leading universities reveals signs of doubt and hesitation. Thus, to sustain current development, leading universities in China have to look for new opportunities and learn to be self-sufficient.

Over nearly 30 years of reform, China's economy has gradually changed from a labor-intensive to a knowledge-based one. This change requires the leading universities to focus on more complicated knowledge creation, rather than simple technology transfers by establishing enterprises and companies. Past experiences have proved that universities, even leading ones, have no such ability to run businesses, and the overall returns to the universities from university enterprises or companies are actually limited. So for future development, leading universities have to give up the idea of establishing companies or enterprises or heavily involving themselves in science parks and instead focus on basic research, because only basic research can provide new ideas and insights for knowledge innovation. Leading universities in China have already built up the capacity for basic research with national key laboratories, and what is needed is to make full use of their capacities.

In describing the role of the leading universities in China's economic development, the term *locomotive* or *engine* has been used as a metaphor. While universities have a responsibility for scientific research and knowledge transfer, they should distinguish themselves from research institutes because they also have other responsibilities. Embodying and integrating national cultural heritages, denouncing social injustices and supporting a harmonious society, and developing socially responsible and committed students are all parts of the mission of education institutions, especially for the leading universities. Furthermore, modern knowledge creation is a complicated process, and sometimes faculty members from science have to work with colleagues from the social sciences and humanities for new ideas and insights. The current practice of overemphasizing the importance of science has already downplayed the importance of the social sciences and humanities. Consequently, unequal distribution of resources, limited access to higher education for the rural poor, disparity in regional development, lack of employment opportunities, and an increase in social crimes may lead to social instability. The leading universities have the responsibility to address these issues with the expert knowledge from the social sciences and humanities. It requires leading universities in China to reconsider their development policy in academic planning.

In research universities in the United States, how to claim preeminence in scientific research with teaching excellence has been a longtime debate. The debate has been focused on a proper balance between the demands of research and demands of teaching in faculty evaluation. In China, the leading universities face the same dilemma: "publish or perish" is a familiar phrase, but overemphasizing research and knowledge production has already resulted in student complaints of being neglected by the faculty. The recent rise in student suicide rates at leading universities might indicate that something is missing. It is high time for the leading universities in China to balance their multifaceted roles for the well-being of students, because it is the students who are the future resources for sustainable social and economic growth.

In discussing the many functions of the modern university in the United States, Clark Kerr used the term *multiversity* and the term can also be applied to the leading universities in China. How to balance those multiple functions is more than a matter of university development; it concerns social well-being as well. It is therefore of crucial importance that the leading universities in China carefully reconsider their missions and functions when they are besieged by different social, political, and economic demands.

REFERENCES

Central Committee of the Communist Party and the State Council of the People's Republic of China. 1993. Outline for education reform and development in China. Beijing: State Council.

Chen, Jia'er. 1998. Mission and role of the university in an information society. In *The university of the 21st century: Proceedings of the forum of higher education in conjunction with the centennial of Peking University May 2–4, 1998*, ed. Xin Wei and Wanhua Ma, 11–16. Beijing: Peking Univ. Press.

Ding, Xueliang. 2004. *What is a world-class university?* Beijing: Peking Univ. Press.

Hawkins, John N. 2000. Centralization, decentralization, recentralization: Educational reform in China. *Journal of Educational Administration* 38 (5):442–54.

Liu, Zhihua. 2002. Zhongguancun—the most dynamic regional technological innovation base. A survey of achievements scored in three-year construction of Zhongguancun Science Park. www.zgc.gov.cn/cms/template /item_english.html.

Ma, Wanhua. 2003. Economic reform and higher education in China. Higher Education Series, CIDE Occasional Paper no. 2.

———. 2004. *From Berkeley to Beida and Tsinghua: The building of public research universities in China and the United States* [in Chinese]. Beijing: Educational Science Press.

———. 2005. Transnational education: More than a new tendency for higher education internationalization [in Chinese]. *Higher Education in China* no. 21:23–24.

Min, Weifang. 2004. Chinese higher education: The legacy of the past and the context of the future. In *Asian universities: Historical perspectives and contemporary challenges*, ed. P. Altbach and T. Umakoshi, 53–83. Baltimore: Johns Hopkins Univ. Press.

Ministry of Education. 2001. A statistical report of the country's university enterprises in 2001 [in Chinese]. www.edu.cn/20020809/3063829.shtml.

———. 2004. The action plan for education revitalization between 2003–2007. Beijing: Ministry of Education, People's Republic of China.

United Nations Conference on Trade and Development (UNCTAD). 2003. *World report 2000: Cross-border mergers and acquisitions and development*. New York: UNCTAD.

Wang, Dazhong. 1998. Toward a new partnership between universities and society in a global knowledge economy [in Chinese]. In *The university of the 21st century: Proceedings of the forum of higher education in conjunction with the centennial of Peking University, May 2–4, 1998*, ed. Wei Xin and Wanhua Ma, 173–78. Beijing: Peking Univ. Press.

Wang, Zhanjun. 2003. Why should we build research universities? [in Chinese] *Degree and Graduate Education* 2:10–13.

Zhang, Xumei. 1998. Current situation and future development for university and industry relations in China [in Chinese]. Paper presented at the conference on university linkage with industry in Asia and the Pacific. Kunming, China.

Zhao, Xinping. 2003. To explore the Chinese way of building research universities [in Chinese]. China's Higher Education nos. 15–16:4–5.

3
Research Universities in China

Differentiation, Classification, and Future World-Class Status

Nian Cai Liu

Chinese higher education has undergone rapid developments since the 1980s. By the 1990s, the research university had become a popular topic in China, and hundreds of articles on the phenomenon have been published. Although no clear definition and classification criteria exist for research universities in China, these universities have been differentiated from others through government policies and university rankings. Strengthening the concept and quality of the Chinese research university will require the establishment of classification criteria.

Building world-class universities has been the dream of generations of Chinese. This chapter discusses the gap between top Chinese research universities and world-class universities, the major challenges that top Chinese research universities face, and the time frame within which the top Chinese research universities could become world-class universities. Unless otherwise noted, the chapter concentrates on mainland China.

OVERVIEW OF CHINESE HIGHER EDUCATION

Undergraduate Education

Higher education in China has experienced rapid developments since the 1980s, particularly since the late 1990s. China now has more than 1,700 universities and colleges, about 38 percent of which award bachelor's degrees. The total number of undergraduate admissions in 2004 was over fourfold that of 1998. The total number of students in Chinese higher education reached 20 million in 2004, making the system the largest in the world. Undergraduate admissions increased by another 8 percent in 2005 (Ministry of Education 2005).

Private higher education in China has especially experienced rapid growth. The number of students enrolled at private higher education institutions reached 1.4 million in 2004, about 10 percent of the national total (Ministry of Education 2005). Almost all private higher education institutions provide undergraduate education; most award only undergraduate certificates and lack the power to grant bachelor's degrees.

Graduate Education

Graduate education in China was started in 1981. The total number of doctoral degrees awarded increased from 19 in 1983 to 18,625 in 2003. More than 90 percent of doctoral degrees are awarded by universities and colleges and less than 10 percent by independent research institutes, such as the Chinese Academy of Sciences. The number of doctoral degrees awarded in various fields from 1983 to 2003 are listed in table 3.1. About one-third of all doctoral degrees are awarded in engineering. Rapid increases in the total number of doctoral degrees are anticipated since the number of admissions to doctoral programs has been experiencing major increases. In 2005 the number of students admitted to doctoral programs was 54,000 (Ministry of Education 2005).

Table 3.1 Doctoral Degrees Awarded in China, 1983–2003

Doctoral Degrees	1983	1988	1993	1998	2003
Philosophy, history, and literature	2	156	121	546	1,580
Social sciences (including law and management)	0	93	171	800	3,094
Science fields	12	510	584	2,246	3,580
Engineering	4	704	756	3,250	6,242
Medicine	1	157	406	1,240	3,073
Agriculture	0	62	76	416	742
Other fields	0	0	0	20	314
Total	19	1,682	2,114	8,518	18,625

Source: Ministry of Education. 2004. www.moe.edu.cn/edoas/website18/siju_xuewei.jsp.

The first professional degree offered in China, the master of business administration (MBA), was started in 1990. In the past 15 years, 20 types of professional master's degrees have been developed. The degree programs with enrollments of more than 1,000 include those in engineering, business administration, education, law, public administration, agriculture extension, and medicine.

Graduate education has always been closely related to research. Graduate students in China are playing significant roles in research. For example, more than half of the first authors of cited articles from Shanghai Jiao Tong University are graduate students (Shanghai Jiao Tong University 2004). The situation is similar at the top Chinese universities.

Research as a Major Function

In the 1950s, China adopted the Soviet model of establishing independent research institutes outside universities, including the Chinese Academy of Sciences, the Chinese Academy of Social Sciences, and the Chinese Academy of Agricultural Sciences, among others. These academies have several hundred research institutes, covering all the major disciplines. Until the 1980s, most research activities in China were carried out at these independent research institutes; the focus of Chinese universities was on teaching.

The establishment of the National Natural Science Foundation of China in 1986 offered Chinese universities the opportunity to compete for research funding. The founding of many research initiatives by the Ministry of Science and Technology and other Chinese government ministries in the 1980s and 1990s also provided Chinese universities major opportunities. At the same time, Chinese universities have been paying more attention to research, which has become a major function of many top Chinese universities.

Chinese universities publish about three-quarters of the articles indexed in the Science Citation Index Expanded (SCIE), the Social Science Citation Index (SSCI), and the Engineering Index (EI). Chinese universities have about two-thirds of all the "state key laboratories" (China's top-quality research centers). More than half the National Awards of Natural Sciences are won by universities.

Professors at the top Chinese research universities spend more time on research than on teaching. A significant proportion of full professors and associate professors do not teach any undergraduate courses. In order to improve undergraduate education, the Ministry of Education issued a directive in 2003, stating that full professors and associate professors must teach undergraduate courses. In addition, the percentage of professors teaching undergraduate courses has been selected as a major indicator in the national evaluation of the quality of undergraduate education in Chinese universities.

University Funding

In 1993, the central government of China set the goal of educational spending as 4 percent of gross domestic product (GDP). Nevertheless, the percentage of educational spending has stagnated at about 3.3 percent in the past few years (Ministry of Education 2005). However, the actual amount of educational funding has been increasing significantly with the rapidly growing GDP in China. For a few years following 2005, increases in educational spending, as a result of the rise in GDP, will be mainly used to improve primary and secondary education, particularly in the countryside.

There are about 100 national universities in China, which are funded by the central government. The rest of the public universities are funded by provincial governments. Both the central and provincial governments allocate their regular educational funding to universities based mainly on the number of students. Per capita funding standards differ for undergraduate and graduate students. However, there is no difference between research universities and other universities. In addition, universities can apply for infrastructure funding from governments for specific projects.

There are many special initiatives for universities in China, such as the well-known 211 Project and 985 Project. Most of the initiatives are aimed at top universities to improve their research capability; most of their funding is spent on research-related activities. Most of the initiatives allocate funding to universities by block grants based mainly on the strategic plans of universities. In most cases, the central and provincial governments negotiate so as to share responsibilities.

In the mid-1990s, the central government set up a plan of building 100 universities by the early 21st century—the 211 Project. At the 100th anniversary of Peking University (May 1998), the president of China declared that the country should have several world-class universities—the 985 Project. The total funding for the 34 universities in phase one of the 985 Project was 28.3 billion yuan (US$3.4 billion) for a period of three years, between 1999 and 2001—more than 50 percent of which came from the central government. Unfortunately, the level of support was significantly lower in the second phase of the 985 Project.

Chinese universities compete for research funding from various funding agencies. Between 2001 and 2005, the total R&D funding of all Chinese universitics more than doubled and is continuing to increase at similar rate. The R&D funding of universities as a percentage of the total national R&D funding is also increasing steadily. For example, universities obtain about three-quarters of research grants from the National Natural Science Foundation of China.

Major Reforms in Chinese Higher Education

China followed the Soviet model of specialized universities in the 1950s. Since most world-class universities are comprehensive and have a wide range of disciplines, the Chinese government has been restructuring its higher education institutions in an effort to improve their efficiency and build world-class universities. Since 1992, more than 200 specialized institutions have been merged into comprehensive or multidisciplinary universities. During the restructuring process, almost every leading research university acquired a top medical university or other specialized universities. For example, Beijing Medical University has been merged into Peking University, and the Central University of Fine Arts has been merged into Tsinghua University.

THE DIFFERENTIATION OF CHINESE UNIVERSITIES

Government Policy

There have been "national key universities" since the early period of the People's Republic of China. Six universities were named national key universities by the central government in 1954, an additional 16 and 44 universities were named in 1959 and 1960, respectively, and another 4 universities were added to the list in 1963. After the Cultural Revolution, national key universities were renamed; more universities were added to the list, and there were 96 national universities in 1981. Preferential financial treatment was given to these national key universities.

Since 1984, 10 universities have been given additional financial support by means of the National Key Project: Peking University, Tsinghua University, Fudan University, Shanghai Jiao Tong University, Xi'an Jiao Tong University, University of Science and Technology of China, Beijing Medical University, Remin University, Beijing Normal University, and Agriculture

University of China. In the late 1980s, 416 national key programs at 107 universities were selected and given additional financial support as part of the National Key Project.

There are about 100 universities involved in the 211 Project, while only 38 universities obtain funding from the 985 Project. Tsinghua University, Peking University, Zhejiang University, Fudan University, Shanghai Jiao Tong University, Nanjing University, University of Science and Technology of China, Xi'an Jiao Tong University, and Harbin Institute of Technology are the top 9 universities with the strongest support from the 985 Project.

In addition to the differentiation by financial policies, differentiation also occurs through academic policies, the most influential one of which is the graduate school policy. So far, 53 universities (among the more than 400 universities offering graduate programs) have been approved to receive the status of a graduate school by the central government; other universities are not allowed to use the name of *graduate school* (*graduate division* or *graduate section* is used instead). Only universities with a reasonably large enrollment of graduate students, a relatively wide range of graduate programs, and high-quality graduate education can receive approval to have the status of graduate school. In fact, more than three-quarters of all doctoral students are enrolled at universities with graduate school status. Being recognized as a graduate school not only enhances the status and reputation of a university but also results in more power and flexibility to establish new programs and curricula.

A surprising aspect of the system, to most Westerners, is that the leaders of Chinese universities acquire civil service ranks. The president of a university offering baccalaureate education receives the departmental rank, which is equivalent to the level of a departmental director in a ministry of the central government. Recently, the presidents of 31 universities were given the vice ministerial rank by the central government, which is equivalent to the level of vice ministers in the central government. The civil service ranks do not have much influence on the 31 universities, however.

University Rankings

Since the mid-1990s, university rankings in China have become a popular phenomenon. There are five influential ranking programs, four of which are institutional rankings. The rankings are widely used by students and their parents as important sources of information. Universities and governments are also paying attention to the rankings. Although there are many problems with the university rankings in China, particularly concerning the availability and reliability of data, they do offer rough ideas on the standing of each institution.

Table 3.2 shows the average ranks of top Chinese universities by the 4 major rankings in 2004. All of the top 20 universities are supported by the 985 Project. Seven of the top 9 universities in the 985 Project, which are located in the more developed regions of China, are ranked among the top 9. The 2 exceptions are Xi'an Jiao Tong University in the western part of China and the Harbin Institute of Technology in the northeastern part of China; both are suffering brain drain due to unfavorable locations.

Table 3.2 The Top 20 Chinese Universities, 2004

Rank	Institution	Location	Average Ranks
1	Tsinghua Univ.	Beijing	1.3
2	Peking Univ.	Beijing	1.8
3	Fudan Univ.	Shanghai	3.5
4	Zhejiang Univ.	Hangzhou, Zhejiang	4.0
5	Nanjing Univ.	Nanjing, Jiangsu	4.8
6	Shanghai Jiao Tong Univ.	Shanghai	7.0
7	Wuhan Univ.	Wuhan, Hubei	8.8
8	Univ. of Science and Tech. of China	Hefei, Anhui	9.5
9	Huazhong Univ. of Science and Technology	Wuhan, Hubei	10.3
10	Zhongshan Univ.	Guangzhou, Guangdong	11.8
11	Xi'an Jiao Tong Univ.	Xi'an, Shanxi	12.3
12	Nankai Univ.	Tianjin	12.5
13	Jilin Univ.	Changchun, Jilin	13.3
14	Harbin Institute of Technology	Harbin, Heilongjiang	14.0
15	Sichuan Univ.	Chengdu, Sichuan	15.0
16	Beijing Normal Univ.	Beijing	15.8
17	Renmin Univ.	Beijing	16.3
18	Tianjin Univ.	Tianjin	18.3
19	Tongji Univ.	Shanghai	19.5
20	Shandong Univ.	Jinan, Shandong	19.5

Source: The rankings are the results of four major 2004 university rankings in China. Their sources are: NETBIG.com (China) Ltd., http://rank2004.netbig.com/; Guangdong Institute of Management Science, *Ke Xue Xue Yu Ke Xue Ji Shu Guan Li* (1):61–68; Research Center for China Science Evaluation, rccse.whu.edu.cn; China Universities Alumni Association, www.cuaa.net.

Characteristics and Indicators of Top Research Universities

The top 9 universities in the first group involved in the 985 Project account for 42.1 percent of articles indexed in SCIE and SSCI, 47.3 percent of the state key laboratories, and 20.2 percent of the research income. The 53 universities with approved graduate school status account for 73.8 percent of articles indexed in SCIE and SSCI, 92.0 percent of the state key laboratories, and 60.0 percent of the research income of all higher education institutions.

The top 9 universities in the first group in the 985 Project account for 20.0 percent of enrolled doctoral students, 10.1 percent of the enrolled master's students, and 30.6 percent of the national key programs. The 53 universities with approved graduate school status account for 78.0 percent of enrolled doctoral students, 55.4 percent of the enrolled master's students, and 75.2 percent of the national key programs. The number of graduate students has been controlled by the central government, which approves the annual admissions plans of each university. After the rapid increase in the number of graduate students in the early 21st century, relatively strict control on increases in graduate admissions continues to be set by the central government.

The top 9 universities in the first 985 Project group account for 41.5 percent of the academicians in the Chinese Academy of Sciences and the Chinese Academy of Engineering (these organizations are equivalent to the National Academy of Sciences and National Academy of Engineering in the United States). The proportion of faculty members with doctoral degrees at the top 9 universities is now close to 50 percent. Since the top 9 universities require that all their new faculty members have doctoral degrees, the proportion of faculty members with doctoral degrees is expected to reach 90 percent in 10 years.

THE CLASSIFICATION OF HIGHER EDUCATION INSTITUTIONS

The classification of Chinese higher education institutions attracts extensive attention from governments, higher education institutions, and the academic community. Several dozen papers on the theoretical aspect of the subject have also been published, including several scenarios of the arrangement. However, as of 2006, no practical standards have been established (Ma 2004).

The Carnegie classification of higher education institutions in the United States has long been well known throughout the world. It classifies higher education institutions by the characteristics of institutions and the number or percentage of degrees awarded. For example, its 2000 edition defines "research/doctoral-extensive" universities as those awarding 50 or more doctoral degrees per year across at least 15 disciplines.

Amano (Amano and Chen 2004) once divided Japanese universities into five types, including research universities, doctorate-granting universities I, doctorate-granting universities II, master's degree–granting universities, and colleges. A major characteristic of research universities is that the ratio between doctoral students and baccalaureate students is higher than 9 percent and 6 percent for public universities and private universities, respectively.

Classification Criteria

By considering the criteria of the Carnegie classification in the United States and Amano's classification in Japan, as well as the Chinese reality, four criteria were selected to classify Chinese higher education institutions. The criteria included the total number of degrees awarded at various levels, the ratio between doctoral and baccalaureate students, annual research income from governments, and per capita articles indexed in the SCIE and SSCI. Chinese higher education institutions are then classified into nine categories, including research universities I, research universities II, doctoral universities I, doctoral universities II, master's universities I, master's universities II, baccalaureate colleges I, baccalaureate colleges II, and associate colleges (Liu and Liu 2005).

The criterion of per capita articles indexed in the SCIE and SSCI was introduced to reflect the growing phenomenon of international competition and put Chinese research universities in the international context. The lowest number of per capita articles indexed in SCIE and SSCI among the 60 US members of the Association of American Universities was chosen as the standard in China, which in 2004 was determined to be 0.7. There are only 10 Chinese universities with a number of per capita articles above the US minimum rate.

Research universities I. These institutions offer a wide range of baccalaureate programs. They are committed to graduate education through the doctorate, emphasize fundamental research, and are able to compete for government research funding.

Research universities II. These institutions offer a wide range of baccalaureate programs, are committed to graduate education through the doctorate, and able to compete for government research funding.

Doctoral universities I. These institutions offer a wide range of baccalaureate programs, are committed to graduate education through the doctorate, and consider research an important function. Seventy or more doctoral degrees are awarded in a year.

Doctoral universities II. These institutions offer a wide range of baccalaureate programs, are committed to graduate education through the doctorate, and consider research to be an important function. Less than 70 doctoral degrees are awarded in a year.

The Results of Classification

The distribution of Chinese higher education institutions, according to the above classification criteria, is shown in table 3.3. Research universities I include Tsinghua University, Peking University, Science and Technology University of China, Nanjing University, Fudan University, Zhejiang University, and Shanghai Jiao Tong University—accounting for a small portion of the total number of institutions.

Table 3.4 shows the average student admissions of Chinese universities in 2004. The average number of doctoral students admitted to research universities I and research universities II is 1,104 and 553, respectively—much higher than that of research universities in major developed countries. On the other hand, the average research income of research universities I and II is only 289 million yuan (US$35 million), which is much less than the levels at the top research universities in developed countries.

Table 3.3 Distribution of Chinese Higher Education Institutions, 2004

Institutions	Category	Number	Percentage
Research universities	I	7	0.4
	II	48	2.8
Doctoral universities	I	74	4.3
	II	116	6.8
Master's universities	I	83	4.9
	II	126	7.4
Baccalaureate colleges	I and II	201	11.8
Associate colleges		1,047	61.5
Total		1,702	100

Source: Liu and Liu (2005).

Table 3.4 Average Number of Students Admitted, 2004

Institutions	Category	Doctoral Students	Master's Students	Bachelor's Students
Research universities	I	1,104	2,819	3,600
	II	553	2,166	4,200
Doctoral universities	I	132	896	4,000
	II	27	380	3,200
Master's universities	I	n.a.	237	3,300
	II	n.a.	69	2,300
Baccalaureate colleges	I and II	n.a.	n.a.	2,000

Source: Liu and Liu (2005).
Note: n.a. = not applicable.

BUILDING OF WORLD-CLASS UNIVERSITIES IN CHINA

The building of world-class universities has been the dream of generations of Chinese, including politicians, university administrators, staff, students, and the ordinary public. As mentioned earlier in this chapter, the Chinese government started the 985 Project to build several world-class universities. The amount of support from the 985 Project for the top nine research universities is significantly greater than their regular government educational funding. Recently, government officials expressed the explicit hope of transforming several Chinese research universities into world-class universities by 2020.

Several dozen Chinese universities have established strategic goals of becoming world-class universities or world-renowned universities. For example, Tsinghua University and Peking University are committed to becoming world-class universities by 2020 and 2016, respectively. Unfortunately, there is no universal standard for world-class universities. It is unclear to most Chinese universities what constitutes a world-class university and what has to be done to become one.

The Top Chinese Research Universities versus World-Class Universities

To discover the gap between Chinese universities and world-class universities, the Institute of Higher Education at Shanghai Jiao Tong University has ranked research universities in the world by their academic or research performance, based on internationally comparable data that everyone could verify. Only eight Chinese universities are ranked in the top 500 of world universities. The best position of Chinese universities is in the range of 151 to 200 (Institute of Higher Education 2005). The Shanghai Jiao Tong University ranking group defined "world-class universities" as the top 100 in the world.

The main distinction between top Chinese research universities and world-class universities is the quality of faculty and research, indicated by the number of faculty winning major international scientific prizes, highly cited researchers in major academic fields, faculty members having doctoral degrees from world-class universities, and citations of published articles, among other factors.

World-class universities have an average of 4.4 faculty members winning Nobel Prizes and Fields Medals and an average of 56 highly cited researchers in major academic fields, whereas no Chinese universities have any faculty members winning Nobel Prizes or Fields Medals and lack any highly cited researchers in the major academic fields (Liu, Cheng, and Liu 2005).

More than 85 percent of the faculty members at world-class universities have doctoral degrees from the top 100 universities in the world, as compared to only about 10 percent of faculty at top Chinese research universities, such as Tsinghua University and Peking University (Jiang 2004). The average citations per article in the Science Citation Index (SCI) are between 2 and 3 for top Chinese research universities such as Tsinghua University and Peking University, as compared to about 25 for Harvard University (China Institute for Science and Technology Information 2005).

Although financial support for top Chinese research universities has increased significantly since 1999, their annual budgets are still much smaller than those of world-class universities. Top Chinese research universities do not have the financial strength to attract world-class professors. In addition to the gap in academic performance and financial resources, top Chinese research universities also lag behind world-class universities in nonacademic matters such as university management and academic culture.

The Main Challenges

Government control over Chinese universities has declined. However, Chinese governments have retained their strong influence through resource allocation, program approval, project evaluation, campus visits, and numerous meetings. There is still a long way to go before Chinese universities gain the desired extent of autonomy. Since the capability of technology innovation in Chinese industries is weak, Chinese governments encourage research universities to serve the economic development of the nation. The majority of research undertaken at Chinese universities is applied and a significant proportion involves industrial development. Basic research is still a luxury for Chinese research universities.

Only a small percentage of university professors are conducting research for purely academic interests. Most of them are teaching and doing research as a way of making a living. The quality of faculty, promotion criteria, and evaluation procedures are far from desirable for the building of world-class universities. Radical reforms are essential.

The competition of the Chinese Academy of Sciences with universities is becoming stronger. The academy has been granted the power of awarding graduate degrees, and its goal is to reach 50,000 graduate enrollments by 2010. Furthermore, it has obtained extra financial support from the central government in addition to its regular funding. Therefore, its capacity to compete for major research grants and fulfill the needs of the country will grow.

Although the top Chinese research universities are seeking to become world-class universities, they are paying more attention to national rather than international competition in order to maintain their status and compete for necessary resources. World-class universities are making progress, and top Chinese research universities need to focus their efforts on international competition.

Progress at Top Chinese Research Universities

Along with the rapid development of higher education in China and the strong financial support from Chinese governments, the country's top research universities are taking important steps to improve their academic performance and are making significant progress toward their strategic goal of becoming world-class universities.

Between 2000 and 2005, the articles indexed in the SCI more than doubled for the top research universities. For Tsinghua University, about 2,700 of its articles were indexed in the SCI in 2003, which is close to the levels at the top 50 universities in the world. The top Chinese research universities have started to emphasize the quality of published articles by rewarding publications, with high citation rates, that appear in top journals.

As mentioned earlier in this chapter, the proportion of faculty members with doctoral degrees has already reached about 50 percent for the top Chinese research universities and is expected to reach 75 percent by

2010. These universities are committed to raising the proportion of faculty members with doctoral degrees from world-class universities. In addition, they are making special efforts to attract world-class professors in a variety of ways.

The ratio of graduate students (including professional students) to undergraduate students is already close to 1:1. Again, the universities are now struggling to improve the quality of graduate education, especially regarding the capacity for innovation and creativity on the part of doctoral students. Doctoral students are often required to publish in refereed international journals before they can defend their dissertations.

Committed to positioning themselves actively in the global context, the top research universities are engaging in international collaboration. Success has been achieved in a variety of student-exchange and joint-degree programs. The institutions are making significant progress in attracting international students and establishing joint research programs. They are trying to introduce international evaluation of their faculty members and academic programs.

Prediction of the Outcome

The building of world-class universities involves the economic, political, and cultural development of their countries or regions. Some earlier studies have shown that the per capita GDP and GDP for most of the countries with universities among the top 100 universities in the world are higher than US$210 billion and US$25,000, respectively (Cheng, Liu, and Liu 2005). A couple of countries with world-class universities did not meet the basic criteria of GDP and GDP per capita linked to world-class universities. These few countries have favorable policies toward higher education, science, and technology. Their investment in higher education, science, and technology is among the highest in the world.

According to the strategic plans of the Chinese government, the total GDP in 2020 will reach four times the GDP in 2000. The total GDP of developed Chinese regions such as Shanghai and Beijing is expected to exceed US$210 billion, and their GDP per capita is expected to be around US$25,000 in 2020. In addition to the development of the Chinese economy, Chinese governments are expected to continue to support the top research universities. Therefore, Tsinghua University and Peking University in Beijing and Fudan University and Shanghai Jiao Tong University in Shanghai could become world-class universities by 2020.

CONCLUSION

In an era of knowledge-based economies, research universities are becoming more important in the international competition between countries. As an emerging economic world power, China must strengthen its research universities through preferential policies and financial support. Classification of Chinese higher education institutions and establishing a set of criteria for Chinese research universities are essential factors. The Chinese higher education system—the largest in the world—is complex; its classification criteria cannot be borrowed from other countries and must have their own unique characteristics. Chinese governments should gradually establish their preferential policies toward research universities.

In spite of central and local governments' great efforts to improve research universities through financial support and restructuring, large gaps still exist between top Chinese research universities and world-class universities, and the challenges in transforming top Chinese research universities into world-class universities remain serious. The key for success includes, first, the selection of university presidents from all over the world by transparent processes; second, the recruitment of world-class scholars as faculty members, particularly established scholars, with Chinese backgrounds, from developed countries; third, sustainable financial support and continued preferential policies for a small number of selected top research universities; fourth, the merging of selected institutes of the Chinese Academy of Sciences into top research universities; and, fifth, the internationalization of universities' activities.

REFERENCES

Amano, I., and W. Y. Chen. 2004. Classification of higher education institutions in Japan [in Chinese]. *Fudan Jiaoyu Luntan* [Fudan education forum] 2 (5): 5–8.

Cheng, Y., S. X. Liu, and N. C. Liu. 2005. When will Chinese universities be able to become world-class [in Chinese]? *Journal of Higher Education* 26 (4): 1–6.

China Institute for Science and Technology Information. 2005. 2004 statistical analysis of science and technology articles of China. December.

Institute of Higher Education, Shanghai Jiao Tong University. 2005. *Academic ranking of world universities—2005*. http://ed.sjtu.edu.cn/ranking.htm.

Jiang, Y. P. 2004. The origins of doctoral degrees of faculty members in world-class universities [in Chinese]. *Jiangsu Gaojiao* no. 4:106–09.

Liu, N. C., Y. Cheng, and L. Liu. 2005. Academic ranking of world universities: Present and future [in Chinese]. *Tsinghua Journal of Education (China)* 26 (3): 8–15.

Liu, S. X. and N. C. Liu. 2005. Classification of Chinese higher education institutions [in Chinese]. *Journal of Higher Education* 26 (7): 40–44.

Ma, L. T. 2004. *The classification and management of tertiary educational institutions* [in Chinese]. Guangzhou: Guangdong Education Press.

Ministry of Education. 2005. *Education development in 2004 and prospect of 2005* [in Chinese]. www.moe.edu.cn.

Shanghai Jiao Tong University. 2004. International publications of graduate students. Unpublished reports, Graduate School.

4

Beyond Retailing Knowledge

Prospects of Research-Oriented Universities in India

N. Jayaram

The most important reform that we envisage is the development of five or six of what we may call "major" universities where conditions may be provided, both as to staff and students as well as to the necessary equipment and atmosphere, to make first-class postgraduate work and research possible. The standards of these major universities should be comparable to the best institutions of their type in any part of the world. . . . We consider that the development of a few of the most promising universities in India . . . to such a standard within the next ten years is definitely practicable and should be taken up as a matter of high priority.

—EDUCATION COMMISSION

In recommending the establishment of "major universities" in India, the Education Commission (1964–1966) had apprehended the mire into which higher education in the country was soon to land (Ministry of Education 1971, 506–07). This recommendation was summarily rejected in 1968 by India's Ministry of Education, which processed the commission's report. The ministry's tinkering with the university system did not help much, and the country is now back to square one—discussing what the eminent astrophysicist and cosmologist Jayant V. Narlikar has described as "the gathering of real danger clouds on the horizons of our higher education scene" (2003, 17) and ruing the lost time and opportunities.

India has the third largest system of higher education in the world (behind China and the United States),[1] with 323 university-status institutions (178 state and 18 central universities, 18 medical and 40 agricultural universities, 52 institutions "deemed-to-be universities," 12 institutions of national importance, and 5 institutions established under state legislature acts), 13,150 colleges, and about 900 polytechnics. The system employs about 411,600 teachers and caters to about 8.4 million students.[2] It is also noteworthy that this system has a history of nearly 150 years and has been producing graduates and doctorates in science and technology, arts and humanities, medicine and law, and other fields by the thousands every year, making India the second largest repository of university credential holders and the fourth largest science and technology workforce in the world.

Paradoxically, such a large and experienced system of higher education is hardly known for its excellence in research. The number of Indians among Nobel Laureates in science is negligible (only three—C. V. Raman, H. Khurana, and S. Chandrashekar), and in economics, only one (Amartya Sen). The number of renowned scientists—such as J. C. Bose, S. Ramanujan, S. N. Bose, Homi Bhaba, S. S. Bhatnagar, P. C. Mahalnobis, P. C. Roy, Vikram Sarabhai, and M. N. Saha—can be counted on one's fingertips. Only 46 Indians—3 engineers and 43 scientists—have become fellows of the Royal Society. The well-reputed scientists of the contemporary generation are mostly working outside India. The scientific journals published in India are not generally of international quality. Research publications by Indians in well-reputed international journals are few and far between. Not surprisingly, Indian scientists have a poor citation index,[3] and according to Human Development Report 2000, "India could claim only one patent per million residents in 1998" (cited in Vijayakumar 2003, 4). More important, rather than in the universities,[4] whatever significant research credited to Indian scientists has been conducted in institutes—like the Indian Institute of Science (IISc) (Bangalore), the Tata Institute of Fundamental Research (TIFR) (Mumbai), and the Indian Institutes of Technology (IITs) (Chennai, Delhi, Kanpur, Kharagpur, and Mumbai)—and the laboratories under the umbrella of the Council of Scientific and Industrial Research (CSIR).

This chapter deals with the peculiar disjunction in Indian higher education: the concentration by the expanding university system on "retailing knowledge" rather than on creating and refining knowledge—a function assigned to specialist institutes and laboratories outside the university system. After tracing this disjunction to the colonial legacy of the Indian university system, the chapter examines the rejected proposal for establishing "major universities," the question of quality raised by massification of the university system, science and education policy perspectives, the efforts of the University Grants Commission (UGC)[5] to take the university system beyond retailing knowledge, and the portents of the post-SAP (structural adjustment policy) scenario.[6]

THE COLONIAL LEGACY: UNIVERSITIES AS RETAILERS OF KNOWLEDGE

The foundation for India's present system of higher education was laid by the British colonial regime in the mid-19th century (Ashby and Anderson 1966, 54–146). The initial efforts of the Christian missionaries and the East India Company generated a protracted controversy between the "Anglicists," commending a Western course, and the "Orientalists," favoring an indigenous direction. William Bentinck finally resolved this controversy in favor of the Anglicist orientation, barely a month after Thomas Babington Macaulay had penned his (in)famous *Minute* (on February 2, 1835). Charles Wood's *Despatch* (of July 19, 1854) reaffirmed his policy. Upon the recommendation of the committee appointed on January 26, 1855, the first three universities were established in Bombay (now Mumbai), Calcutta (now Kolkata), and Madras (now Chennai) in 1857.

Modeled after the University of London (established in 1836), these pioneer universities were largely affiliating and examining bodies with little intellectual life of their own. All the universities that were subsequently established developed in an isomorphic fashion after the pattern of the original universities. The British educational implantation in India was conceived to serve the economic, political, and administrative interests of the British and, in particular, to consolidate and maintain their dominance in the country.[7] Its contents were biased in favor of languages and the humanities, and against science and technology.

It is not as if the British rulers did not realize the problems associated with such an educational implantation or its adverse consequences for the colonized society. Yet, it was only during the early years of the 20th century—thanks to the initiative of Lord Curzon, the viceroy of India (1898–1905)—that efforts were made to "rescue the original concept of the university from its corrosive narrowness." Several inquiries were instituted during the last three decades of colonial rule, but "hardly any of their major recommendations were translated into university policy or practice" (Tickoo 1980, 34).

Thus, the legacy of higher education inherited by India at the time of independence in 1947 was already "anemic, distorted and dysfunctional" (Raza et al. 1985, 100). While the obsolescence of the inherited system of higher education persisted, the system itself underwent phenomenal expansion. The bulk of the expansion in enrollments at the postsecondary level took place during the 1950s and 1960s, when the rate of expansion was as high as 13 to 14 percent per annum. During the past few decades, the rate of expansion has come down markedly. It was 6.1 percent in 1982/83, peaked at 7.4 percent in 1989/90, and has declined to remain stable at 4 to 5 percent since then. Despite the massive growth in higher education, barely 8 to 9 percent of the 18- to 23-year-old age group is currently enrolled in higher education institutions. Analyzing the data for colleges and their enrollments in 2001,[8] we find that nearly 74 percent of these colleges offered first-degree courses in arts, science, and commerce and that more than 69 percent of their enrollments were in arts, commerce, education, law, and other programs, and a meager 20 percent enrolled in science courses. The lasting imprint of the colonial legacy is clearly evident in these data.

Research as an essential part of the university system was not emphasized during the colonial era. The University of Calcutta (established in 1857) awarded its first doctoral degree in economics in 1911 to Jajneswar Ghosh on his thesis, "The History of Land Tenures in England, France, Germany and Russia and the Agrarian Question." This doctorate has been cited as the first PhD degree in the social sciences awarded by an Indian university (Datta 1989, 78 and 79). No wonder that the best of Indian scientists and scholars of the post-Macaulay colonial era, and immediately after independence as well, went abroad, mostly to England, for research-oriented or high-quality higher education.

The colonial legacy of universities as retailers of knowledge has persisted. Thus, the director general of CSIR, R. A. Mashelkar notes, "Despite the two-fold increase in the number of universities and rise in expenditure on research and development by 16 times during 1980-2000, the quantum of research has gone down" (as reported to the United News of India [2002, 11]). According to the 2000 report of the World Bank's Task Force on Higher Education and Society, the number of papers in sciences and social sciences from India increased only marginally, from 13,623 in 1981 to 14,883 in 1995 (i.e., by 9.25 percent in 15 years). This is negligible compared to the phenomenal 784.38 percent (from a meager 1,293 to 11,435) increase registered by China during the same period (Task Force on Higher Education 2000, 124–25).

Mashelkar also cites a report that records India's decline in the number of scientific papers cited in the International Science Citation Index from 15,000 to 12,000 during the 1980–2000 period: whereas India slipped from 8th rank in the world in 1980 to 15th in 2000, China improved its position from 15th to 9th. In absolute terms, there was, no doubt, an increase in the number of citations of Indian scientific papers—from 56,464 in 1981–1985 to 90,162 in 1993–1997 (i.e., by 59.68 percent). But this increase appears to be infinitesimal compared to the stupendous increase in the number of citations of Chinese scientific papers for the corresponding period—from 8,517 to 77,841 (i.e., by 813.95 percent) (Task Force on Higher Education 2000, 124–25). Quoting a CSIR report, B. Vijayakumar (2003) notes that "in the entire history of CSIR of India, only three out of over 20,000 papers published by the scientists have been cited 100 times against a world average of one in every 250." He further states that a paper with a "thousand citation counts" (i.e., a paper that has been cited 1,000 times) is either nil or extremely rare (Vijayakumar 2003, 4 and 5). No wonder that there has been a growing disquiet over the declining quality of science education and research in the country.

THE KOTHARI COMMISSION AND THE IDEA OF "MAJOR UNIVERSITIES"

After independence, the government of India appointed the University Education Commission (1948–1949)—popularly known as the Radhakrishnan Commission—to examine the development of higher education and make proposals for its future expansion and improvement. This commission viewed the universities as the "organs of civilization" and the "homes of intellectual adventure"; it reflected on the philosophy of higher education and suggested measures for improving the standards of teaching. However, it had little to say about how to reorient the university system toward research, except for noting the teachers' obligation "to engage in research" and "to keep themselves up-to-date in their knowledge" (University Education Commission 1985, 240–47).

The Education Commission (1964–1966)—popularly known as the Kothari Commission—was the first commission in India's educational history to look comprehensively at almost all aspects of education and to develop a blueprint for a "national system of education." Having influenced the two statements on the National Policy on Education (1968 and 1979) and, through them, the policies and programs adopted in the fourth, fifth, and sixth Five-Year Plans (1968–1983), the report of the Education Commission (Ministry of Education 1971) was on the anvil for nearly two decades. This report presents a well-articulated proposal for reorienting the university system toward research.

Perhaps the most important reform that the Kothari Commission envisaged was the development of five or six "major universities," "where conditions may be provided, both as to staff and students as well as to the necessary equipment and atmosphere, to make first-class postgraduate work and research possible." The standards of these universities, it was emphasized, "should be comparable to the best institutions of their type in any part of the world." The commission was confident that, if given top priority, the idea of "major universities" could be realized in 10 years (Ministry of Education 1971, 506–07). The commission expected these universities to play a "vital and catalytic role" in higher education, as they would:

- make their existence felt by their research and by the high standards of training that they would provide for their students
- supply a goodly portion of the outstanding personnel needed for the staffs of universities, colleges, and other institutions of higher education
- provide, within the country itself, first-rate postgraduate education comparable to that in educationally advanced nations
- help Indian academic life to come into its own. (Ministry of Education 1971, 507 and 508)

Apart from shifting the "center of gravity" of Indian academic life—which then largely existed outside India—to the country, the "major universities" could also save scarce foreign exchange being spent on Indian scholars going abroad for higher studies and research. This proposal found strong support from F. Seitz, the president of the US Academy of Sciences, and P. M. S. Blackett, the president of the British Royal Society.

Given the large capital expenditure involved and also the delay the process of establishing such universities from scratch would entail, the Kothari Commission recommended that the UGC select "from amongst the existing universities, about six universities (including one of the IITs and one agricultural university) for development as major universities." It spelled out guidelines for the recruitment of "an intellectually distinguished group of teachers who will be able to provide the requisite training and make valuable research contributions" and for the enrollment of qualified students who would benefit from the superior training to be given and recommended the provision of "adequate facilities and satisfactory conditions of work" (Ministry of Education 1971, 510ff.).

As an adjunct to its idea of "major universities," the Kothari Commission recommended the expansion and strengthening of the UGC program of "centers of advanced study." The commission thought this approach could be undertaken as a preparation to the establishment of major universities or as a consequence of their establishment. Ideally, "clusters" of advanced centers would be established in select universities, as had been done in the University of Delhi. Such a cluster of advanced centers, the commission hoped, would lead centers to strengthen and enrich one another and promote interdisciplinary research. Where such clusters were not possible, the UGC could begin with the establishment of single centers of postgraduate teaching and research, especially in areas where such centers did not exist. The commission suggested measures for the selection, periodical review, and management of the centers of advanced study and steps to be taken to extend their standards to other departments and affiliated colleges (Ministry of Education 1971, 512). The commission was not oblivious to the need for improvement in the facilities and standards at other universities and affiliated colleges, and it dwelled at length on how to go about it (Ministry of Education 1971, 514–18).

The Kothari Commission's eloquent proposal for the establishment of "major universities" was, however, opposed from all quarters. It was summarily rejected by the Parliamentary Committee and the Vice Chancellors' Conference. While scholars like D. R. Gadgil,[9] who opposed elitism in all its forms, were extremely critical, the proposal did not find favor even with academics who generally favored a selective approach to higher education (see Naik 1982, 111–13). A rhetorical ground on which the proposal was opposed and rejected was that it was elitist and antithetical to the egalitarian ethos of a socialist-democratic polity. The commission had anticipated such criticism of the proposal, and it conceded that its proposal would, at that stage, involve a differentiation between universities. "This," the commission held, "is not only inevitable in an economy of scarcity but is also the only sure and practicable way to benefit all ultimately in the shortest time possible." It went on to argue that "we must recognize that pursuit of excellence implies and requires a discriminatory approach; and that to provide equal resources to all irrespective of the quality of their performance and potentiality for growth merely promotes mediocrity" (Ministry of Education 1971, 509).

Even those who accepted the principle of selective approach for qualitative improvement argued against the concept of major universities on the ground "that a *department*, and not a university, should be taken as the unit, that *all* departments of *all* universities should be eligible for selection as Centers of Advanced Study" (Naik 1982, 113). They, however, accepted the idea of clustering a number of advanced centers into some selected universities where conditions were favorable. This idea was also endorsed by the Parliamentary Committee that reviewed the report. While the concept of "major universities" was shelved, the idea of clustering centers of advanced study found a place in the National Policy on Education 1968. However, as J. P. Naik, member secretary of the Education Commission, observes, this "was of no avail and no effective steps were taken to implement the proposal even in this modified form." In March 1987, there were as many as 25 independent centers for advanced study in science subjects and 15 in the humanities and social sciences. However, the "prestige and glamor" that the idea of centers of advanced study had in 1966 were lost (Naik 1982).

MASSIFICATION OF THE UNIVERSITY SYSTEM AND THE QUESTION OF QUALITY

Rapid expansion of higher education in postindependence India has occurred at the cost of its quality.[10] Despite the general deterioration of quality, some institutions have maintained high standards. These institutions include the IITs (Chennai, Delhi, Kanpur, Kharagpur, and Mumbai), the Indian Institutes of Management (at Ahmedabad, Bangalore, and Kolkata), the Indian Institute of Science (Bangalore), the Tata Institute of Fundamental Research (Mumbai), the National Law School of India University (Bangalore), and a few exceptional departments at some universities. Some affiliated colleges have also maintained high standards.

The deterioration in quality is most glaring at the state universities in general and at the undergraduate level in affiliated colleges in particular. This crisis now encompasses the conventional postgraduate (MA, MSc, and MCom) programs offered in the university departments as well. These courses are now performing an extended "babysitting" function. This is understandable considering the relatively low unit cost of running these courses and the fact that the students entering this stream pay little for their education—far less than what students in private-sector primary schools pay. The unregulated expansion of this sector of education has been invariably identified as the main cause of its quality crisis.

What goes on in the name of higher education at many state universities and colleges is pathetic. The deplorable physical facilities and the woefully inadequate libraries and laboratories have earned many institutions the sobriquet *academic slums*. While lack of resources—a general refrain heard in this context—is primarily responsible for this dilemma, we cannot blame it alone. Another serious factor is that even the prescriptions governing the minimum qualifications for the appointment and promotion of academic staff are violated, the minimum number of working days is not met, the calendar of academic activities exists only on paper, and the administration has virtually collapsed. All this has adversely affected the quality of education offered at India's colleges and universities. The undue emphasis on certification rather than on the teaching-learning process seems to have distorted the orientation of university education. Naturally, there is little in the university system to attract the best talent.

As an illustration of the decline in quality, we could take the special instance of the PhD, the highest academic certificate awarded by the university system. During the past two decades, on average Indian universities (including institutions deemed-to-be universities) are turning out 10,000 doctorates per year.[11] During 1999–2000, a total of 11,296 doctoral degrees (PhD/DLitt/DSc) were awarded: arts/social science (4,280, 37.89 percent) and science (3,885, 34.39 percent) faculties together accounted for over 72 percent and the remaining 28 percent by commerce (571, 5.05 percent), education (364, 3.22 percent), engineering/technology (723, 6.40 percent), medicine (228, 2.02 percent), agriculture (787, 6.97 percent), veterinary science (146, 1.29 percent), law (74, 0.66 percent), and others (including music/fine arts, library science, physical education, journalism, and social work) (238, 2.11 percent) (UGC 2002, 1).

A subject-based analysis of these doctorates reveals that in arts/social sciences, of the 4,280 degrees awarded, languages and literature alone accounted for nearly 40 percent (1,685, 39.37 percent), followed by economics (830, 19.39 percent), political science (362, 8.46 percent), sociology (257, 6.00 percent), psychology (199, 4.65 percent), and others (947, 22.13 percent). Similarly, of the 3,885 degrees awarded in the science faculty, more than 76 percent (or 2,954) were in 7 disciplines: chemistry (965, 24.84 percent), physics (533, 13.72 percent), botany (495, 12.74 percent), zoology (438, 11.27 percent), mathematics (265, 6.82 percent), biochemistry (142, 3.66 percent), and home science (116, 2.99 percent) (UGC 2002, 27–30 and 31–33).

The large-scale awarding of doctoral degrees in conventional fields does not, however, reflect a genuine interest in research. It is better explained by the fact that the UGC has made the doctoral degree in a given subject mandatory for appointment to a teaching job in universities and colleges and for career advancement from the lecturer's position to that of the reader.[12]

Besides, lecturers who did not have doctoral qualifications at the time of their recruitment are given paid leave under the Faculty Improvement Program to work on a doctoral thesis and are given two increments on obtaining that degree. Making a doctoral degree mandatory for appointments to and career advancement in the teaching profession, without regard to its quality, has eroded its status and quality.

Based on a review of the situation, C. P. S. Chauhan observes that "the topics undertaken for investigation are normally repetitions or linguistic transformations of some old topics of other Indian or a foreign university." Replications apart, "the topics [chosen] are not based on genuine problems of the discipline or of society, rather they involve futile mental exercise in theoretical subject matter resulting in no practical utility" (Chauhan 1990, 183). This is evident if one glances at the list of theses that have been accepted for the award of doctorates published in the *University News*, the weekly journal of the Association of Indian Universities.

For most postgraduates, obtaining the doctoral degree marks the end of their association with research. They typically do not even publish an article based on it; their theses, thus, get stacked up in university libraries or some documentation center. With extra-academic considerations entering the scene, doctoral research, therefore, can hardly be viewed as a genuine indicator of the research orientation of an Indian university. Another neglected issue in this context is the high rate of stagnation and dropout in doctoral research, as many students take it up as a stop-gap arrangement until they get a job.

Unlike its British counterpart, the UGC in India has the responsibility of regulating the quality of education in universities and colleges.[13] However, considering the inordinate number of universities and colleges it is required to oversee, and being endowed with little power, the UGC has been virtually reduced to a fund-disbursing agency, incapable of enforcing its own recommendations. As a step in the direction of quality control in higher education, following the national policy of education (MHRD 1986), in 1994 the UGC set up an autonomous body called the National Assessment and Accreditation Council (Stella and Gnanam 2003). Initially, the scheme of assessment and accreditation was voluntary, but the idea of an external institution doing this was not well received by universities and colleges. By November 2004, the council had assessed and accredited only 113 universities and 2,088 colleges; it has commenced reaccreditation of 20 institutions—one university and 19 colleges—that had been assessed first in 1998/99 (NAAC 2005, 16). The scheme is now mandatory, and the universities and colleges failing to get assessed and accredited will be deprived of developmental grants. How far this will improve the state of affairs in the university system, even if indirectly, remains to be seen.

SCIENCE POLICY VIS-À-VIS UNIVERSITIES: A FLAWED MODEL

It is not that Indian political leaders did not recognize the importance of science in national development. The science policy resolution of March 4, 1958, moved by Prime Minister Jawaharlal Nehru, clearly stated that Indians should get all the benefits that can accrue from the acquisition and application of scientific knowledge. However, neither this resolution nor its successor, the science and technology policy of 1983, made any reference to the role of either universities or higher education in the development of science. Only the latest resolution—the science and technology policy of 2003—makes an explicit reference to the role of universities and higher education in the development of science.

The neglect of the university in science policy formulation has often been interpreted as a failure on the part of scientific leadership and management (Dadhich 2004, 2181). Narlikar holds the view that, paradoxical as it may sound, "the manner of establishment of institutes like the TIFR [the Tata Institute of Fundamental Research] . . . has been largely responsible for the present decline in the following of basic sciences amongst the students today" (Narlikar 2003, 8–9). The Tata Institute of Fundamental Research was established in 1946 on the eve of India's independence, and the research institutes and laboratories founded after independence were all based on this model: they enjoyed considerable autonomy and generous funds and facilities, and they were "decoupled from universities so that teaching undergraduate or postgraduate students should not come 'in the way' of the researcher" (Narlikar 2003, 9). The catch in this was that the researcher was not only decoupled from university/college teaching but also from students. "So while research got progressively to the back seat in universities, teaching became noticeably absent from the research institutions" (Narlikar 2003, 9).

This has happened not only in the case of commonly known basic sciences but also in the fields of medicine and engineering. Well-known hospitals may declare themselves as "research centers," but they seldom pursue research. In most medical colleges, medical students never get any exposure to research being done on their campuses. The students perceive themselves as medical practitioners or surgeons, rather than as medical researchers. The likes of Dr. Pramod Karan Sethi (of artificial limb fame), Dr. Durga Dutt Gaur (known for laparoscopic operative retroperitonescopy), and Dr V. N. Shirkhande (known for innovations in surgery) are few and far between, and their examples hardly influence the typical medical student (Narlikar 2003, 10–11).

Thus, while research got an enormous boost from the creation of such specialist institutes, facilities, and laboratories, the fact that such sites were developed outside the university system undermined whatever research potentialities the universities had by contributing to an "internal brain drain" of science talent from the universities to institutes and laboratories. One may recall, as Sushanta Dattagupta does with reference to physics, that J. C. Bose worked at Presidency College before he founded the Basu Vigyan Mandir (now under the Department of Science and Technology), C. V. Raman was at Calcutta University and the Indian Institute of Science (Bangalore) before establishing the Raman Research Institute (also under the Department of Science and Technology), and M. N. Saha moved from Allahabad University to create the Saha Institute of Nuclear Physics (now under the aegis of the Department of Atomic Energy) (Dattagupta 2005, 19–20).

The divorcing of teaching from research by building research institutes outside the university system seems to have had adverse consequences for the former, too. Autonomous research institutions are finding it "increasingly difficult to attract young talent, with the problem that a vacuum is slowly but steadily being created at the younger age of the spectrum. Since it is this young age-group that eventually grows to take up higher responsibilities, scientific projects which proceed in a mission mode . . . are experiencing serious humanpower shortages" (Narlikar 2003, 11). With research retreating increasingly to the back seat in universities, "the very lifeline of science graduates from universities that fed young scientists to [the research] institutions began to get more and more tenuous and is now close to becoming extinct" (Narlikar 2003, 11).[14] Thus the divide between teaching and research has perhaps done the most damage to the universities as centers of creation of knowledge.

The best students in science at Indian universities invariably go abroad, mostly to the United States, to pursue higher studies and research, and many of them do not return. While brain drain is a more general phenomenon, experienced by some developed countries as well, its socioeconomic impact on developing countries like India is serious. As the Task Force on Higher Education and Society observes, often the returning experts transport with them the research agenda of industrialized countries, which may not have much relevance to their native country. Thus, this "camp-follower" phenomenon implies that, "effectively, 'brain drain' can take place in the absence of actual emigration" (2000, 73).

NEW EDUCATION POLICY: TOWARD A RESEARCH ORIENTATION IN UNIVERSITIES

In 1985, the new Congress government proposed to embark on the complex task of "restructuring the system of education." Toward this end, in August of that year the Ministry of Education (since reorganized as the Ministry of Human Resource Development) presented to Parliament a 119-page document titled *Challenge of Education: A Policy Perspective*. This document placed the utmost emphasis on higher education and noted that because "major national inputs have gone to laboratories outside the universities," there has been "great deprivation in terms of facilities for frontline work" in the university system. It called for correcting this anomaly (Ministry of Education 1985, 49), while at the same time recommending a moratorium on the expansion of the conventional pattern of colleges and universities and the establishment of new centers of excellence.

The "program of action of the national education policy" (Ministry of Human Resource Development 1986) was reviewed by the Acharya Ramamurti Committee (MHRD 1991). The recommendations of the Central Advisory Board on Education that considered the review report were adopted by Parliament in May 1992. The revised *Program of Action—1992* (Ministry of Human Resource Development 1992) emphasized the need for strengthening research. Outcomes of the new education policy of 1986 included the setting up of interuniversity centers to provide common facilities for research in key areas of science, support to departments under the scheme of "Strengthening of Infrastructure in Science and Technology," and the signing of a memorandum of understanding between the UGC and CSIR in 1991 for providing scientists in universities access to research facilities in CSIR and vice versa (MHRD 1992, 66–67). The revised *Program of Action–1992* also recommended the establishment of university-industry linkage on "a priority basis in metropolitan areas, cities and regions with a concentration of industry," and "inter-institutional links between universities in India and 'state of the art' research institutions abroad." More important, it recommended the constitution of "a high powered committee," with representatives from the Department of Science and Technology, the Council of Scientific and Industrial Research, the Indian Council of Social Science Research, the Indian Council of Historical Research, and others, "to assess the quality of research" in the universities. However, not all these recommendations have received the serious attention that they deserve.

FOSTERING RESEARCH IN UNIVERSITIES: THE EFFORTS OF THE UGC

Appreciating that teaching without research is sterile, on its own part and in accordance with the changing educational policies, the UGC has undertaken several schemes to provide substantial support to universities and colleges to strengthen their teaching and research activities. To start with, it launched programs for improvement of education in science, and in the humanities and social sciences, called respectively the College Science Improvement Program (introduced in 1970/71) and the College Humanities and Social Science Improvement Program (introduced in 1974/75). These programs were taken up at two different levels: (1) at selected colleges covering the entire respective faculty and (2) by way of a University Leadership Project in one subject at all colleges affiliated to a university. Besides the centers of advanced studies referred to earlier, the UGC gives financial support to select well-established departments under the Special Assistance Program for undertaking academic programs in specific fields. The UGC also extends financial assistance to "major" (long-term) and "minor" (short-term) research projects undertaken by individual teachers or a group of teachers or by a department as a whole. Promising young teachers with a research proclivity are offered funds under the Career Award Scheme, and the renowned among senior teachers are given a National Associateship. Financial assistance is also extended to individual teachers to complete their doctoral research and attend seminars, symposia, and workshops.

To derive the best research potentialities of university teachers, the UGC has several schemes: through National Fellowships (limited to 30 at any point of time), eminent teachers can take a year off from their normal duties to devote time exclusively to research; through National Lecturerships, outstanding teachers and researchers can visit other universities or colleges to deliver a series of lectures and participate in other academic programs; and through Emeritus Fellowships (initiated in 1983), universities can utilize the expertise of superannuated professors below the age of 65.

With a view to provide the option of research as a career to bright scholars in science, social science, and humanities, the UGC had launched (in 1983–1984) a Scheme of Research Scientists. Under this scheme, 100 positions each in science and social sciences and humanities were created in the grades of lecturer, reader, and professor (categories A, B, and C, respectively) in a ratio of 60:30:10. In addition to pay and allowances, these research scientists were given a contingency grant. The appointment was made for five years in the first instance and extended for another term after review. The awardees were also promoted to the next higher grade depending on the quality of research conducted by them. In March 2003, 78 scientists were working under this scheme, which has since been discontinued (UGC 2003a, 141–42).

For research to go on and a major breakthrough to come about, there should be a symbiotic relationship between research and teaching. As a follow-up of the New Education Policy's revised *Program of Action–1992*, the UGC has established specialized interuniversity centers as world-class facilities that can be used by university teachers and students. The Inter-University Center for Astronomy and Astrophysics at Pune, the Nuclear Science Center in New Delhi, and the Inter-University Consortium for Department of Atomic Energy Facilities in Indore are such common facilities. Modern computer-based information centers have been set up at the Indian Institute of Science (Bangalore), SNDT Women's University (Mumbai), and M. S. University of Baroda. The UGC's Inter-University Center for Information and Library Network in Ahmedabad is now providing access to current literature through e-subscriptions of journals. Through this network, most of the important journals in sciences and social sciences and humanities are now accessible at more than 100 universities, and the plan is to cover all universities. Such centers, of course, are no substitute to establishing "research universities," but considering the general state of affairs at universities, these and similar initiatives are welcome developments.

Perhaps the most significant effort of the UGC in the direction of research-oriented universities—à la "major universities" recommended by the Kothari Commission almost four decades earlier—is its heavily funded scheme of "Universities with Potential for Excellence" (UGC 2003a, 127–28). Based on the proposals submitted by several universities and presentations made by their vice chancellors on their achievements and promise, the UGC has selected five universities—Jadavpur University, Jawarhalal Nehru University (New Delhi), University of Hyderabad, University of Madras (Chennai), and University of Pune—and given each a development grant of 300 million rupees for five years.[15] While three of them have definite thrust areas, two have a general spread. The UGC further proposes to select 100 colleges with potential for excellence and give each a development grant of 10 million rupees.

The Bharatiya Janata Party–led National Democratic Alliance government (in office during 1999–2004) had conceived the idea of establishing four national institutes of science (NIS)—one each in Allahabad, Bhuvaneshwar, Chennai, and Pune—to work in tandem with Allahabad University, Utkal University, Anna University, and Pune University, respectively. After detailed deliberations with these "link universities," in May 2004 the UGC had prepared a detailed project report with an initial outlay of 745 million rupees for each NIS. But that was the last time that the four universities heard about the project. The NIS was touted to be for science education what the IITs are for technology and Indian Institutes of Management for management education. The idea was to attract the brightest science students from all over the country and enroll them for a five-year integrated MSc program in basic and applied sciences. This was intended to meet the requirement for top-notch science postgraduates to staff and lead the national laboratories and mission-oriented agencies that are likely to face a crisis in the coming years with a large number of senior hands retiring.

This proposal, which would have helped blur the superficial divide between pure and applied sciences, would have been a landmark—again à la "major universities"—in India's science education system. In June 2005, President A. P. J. Abdul Kalam—himself a renowned missile scientist and academician–announced the setting up of these institutes on the occasion of the concluding ceremony of the Golden Jubilee of UGC on December 28, 2003, but the Congress-led United Progressive Alliance government (which came to power in May 2004) seems to have put the project in cold storage (Kumar 2005).

The shelving of the NIS project is a typical instance of how politics has affected higher education in India. But there is another dimension to the politics of higher education that acts as a hindrance to innovative initiatives. With the 42nd constitutional amendment (January 1977), the central (federal) government was empowered to legislate on education concurrently with the states. With the gradual deterioration of the relationship between the center and some states, no government at the center can confidently take any bold steps in the realm of education.

THE POST-SAP SCENARIO

Decline of State Patronage

While public expenditure on education in India has always been inadequate for meeting the needs of "education for all,"[16] throughout its history the state has highly subsidized higher education (Tilak 2004b). Structural adjustment has meant a drastic cut in public expenditure on higher education: between 1989/90 and 1994/95, the share of higher education in development (plan) expenditure decreased from 12.6 to 6 percent, whereas the same in maintenance (nonplan) expenditure declined from 14.2 to 11 percent (Tilak 1996). Overall, the allocation for higher education, which had peaked at 28 percent in the fifth Five-Year Plan (1974–1979), has steadily declined in the successive plans to just 8 percent in the tenth Five-Year Plan (2002–2007), which is the same as the allocation in the first Five-Year Plan (1951–1956).

The annual growth rate of public expenditure on universities and higher education, which was 13.1 percent between 1980/81 and 1985/86, had fallen to 7.8 percent between 1980/81 and 1995/96 (Shariff and Ghosh 2000, 1400). As a proportion of total government expenditure, the share of higher education declined from 1.57 percent in 1990/91 to 1.33 percent in 2001/02. Considering the trends in per student expenditure—from 7,676 rupees (US$154) in 1990/91 to 5,873 rupees (US$117) in 2001/02 (in 1993/94 prices) (by 23.49 percent)—the decline in public expenditure on higher education would appear even more drastic (Tilak 2004a, 2160–61). The money that universities get from the UGC and the state governments would only ensure their mere survival. With much of the funds being spent on staff salary, the shortages in the infrastructure have become ever more magnified. This obviously has affected the quality of higher education and research adversely.

Coterminous with the gradual withdrawal of state patronage for higher education has been a trend toward privatization of that sphere. However, the new breed of private initiatives in higher education—establishment of private universities[17] and institutes, "twinning programs," and international collaborations—have all invariably been in areas of high-demand programs (management, information technology, biotechnology, etc.) and have no interest in research per se. Even if they are research focused, the private initiatives are in the area of applied technology, which can yield quick returns. The initiative of Google (which recently opened its R&D center in Bangalore) to promote research in computer science and engineering at Indian universities is a case in point (see www.webindia123.com).

The Changing Demand for Courses

Since the early 1990s there has been a dramatic shift in Indian students' career choices. The expansion of traditional programs of study seems to have outstripped the demand for them by students. The unemployment situation, particularly among conventional degree holders, has worsened over the decades, with the government no longer able to absorb them in public employment. Aggravating the situation is the economic liberalization program, which demands knowledge and skills generally not possessed by conventional degree holders. It is only natural that those who have been using conventional programs as waiting rooms are either seeking early entry into the job market at lower levels or entering programs that carry better job prospects. Those who still seek conventional graduate programs are generally the leftovers and dregs or the first-generation students from rural and indigent backgrounds (the "scheduled castes" and "scheduled tribes"), especially those who are supported by financial assistance from the government.

While the demand for conventional programs has tapered off, the demand for professional and other allied ones—such as medicine, dentistry, nursing, engineering and technology, computer science and information technology, and business management—has been incessantly increasing, in spite of escalating unemployment even among the professional degree holders. Those who cannot make it to any professional programs would rather try something with narrow but specialized job prospects, such as packaging, plastic technology, fabric designing, air conditioning and refrigeration, among others. To enhance their marketability and employment prospects, students in professional programs try to specialize in a given field or obtain qualifications and skills in some sophisticated programs not generally offered by the universities.

The fact that talented students are no longer taking basic science programs has become a cause for concern. According to a report submitted to the Central Cabinet's Scientific Advisory Committee in July 2004, the percentage of students opting for science after class 12 dropped from 31 percent in the 1950s to 20 percent in the 1990s. Also, those who opted for science programs in the 1950s were the top students, whereas those who opt for these programs today are from the lower-middle academic bracket (Batra 2005, 7). This has seriously affected the academic programs of reputed science institutions such as the IISc (Bangalore), which for many years had enrolled students only for the PhD program, but then started a five-year integrated MSc program in the early 1990s. According to R. Chidambaram, scientific adviser to the Central Cabinet, the institute is now contemplating starting undergraduate science programs beginning with a BSc program in physics (Ray 2005, 7). The Ministry of Human Resource Development's proposal that the IITs should open up by starting courses in pure sciences (and also in economics and business administration) is under consideration by the IIT Council (see Times News Network 2005, 18).[18]

CONCLUSION

Notwithstanding the good work done by select higher education institutions in India, especially in nuclear and space sciences, it can hardly be denied that the gap between India and advanced countries has significantly widened in terms of scientific and technology capabilities. While some sincere effort is now being made to give a research orientation to select universities in the country, the Indian university system has largely remained content with retailing knowledge. With quality control yet to take off beyond the notional stage, the universities in India have declined in quality. Unsurprisingly, not even one Indian university or institute found a place in a recent academic ranking of top 100 universities and institutions of higher education in the world, and only two institutes and one university found listing under ranks below 200: IISc (Bangalore) (ranked in the 202–301 bracket), IIT (Kharagpur) and University of Calcutta (Kolkata) (both ranked in the 404–502 bracket) were the top three Indian institutions of higher education, in that order.[19]

Considering the disjunction between teaching and research in Indian higher education and the consequent absence of research orientation in the university system, it would be tempting to make radical suggestions. However, with the rejection of the concept of "major universities" proposed by the Kothari Commission in the mid-1960s on grounds of elitism, the adoption of the strategy of tinkering with the system since the new education policy of the 1980s and its *Program of Action* of the 1990s, and constraints of the compulsions of coalition politics now, such radical reform proposals are sure to remain only on paper. Without disagreeing with the need for such radical restructuring of higher education, therefore, we can only turn to proposals deemed practical and institutionally viable to move the Indian university system beyond retailing knowledge.

There has been no dearth of suggestions for improving the state of affairs. According to Narlikar (2003), improvement of teaching basic science is the need of the hour as the prospects not only of higher education but also of science and technology in the country are dependent on that progress. Among others, he suggests (1) interactive classrooms with distinguished scientists acting as resource persons; (2) networking of resource libraries with electronic transfer of information; (3) sharing of facilities by universities and institutions; and (4) bringing autonomous research institutions closer to universities through exchange of faculty. Similar suggestions have been made with reference to the social sciences by the Social Science Research Council report on social science research capacity in South Asia (Chatterjee 2002, 140–53). Whether any policy recommendations work if the state is not committed to enhancing its financial support to higher education, however, is a moot question.

It is clear from the work of J. C. Bose, C. V. Raman, M. N. Saha, S. N. Bose, and K. S. Krishnan (and many Indian scientists and scholars who have shined abroad) that India does not lack indigenous talent. Although all these scholars worked in colonial Calcutta and were influenced by the English concept of scientific approach, it is important to emphasize that they were "individual giants with little support from the British government" (Dattagupta 2005, 19). Whether the UGC's support of "the centers of excellence" in the past few years will convert them into India's first "research universities" and act as incubators for more Boses, Ramans, and Sahas is a question for which answers will have to wait. If the history of the Indian university system is any guide, one cannot be too optimistic.

NOTES

Epigraph. Ministry of Education 1971, 506–07.

1. The universities in India are established by an act of Parliament (central universities) or state legislatures (state universities). Several institutions that specialize in some area of knowledge or are heirs to a tradition, but not expected to grow to be multidiscipline universities of the general type, have been recognized as "institutions deemed-to-be universities" under the University Grants Commission (UGC) act of 1956. The government of India has conferred upon 12 university-level institutions the status of "institutions of national importance"; they are empowered to award degrees that, according to the UGC act of 1956, can be granted only by a university. The Indian Institutes of Management, which are also national-level institutions, are not vested with the power to award degrees, though their "fellowships" are treated on par with university degrees.

As for their structure, the largest number of Indian universities belong to the *affiliating* type. They have a central campus housing departments or schools of study that offer instruction at the postgraduate level and undertake research. In addition, a large number of colleges generally offering first-degree-level education are affiliated to them. A major task of such universities is to determine and oversee the academic standards of these affiliated colleges and conduct centralized examinations for the candidates enrolled in them. These affiliated colleges may be dispersed geographically but are under the jurisdiction of a university as determined by law. In contrast, the *unitary* type of university is self-contained and has no colleges. Most of them offer both undergraduate and postgraduate courses and undertake research. A few universities are in some sense a mixture of these two types.

2. The statistical data cited in this chapter are drawn from the Institute of Applied Manpower Research (2002), Kaur (2003), University Grants Commission (2003b), and Association of Indian Universities (2004).

3. The average impact factor per paper (Avgif is the ratio of the number of citations received by the Philadelphia-based Institute for Scientific Information [ISI] for the current year to the number of papers of a particular research center printed in journals of the institute during the preceding two years) for CSIR went up to 1.70 in 2001 against 1.47 in 1999 (15.65 percent), and the number of papers increased from 1,563 to 1,700 (8.77 percent) during the period. Similar trends are noticed for two prestigious research institutes—the Indian Institute of Science (IISc), Bangalore, and the Tata Institute of Fundamental Research, Mumbai. The Avgif increased for IISc from 1.86 in 1997 to 2.15 in 2001 (15.59 percent), and for TIFR, from 2.52 to 2.67 (5.95 percent). As many as 845 papers of the IISc got into print in the ISI journals in 2001 compared to 542 in 1997 (55.90 percent); the corresponding figures for the Tata Institute being 415 and 280 (48.21 percent) (R. A. Mashelkar, cited in *The Navhind Times*, Panjim, November 2, 2002, 11). Implicitly, at least, the Avgif is an indicator of the quality of the research papers, as it reveals the impact of such papers on international science circles.

4. Recently, the UGC has conferred the "deemed-university" status on CSIR (*Times of India*, Mumbai, May 27, 2005, 7). However, how this umbrella organization will function as a "university" is unclear.

5. The University Grants Commission was established by an act of Parliament in 1956 as a centralized authority vested with the power to provide funds and to set and coordinate standards of higher education (Singh 2004). It was modeled after the British UGC (established after World War I—since abolished).

6. For the discussion on colonial legacy, massification, and the post-SAP scenario, I have drawn from my essay "Higher Education in India: Massification and Change" (Jayaram 2004).

7. The expectations underlying the English implantation of education in India is succinctly summarized in Macaulay's oft-quoted words: "to form a class who may be interpreters between us and the millions whom we govern; a class of persons Indian in blood and color, but English in taste, in opinions, in morals, and in intellect" (Young 1935, 359). The Indian urban elite, too, welcomed this education as it was viewed not only as an avenue to jobs but also an instrument for social and political regeneration of India (Basu 2002, 168).

8. In March 2001, the distribution of colleges in the country was as follows: arts, science, commerce, and oriental learning, 73.92 percent; teacher training, 5.42 percent; engineering/technology/architecture, 5.29 percent; medical sciences, 8.35 percent; agriculture, 0.80 percent; veterinary science/animal science, 0.39 percent; law, 3.62 percent; and others, 3.22 percent. Student enrollments were as follows: arts, 46.1 percent; science, 19.9 percent; commerce/management, 17.8 percent; education, 1.3 percent; engineering/technology, 6.9 percent; medicine, 3.1 percent; agriculture, 0.6

percent; veterinary science, 0.2 percent; law, 3.2 percent; and others (including music/fine arts, library science, physical education, journalism, and social work), 0.9 percent (UGC 2003b, 9–10 and 20).

9. In his convocation address to the University of Poona (1966), Gadgil used the choicest epithets to describe the proposal: "favors 'elitism,'" "grandiose," "no relevance to an improvement of existing conditions in our universities and colleges," but will "surely worsen these conditions," "monstrous idea that I am prepared to risk the misunderstanding" (Naik 1982, 111–13).

10. Lacking any objective measurement of higher education standards over a period, it is, no doubt, difficult to determine precisely the nature and extent of deterioration. Nevertheless, there is no denying that India's standards compare unfavorably with the average standards in educationally advanced countries. The Education Commission had drawn attention to this as early as the mid-1960s (Ministry of Education 1971, 66). No wonder, then, that degrees awarded by Indian universities are not regarded by many foreign universities as equivalent to their degrees; employers in India, including the government agencies, are wary of these degrees; and the students are resorting to "shadow education," or private tuition conducted through "coaching classes."

11. The number of PhD degrees awarded increased from 18,286 during 1973–1978 to more than 50,000 during 1993–1998 (Bandyopadhyay 2003, 2).

12. This the UGC did as a measure to counter the decline in the academic profession. With the rapid expansion of higher education, many postgraduates churned out by the state university system found in teaching an easy employment avenue, though their academic preparation was deficient and aptitude for that vocation doubtful. The UGC has tried to rectify this by introducing a National Eligibility Test for prospective entrants to the teaching profession, an orientation course for entrants to the profession, and refresher courses for those already in it. With the embargo on recruitment to teaching positions, most academic staff colleges (started by the UGC to improve the quality of teachers) have stopped offering the orientation course and, with the element of compulsion being introduced, the refresher courses have been ritualized (see Jayaram 2003).

Incidentally, with various pressures working on the university vice chancellors and college principals, recruitment of high-quality faculty is their least concern today. In fact, "wooing good candidates by a well-meaning university academic could [even] be considered unfair" (Dadhich 2004, 2181). While nepotism, favoritism, and corruption are often heard of in recruitment to teaching jobs in universities and colleges, talent scouting is generally unheard of in the Indian university system.

13. The standards of academic performance in professional education are coordinated and regulated by statutory bodies such as the Indian Medical Council, the All India Council of Technical Education, the Bar Council of India, the Dental Council of India, the Pharmacy Council of India, and the Nursing Council of India. The Indian Council of Agricultural Research looks after agricultural education. These bodies were created by different ministries of the central (federal) government, and the lack of coordination among them is a problem. The question of jurisdiction between these bodies created by acts of Parliament and the universities established by acts of Parliament or state legislative bodies has often been raised before courts of law.

14. The Giant Metrewave Radio Telescope—the world's most powerful radio tele-

scope, the brainchild of Govind Swarup, former director of the National Centre for Radio Astrophysics (NCRA), located in Khadad near Pune, completed in 2000—ironically "has to scout more for scientists than for astronomical discoveries!" According to Swarup, the national astronomy researchers have done outstanding work but have not proactively reached out to students: "the number of research scholars joining them annually has hovered around 13 for the past 12 years, while the nation spends Rs. 50 crore every year on them. . . . Only one–two research scholars have been joining NCRA annually, even none at times. Only nine have joined it in the last five years, including three this year" (Kabra 2005, 74).

15. In May 2005, one rupee = US$0.023 and US$1 = 43.42 rupees.

16. An international comparison revealed that in a list of 86 countries, India (with an expenditure of 3.8 percent of the GNP on education) ranked only 32nd in terms of public expenditure on education as a proportion of GNP (quoted in Shariff and Ghosh 2000, 1396).

17. The concept of a purely private university (of the American type) is new in India. The bill to provide for the establishment of private universities, introduced in Rajya Sabha (the upper house of Parliament) in August 1995, is still pending. Considering that higher education is a concurrent subject under the constitution, some states (like the newly formed Chattisgarh) had begun enacting private university acts of their own, and private universities had begun to mushroom in these states. However, in its judgment of February 11, 2005, the Supreme Court of India has held certain clauses of the Chattisgarh Private Sector University Act, 2002 as "unconstitutional" and cancelled the registration of 112 private universities as void (see Thomas and Tiwari 2005).

18. What is said about the disjunction between universities (teaching) and institutes (research) with reference to science would hold good for social sciences, too. This is confirmed by a report on the social science research capacity in South Asia commissioned by the Social Science Research Council, New York, in 2001 (Chatterjee 2002; also Datta 1989).

19. This ranking was based on a study of 2,000 universities and institutions of higher education across the world undertaken by the Institute of Higher Education, Shanghai Jiao Tong University, Shanghai, China. For information on the methodology of ranking adopted by this study, see http://ed.sjtu.edu.cn/rank/2004/top500list.htm. As of now, there is no official ranking of institutions of higher education in India. Some news magazines have attempted such a rank of colleges, but their rankings are populist and lack methodological rigor.

REFERENCES

Ashby, E., and M. Anderson. 1966. *Universities: British, Indian, and African.* London: Weidenfield & Nicholson.

Association of Indian Universities. 2004. *Universities handbook.* New Delhi: Association of Indian Universities.

Bandyopadhyay, M. 2003. Quality control of doctoral research: Role of research fellowships. *University News,* 41 (29): 1–5 and 13.

Basu, A. 2002. Indian higher education: Colonialism and beyond. In *From dependence to autonomy: The development of Asian universities,* ed. P. G. Altbach and V.

Selvaratnam, 167-86. Chestnut Hill, MA: Center for International Higher Education, Boston College.

Batra, A. 2005. Fewer students for pure science has government worried. *Indian Express* (Mumbai), March 31, 7.

Chatterjee, P. 2002. *Social science research capacity in South Asia: A report.* With N. Banerjee, A. K. Baruah, S. Deshpande, P. R. de Souza, K. Hachhethu, B. K. Jahangir, M. S. S. Pandian, N. Wikramasinghe, S. Akbar Zaidi, and I. Abraham. SSRC working paper series, vol. 6. New York: Social Science Research Council.

Chauhan, C. P. S. 1990. *Higher education in India: Achievements, failures and strategies.* New Delhi: Ashish Publishing House.

Dadhich, N. 2004. Indian science experiment. *Economic and Political Weekly* 39:2181–84.

Datta, B. 1989. Social science research: Universities and autonomous institutions. In *Higher education in India: The institutional context,* ed. A. Singh and G. D. Sharma, 78–88. Delhi: Konark.

Dattagupta, S. 2005. The state of physics. *Seminar* 547:19–22.

Institute of Applied Manpower Research. 2002. *Manpower profile: India—Yearbook 2002.* New Delhi: Concept Publishing Company.

Jayaram, N. 2003. The fall of the guru: The decline of the academic profession in India. In *The decline of the guru: The academic profession in developing and middle-income countries,* ed. P. G. Altbach, 199–230. New York: Palgrave Macmillan.

———. 2004. Higher education in India: Massification and change. In *Asian universities: Historical perspectives and contemporary challenges,* ed. P. G. Altbach and T. Umakoshi, 85–112. Baltimore: Johns Hopkins University Press.

Kabra, H. 2005. A vacuum in space. *Outlook* (New Delhi) 45 (11): 74–75.

Kaur, K. 2003. *Higher education in India (1781–2003).* New Delhi: University Grants Commission.

Kumar, D. S. 2005. *Indian Express* (Mumbai), April 27, 9.

MHRD. *See* Ministry of Human Resource Development.

Ministry of Education, Government of India. 1971. *Education and national development (Report of the education commission, 1964–66).* Repr. ed. New Delhi: National Council of Educational Research and Training.

———. 1985. *Challenge of education: A policy perspective.* New Delhi: Controller of Publications.

Ministry of Human Resource Development (MHRD). 1986. *Program of action: National policy on education.* New Delhi: Controller of Publications.

———. 1991. *Towards an enlightened and humane society: Report of the committee for review of national policy on education 1986.* New Delhi: Controller of Publications.

———. 1992. *National policy on education—1986: Program of Action—1992.* New Delhi: Publications Division.

NAAC. *See* National Assessment and Accreditation Council.

Naik, J. P. 1982. *The Education Commission and after.* New Delhi: Allied Publishers.

Narlikar, J. V. 2003. How to recapture the thrill for basic sciences in higher education (UGC golden jubilee lecture series). New Delhi: University Grants Commission.

National Assessment and Accreditation Council (NAAC). 2005. *NAAC News* 5 (11): 16.

Ray, K. 2005. Undergraduate science courses at IISc mooted. *Deccan Herald* (Bangalore), March 30, 7.

Raza, M., et al. 1985. Higher education in India: An assessment. In *Higher education in the eighties,* ed. J. V. Raghavan, 95–173. New Delhi: Lancer International.

Shariff, A., and P. K. Ghosh. 2000. Indian education scene and the public gap. *Economic and Political Weekly* 35:1396–406.

Singh, A. 2004. *Fifty years of higher education in India: The role of the University Grants Commission.* New Delhi: Sage Publications.

Stella, A., and A. Gnanam. 2003. *Foundations of external quality assurance in Indian higher education.* New Delhi: Concept Publishing Company.

Task Force on Higher Education and Society. 2000. *Higher education in developing countries: Peril and promise.* Washington, DC: World Bank.

Thomas, P. M., and D. Tiwari. 2005. Two-room university! *The Week* 23 (13): 36–37.

Tickoo, C. 1980. *Indian universities.* Madras: Orient Longman.

Tilak, J. B. G. 1996. Higher education under structural adjustment. *Journal of Indian School of Political Economy* 8:266–93.

———. 2004a. Absence of policy and perspective in higher education. *Economic and Political Weekly* 39:2159–64.

———. 2004b. Public subsidies in education in India. *Economic and Political Weekly* 39:343–59.

Times News Network. 2005. *Times of India* (Mumbai) March 10, 18.

UGC. *See* University Grants Commission.

United News of India. 2002. *Navhind Times* (Panaji, Goa), September 2, 11.

University Education Commission (1948–1949). 1985. Extracts. In *Higher education in the eighties,* ed. J. V. Raghavan, Appendix I, 240–47. New Delhi: Lancer International.

University Grants Commission UGC). 2002. *University development in India: Basic facts and figures (Doctorate degrees awarded, 1999–2000).* New Delhi: University Grants Commission.

———. 2003a. *Annual Report 2002–2003.* New Delhi: University Grants Commission.

———. 2003b. *University development in India: Basic facts and figures (institutions of higher education; students enrolment; teaching staff, 1995–96 to 2000–01).* New Delhi: University Grants Commission.

Vijayakumar, B. 2003. Regeneration of quality research in higher education: Ways ahead. *University News* 41 (41): 3–7.

Young, C. M. 1935. *Speeches of Lord Macaulay.* Oxford: Oxford University Press.

5

Prospects for World-Class Research Universities in India

P. V. Indiresan

Universities generally perform three functions. At the most basic level, they impart knowledge derived from the past to a new generation of students: they teach. At the midlevel, they critically apprise past knowledge and distill its essence: they produce textbooks. At the highest level, they expand the frontiers of knowledge mainly by minute analysis: they do basic research. A few universities make breakthroughs, open completely new vistas of knowledge, or create knowledge revolutions, leading at times to new kinds of industry.

A world-class research university may be described as one that supports teaching and research, preferably but not necessarily covering a wide range of disciplines (from the arts and humanities, to the social sciences, and science and technology);[1] retains the freedom to decide autonomously what to teach, who will teach, and whom to teach; attracts students and recruits faculty from all over the world; and earns international honors like the Nobel Prize. Such a university will also have a vital undergraduate program. It goes without saying that it will be an elite institution, large enough to support a number of scholars in each discipline to stimulate and challenge one another. It will be so richly endowed that it can keep its doors open to brilliant but poor students. In other words, no university can become a research university unless it possesses the following qualities: dedicated, brilliant students; internationally acclaimed faculty; international-level financial support; and full academic freedom.

Another relevant category to consider is institutions ranked a little below the world's most famous, which may be called merely world-class universities because their research output does not compare well with that of the top institutions. These world-class universities offer good teaching, produce textbooks occasionally, and publish scholarly papers in refereed journals but not always based on cutting-edge research.

Distinctions should be offered between a "flagship" university, a research university, and a mere world-class university. Flagship universities set the pace for others and provide a lead that others follow. Every country can have a flagship university (or may not have any) without it being either a research university or even a world-class teaching university. Likewise, not all research universities need to function as flagship universities if a country has many of them.

STATUS OF INDIA'S HIGHER EDUCATION

India's higher education is like the girl in the nursery rhyme, of whom it was said: "when she was good, she was very, very good; when she was bad, she was horrid!" In recent decades, several Indian universities, particularly the Indian Institutes of Technology (IITs), have received worldwide acclaim for producing high-quality graduates.[2] Indian graduates are highly valued all over the world in well-reputed universities and businesses. At times, they even inspire awe. IIT graduates have been pointedly depicted in a popular American cartoon "Dilbert." India's higher education must be good to earn such an accolade.

Indian universities are well endowed with brilliant students, who are highly motivated because education is the fastest way to achieve social and economic advancement. Because of the common custom of the arranged-marriage system, students avoid some of the distractions their Western counterparts face. However, few Indian scholars have written world-class textbooks, and their research output is patchy. No Indian university is anywhere near to becoming a research university; even the IITs are excellent teaching universities but not yet research universities.

This noticeable difference between the quality of students and the poor research (even graduate-level) performance of Indian universities is a matter of concern. Although many scholars express anguish at the poor condition of India's higher education institutions, they have generally been hesitant to take the problem head on. More often than not, they reconcile themselves to the weaknesses of the system.

India has 13,000 to 14,000 colleges—no one can be sure exactly how many there are, as two to three new ones are added every day. This rapid increase is considered necessary because currently barely 6 percent of the cohort reach the tertiary level. Naturally, there is considerable rising social demand for college education—a situation made worse by escalation in entry qualifications required for most employment. This phenomenon, known as "diploma disease," applies more to India than most countries because a university degree has become necessary even for jobs as peons and bus conductors (Institute of Development Studies 1987). That enormous expansion has come generally at the cost of quality. Because of their numbers and political connections, these colleges are a millstone around the neck of good institutions. This expanding sector is an obstacle to India's chances of developing research universities or even world-class teaching universities. For that reason, any discussion of the possibility of India developing research universities should examine the issues quantitative expansion has created. What follows, therefore, is a description of what ails India's higher education rather than whatever parts are functioning satisfactorily.

In India, as a reaction to age-old discrimination against lower castes, social and political pressures have grown against elitism. Draconian legal measures favoring lower castes and stringent restrictions on the admissions and recruitment of students belonging to upper castes have become an impediment to the pursuit of excellence. The problem is aggravated by political and bureaucratic interference, not merely regarding academic issues like student admissions and faculty selections but even in petty purchases. Such micromanagement takes away all freedom and destroys vitality within the system. Paternalist and authoritarian traditions of Indian culture have led to the existence of autocratic administrations that insist everything has to be done according to rules or precedence, with little or no scope for innovation. That authoritarian culture affects student attitudes, too; students tend to accept what is written down without a questioning mind. Hence, Indian students exhibit commendable skills in applying existing rules to produce optimal designs, but they are uncomfortable about questioning the rules themselves. They suffer from economic pressures as well. Their need to get out of poverty is so great that they are mainly interested in studies that lead to lucrative careers as opposed to scholarship. As a result, not many Indian students make good researchers.

Financially, too, Indian universities are in poor shape. Even the much-pampered IITs have an annual budget of about US$20 million (1 billion rupees) each, about US$4,000 to US$5,000 (150,000–200,000 rupees) per student each year. Even after factoring in the much lower salaries in India, the funds are a small fraction of what most universities in the world command. Although they enjoy more autonomy than most other institutions in the country, IITs are not allowed to accumulate endowments in excess of US$20 million. Thus, Indian universities enjoy only one (brilliant students) of the four factors mentioned above as essential for the success of a research university.

It is no wonder, then, that Philip Altbach, who proposed this study on the prospects for research universities, stated:

> Its systematic disinvestment in higher education in recent years has yielded neither world-class researchers, nor very many highly trained scholars, scientists, nor managers to sustain high-tech development. . . . India's colleges and universities, with just a few exceptions, have become large, underfunded, ungovernable institutions. At many of them, politics have intruded into campus life, influencing academic appointments, and decisions across levels. . . . India's best universities require sustained state support . . . [and] they also require effective management and an ethos of academic meritocracy. At present, the structures are not in place to permit building and sustaining top-quality programs even if resources are provided. (Altbach 2005)

That is a fair description of what ails Indian education. Though India does have a number of good undergraduate colleges, once we go below the top 2 to 3 percent of institutions, quality deteriorates rapidly. Altbach's hopes—that strong state support and better management will lift India's colleges—can materialize only in a small fraction of the country's 13,000 to 14,000 colleges. For almost all of them, there is no hope of ever reaching world standards; their faculties are so poor that they can only produce virtual illiterates who have to be content with menial jobs, at best at the clerical level.

HIGHER EDUCATION IN INDIA: PACESETTING INSTITUTIONS

General universities in India have steadily declined in reputation. In comparison, professional education in engineering, medicine, and management is doing fairly well. That difference is partly because professional education offers lucrative careers and hence professional colleges attract high-caliber students. Good students alone would not have created high-quality professional education if there had not been pacesetting institutions like IITs, the Indian Institutes of Management, and the All India Institute of Medical Sciences, which provide benchmarks for others to emulate. Until recently, IITs also trained an overwhelming proportion of engineering college teachers and provided the nation's engineering colleges a steady supply of well-qualified teachers.

Management education and medical education in India are similar to the past scene at the IITs—excellent teaching but limited research. The Indian Institutes of Management are the most glamorous of the lot. Many of their alumni occupy top positions in Fortune 500 companies and have contributed as much to India's reputation in higher education as IIT alumni. As for medical studies, the All India Institute of Medical Sciences in Delhi and the Post-Graduate Institutes of Medicine in Pondicherry and Chandigarh have legal authority to introduce new teaching programs. Thus, in professional education, India has privileged flagship institutions that provide academic leadership and help other institutions to maintain high-quality instruction. However, in research, the institutions' performance is at best modest and not yet world class.

In science education, the Indian Institute of Science (IISc) has the same or even greater attraction as the IITs. However, in propagating science education, the IISc is handicapped compared to the way IITs have promoted engineering education. First, science education is not as fashionable as engineering and does not attract the same quality of students. Next, the IISc is much smaller and lacks any undergraduate programs that could have been a model for other institutions. Feeder colleges for the IISc graduate programs are in poor shape, even poorer than engineering colleges are, with budgets of barely a couple hundred dollars a year per student. Further, research in science is more expensive, and its benefits are less apparent. For all these reasons, science education is not obtaining the patronage it deserves; the condition of science education in India is causing alarm. The government of India has now decided to improve the situation somewhat, launching two new national universities of science based on the IIT model. However, for the time being, both of these institutions will limit themselves to undergraduate education. Any chance of their evolving into a research university could only occur far into the future.

In arts and humanities, the situation is worse because there are no flagship universities. At one time, the University of Calcutta played that role, but it no longer does. Jawaharlal Nehru University never bothered to assume that responsibility by deliberately opting out of the traditional department structure and electing instead to have interdisciplinary centers. Traditional universities are also hamstrung by outdated university management and are held back by teacher-politicians. Fifty years ago, India opted for the socialist pattern of development and decisively rejected market economics. As a result, advocates of socialism gained ideological control in academia. The more their ideology proved to be wanting, the more they resisted change. Thus, resistance to change has become a contagion at Indian universities. The situation is so bad that even such a prestigious institution as the Delhi School of Economics—in which Amartya Sen (India's only Nobel Prize winner in economics) and the current prime minister, Manmohan Singh, used to teach—could not update its syllabus for 25 years. Such no-changers are still powerful institutions, and they will oppose the idea of a research university as it will not accord with their ideology.

STATUS OF INDIAN RESEARCH

The quality of a research paper is usually measured by the number of times it is cited by subsequent researchers. As a further filter, papers that rank among the top one percent of cited publications (selected on the basis of the number of citations) are considered to be of exceptional quality. Then, a country's share of such exceptional publications is an accepted indicator of the extent of its scientific output. The figures for some selected countries are shown in table 5.1, along with the quantum of R&D investment and the percentage of gross national product (GNP) allocated for R&D. The latter is a useful indicator of the country's commitment to R&D.

Table 5.1 International R&D Performance

Indicators	US	UK	Japan	China	India	South Korea	Brazil
Scientists[a]	4,099	2,666	5,095	n.d.	157	2,329	n.d.
Publications[b]	23,723	4,831	2,609	375	205	294	188
Expenditures Total[c]	206	27	120	16	5.5	12	9.5
Per capita[d]	705	450	978	12	5.5	241	56
Per scientist[e]	230	172	192	16	35	104	36
Per publication[f]	8.4	5.6	6.1	4.0	2.7	3.9	5.1

Source: UNESCO (1999); Chidambaram (2005).

Note: n.d. = no data available.

[a]Number of scientists per million/population.

[b]Number of publications in the top one percent of cited publications.

[c]US$ billions.

[d]US$

[e]US$ thousands, total US national R&D expenditure divided by the number of R&D scientists.

[f]R&D expenditures per top-cited publications (US$ millions), total US national R&D expenditure divided by the number of cited papers published.

The figures indicate that developing countries, including India, have far to go before they can catch up with developed nations. The last column in the table indicates the average cost of generating exceptional-quality research papers. It is worth noting that India's costs are the lowest—three times less than in the United States.

While the IITs have acquired much acclaim for undergraduate education, their graduate programs have not been equally successful. Most IIT graduates migrate to management programs or go abroad for graduate studies. Hence, until recently, master's-level courses at the IITs attracted only students from other colleges, who are usually underprepared. The paucity of well-trained students prevented the IITs from introducing state-of-the art programs at the master's level.

This situation has started changing. About a decade ago, some multinational corporations in the information technology field discovered that in this time of the Internet and videoconferencing, distance is no longer a handicap and research groups could be coordinated from far away. Considering that in India top scientists and professors are paid US$10,000 to US$12,000 (450,000–550,000 rupees) a year, it made economic sense to locate Indian scholars in India rather than transport them to the United States and Europe. Hence, those multinational corporations started R&D centers in India as a cheaper option to importing talented scholars. That has set a new trend, with over a hundred such corporations setting up R&D centers in India. Though no Indian firm has any R&D activity worth the name, some interest in R&D can be seen among indigenous firms as well. Thus, there is now a new market for research professionals within the country. As multinationals pay well, by Indian standards, research is also offering lucrative careers. Furthermore, post 9-11, the United States has been imposing severe restrictions on foreign students. For these reasons, migration of Indian students abroad has noticeably decreased. Student counselors at the IITs estimate that migration of IIT students has been almost cut in half and is down to barely 25 percent.

Thus, in the past few years, master's-level enrollments at the IITs have more than doubled, and the quality of master's-level programs at the IITs has risen a notch. The IITs are enlarging their doctoral programs as well; in the past three years, IIT Bombay has almost doubled its PhD enrollments, to 1,200.

IMPEDIMENTS TO DEVELOPING RESEARCH UNIVERSITIES

Limited Finance

Since Independence, salaries of government officials have been raised seven times, and each time, universities have followed suit. These raises are apart from the periodic increments of "dearness allowance," which makes corrections for inflation. As a result, faculty salaries have risen, in nominal terms, 40 to 50 times in the past 50 years, and those of lower staff, as much as 70 to 80 times. Each time, the government has attempted to economize by reducing salary expenditures. As a result, at many colleges, salaries account for 95 to 98 percent of the total budget, leaving next to nothing for non-salary expenditures on other academic inputs like library books or even routine maintenance. Even at the IITs, the disposable income left at the discretion of an institution's administration has generally been less than 10 percent of the total. That is why all government-funded buildings are dilapidated, libraries are shorn of books and journals, and laboratories are bereft of basic equipment and materials. Recently, as a corrective, the University Grants Commission introduced a much sought after scheme of promoting several focus areas of research in selected "centers of excellence." Each of these centers receives special grants, generally less than a couple of million dollars spread over five years. However, this scheme does not support even one percent of the colleges in the country. In this connection, it is important to note that, regarding books, journals, and materials of consumption, India has to pay dollar prices. Often, Western firms provide substantial discounts to their universities as a promotional policy to familiarize future customers with their products. Such gestures are not available to Indian universities. Hence, Indian universities end up paying higher rates than American and European universities.

This state of affairs is best illustrated by a personal experience. Six years ago, when I was a member of the State Planning Commission of Tamil Nadu, I got a request from a government engineering college for a special grant to purchase two personal computers, at a cost of 150,000 rupees (about US$3,000). The college could not believe it when I suggested that they should get at least 100 computers, and finally, the Finance Department cut the allocation down to about 25. In the same city, there is a privately run college that boasted having several hundred computers. This episode is illustrative of two facts: accepting the World Bank's hypothesis that higher education is a non-merit good and having no political courage to raise fees (often no more than by $5.00 per year), the government has been starving colleges of essential needs. Only a few private colleges are funding their institutions on a relatively generous scale. However, not more than 20 institutions in the country can boast of having sophisticated instruments like electron microscopes, which even then are often decades old.

Much excitement was created when the latest (2005/06) budget granted one billion rupees (US$22 million) to the IISc. The IITs, too, have now been permitted to accumulate private endowments for the same amount (about US$5,000 per student). These figures should be contrasted with the figure of US$400,000 per student enjoyed by Harvard. Even if Harvard is an exceptional case, the fact remains that there are tremendous differences in financial resources, even for Indian "centers of excellence," compared to true research universities. Until this is rectified, India cannot expect to make much progress in higher education.

Elitism versus Equity

India suffers from age-old social disparities. India's constitution expressly stipulates that the government should practice social engineering to uplift the backward castes. Indian politics is so obsessed with (current or long-past) disadvantages that there is little concern for promoting merit. Many state governments reserve as much as 50 to 70 percent of student admissions and faculty appointments to members of backward castes. By the force of law, underprepared students must be admitted and unqualified teachers appointed to fill the quota stipulated by the reservation policy.

This issue recently came to a head when the Supreme Court decided that, so long as private colleges do not accept government grants and the admissions process is transparent, the government cannot force them to admit unqualified lower-caste students. The case has created a major controversy. In the Parliament, all political parties, without exception, decided to support legislation to compel private colleges to admit students according to the states' policy decisions. Legal experts have opined that a simple legal enactment will not do but that a substantial amendment of the constitution will be required. The situation is still fluid; it remains to be seen how the issue will unfold.

The situation in the once highly reputed Jamnalal Bajaj Institute of Management at Mumbai University illustrates the consequences of the reservation policy. Due to the increasing disparity of private-sector salaries and academic salaries, many teachers have left that institute. In the past, there were few teachers from reserved castes. To make up for that backlog, only candidates from those castes may now be recruited. As such qualified candidates are not available, there are practically no teachers at the institute. Still, the institute admits students in large numbers and manages to operate somehow with the help of part-time teachers. This is an illustrative case, and this kind of situation is common. As I said in one of my convocation reports at IIT Madras:

> Some [members of the Parliamentary Committee on Scheduled Castes] feel that our standards are too high. Some members have gone so far as to say that what we need is an Indian standard and not an international standard of instruction. . . . It is necessary to debate the fundamental question whether, just because a group of people cannot cope with a certain level of education, they should have the veto power to deny such an education to the rest. (Indiresan and Nigam 1993, 358)

Unfortunately, the privileges given to the scheduled castes have not really helped them and, instead, have cost them much goodwill. What these people need most is good nutrition and good schools. Reservation has not been adequate to meet those basic needs. If the government decides to amend the constitution, it will have to abrogate the principle of equality in law. The fear of the caste vote is so great that it might still take such a drastic step and to do so in spite of strong opposition from private business.

Quantity versus Quality

Fifty years ago, the vice chancellor of a famous Indian university declared "out of quantity will come quality." To this day, Indians are obsessed with quantity—probably because they are so poor that, like Oliver Twist, they merely ask for more, not for something better. Ambitious parents force children to study long hours, not to make them great scholars but to prepare them for lucrative careers in business. State policy, too, gives higher priority to numbers rather than quality. Table 5.2, which gives the figures of the explosive growth in higher education, does not tell the entire story. There is a minor university in the Himalayas that awards 400 to 500 PhDs every year. Even the prestigious Jawaharlal Nehru University is known to have watered down quality to increase the number of doctoral degrees awarded.

Table 5.2 Trends in Higher Education in India, 1981–2002

Indicators	1981/82	1991/92	2001/02
Total enrollments	3,000,000	5,270,000	8,821,000
Intake in engineering	28,500	66,600	359,723
Engineering colleges	158	337	1,208
All colleges	4,886	8,743	13,150
Faculty strength	199,904	264,000	351,000
PhDs awarded	6,080	8,743	11,450
PhDs in engineering	139	299	739
Higher education expenditures (% of GNP)	1.0	0.46	0.40

Source: University Grants Commission (2004); Ministry of Human Resource Development (2003).

The Planning Commission has stated: "The main objective in the Tenth Plan is to raise the enrolment in higher education of the 18–23 year age group from the present 6 per cent to 10 per cent." That is the objective in spite of the fact unemployment among graduates is estimated to be over 20 percent and underemployment probably over 50 percent. Recently, the government renamed Roorkee University as an IIT, and that has led to a proposal to rename six other existing colleges as IITs. That none of these colleges has a research output that is even a fraction of research at an existing IIT is deterring neither the government nor its pliant advisers. In fact, one of the chosen institutions was considered by the University Grants Commission as not worthy of receiving the paltry US$7 million grant to be given to "universities of excellence." Numbers count; quality does not.

There is a real risk that Gresham's law—a bad coin will drive away the good—will apply in this case to the detriment of quality in India's higher education (Tilak 2004). That risk has already materialized in many universities, where through the sheer force of their numbers mediocre students have dumbed down the academic quality.

Bureaucratic Interference

In the Indian Administrative Services (IAS), all officials are deemed interchangeable, and no one is allowed to stand tall. This "bonsai" culture is a critical handicap because great institutions are built by tall leaders. IAS officials often behave like *khedda* elephants (trained elephants that are used in India to capture wild elephants). They deny freedom and professional dignity to others because they themselves are allowed little of either. In particular, they do not care even if the position of the head of the institution is not filled. For instance, a number of colleges in Delhi University have been without principals for a long time, some as long as four years. When an institution does not have a head of its own, the bureaucracy gets extra power to interfere.

In spring 2005, IIT Delhi had been headless for nine months. The government knew that the previous director's term was coming to a close. It had decided months earlier not to extend his term. Yet it took no steps to avoid a break. Likewise, the All India Council of Technical Education remained headless for months. In contrast, when I. G. Patel was made director of the London School of Economics, his appointment was confirmed two years in advance. Developed countries take special care to plan well in advance the future leadership of institutions. In India, vice chancellors are often treated no better than daily laborers in terms of appointments and transfers.

The latest report on IITs by the comptroller and auditor general has severely chastised IIT directors for not fixing the pay of assistant professors according to the proper interpretation of the rules (*Hindu* 2005). The transparent management decisions taken by all six IIT directors have been publicly declared nationwide as corrupt acts. The directors will now have to go through a series of humiliating exercises to clear their names. In developed countries, salaries of junior faculty would be decided by the head of the department and may not even involve the dean. In India, the bureaucracy forces universities to invest more effort on such petty matters than on academic issues.

The IITs have now been brought under the purview of the Central Vigilance Commission. Henceforth, all purchases and administrative decisions of the IITs will no longer be carried out within a peer review culture but will be bound by a culture of policing. Having been director of a public-sector bank, I am personally aware of the intimidation the Vigilance Commission inspires and the way it freezes all initiative and innovation. At a well-reputed state government institution, given the depredations of the Vigilance Commission, purchases have all but stopped and over 80 percent of the equipment budget has been surrendered because nobody wants to take the risk of being hauled up by inspectors.[3] In IIT Delhi, too, some professors have told me that they have decided not to accept projects involving significant expenditures. Only in the past few years have the IITs emerged as major players in technology development. It is unlikely this flower will be nipped in the bud.

In its report on the status of colleges in Tamil Nadu (which has one of the best-run state governments in the country), the National Assessment and Accreditation Council has rated government colleges as low in each and every one of its seven categories of quality (National Assessment and Accreditation Council 2003). In contrast, autonomous private colleges have all received high ratings on all counts. Evidently, bureaucratic control does more harm than good. Yet bureaucrats on the governing boards of IITs cannot resist political pressure that will harm the institution they are supposed to govern. One bad egg among the bureaucrats would be enough to destroy the modest autonomy IITs have enjoyed all these years. The IITs too are now liable to end up at the same sorry level to which state governments have brought India's erstwhile world-class universities.[4]

Faculty Appointments

Under all state governments, faculty appointments and transfers have been politicized. In the past, central (national) universities were comparatively free of that malaise. However, recently, the central government dismissed 11 directors of national IITs by a stroke of the pen on technical, not academic, grounds. Nobody in the government has ever been concerned about the harm such decapitation does to the health of the affected institutions. The really disturbing feature is that this high-handed action has not raised even a whimper of protest. India's academics, even those in the much-admired IITs, have remained mute witnesses.

At most government colleges, faculty appointments are frozen, transfers are frequent (and politically motivated), and discipline is virtually nonexistent.[5] On the other hand, many private colleges are fly-by-night operators. They are corrupt and demand bribes for admissions and are powerful enough to force down academic standards. Apart from the harm these practices inflict on academic performance, they cause irreparable moral damage to impressionable young minds.

Judicial Interference

Judicial delays are common the world over, but in India they are phenomenal in length. Judicial interference, too, is unprecedented. Thus, a decision taken by one college under local pressure has ramifications for the rest of the country. Any aggrieved official can ask for a "stay order," which is usually granted. Unlike in the United States, where the Supreme

Court takes up only issues of significant importance, the Indian Supreme Court entertains applications written even on a postcard. As a result, judicial proceedings can go on for 20 to 30 years, bringing administration to a standstill.

In recent times, the Indian Supreme Court has been intervening actively in relatively minor matters of college administration. It has pronounced on what fees colleges may charge, how students may be admitted, what proportion of students from different castes can get preference, and so on. As these judgments are applicable nationwide but local conditions in India vary enormously, much confusion has resulted, forcing the court to revise its judgments.

On the other hand, the Supreme Court has been a savior in many cases of highhandedness both in government and in private institutions. For instance, just weeks before a general election the state government of Chattisgarh allowed 157 universities to be started. In this mass expansion, some semiliterate promoters appointed themselves as chancellors and their wives as the registrars and stuffed the board of governors with family members. The situation became so scandalous that the Supreme Court was forced to terminate all such universities by a judicial order. By that time, tens of thousands of students had been admitted. The matter has still not been resolved satisfactorily.

Judicial decisions can also be beyond comprehension. Some time ago, the Supreme Court ordered a professor at Delhi University to be reinstated, even though he had not taught for over a dozen years, on the grounds that his appointment order did not specify he should teach. In contrast, the same court ruled recently that the government cannot force colleges to admit underqualified students on the basis of caste on the grounds this action will affect quality. Strange are the ways of the Indian legal system.

Internal Politics

University academics as well have not covered themselves with glory. Teachers unions are often politically powerful and strongly affect academic functions like student admissions or modernization of syllabi. At Indian universities, it is not unusual for teachers to schedule their classes for only two to three days a week so that they can absent themselves the rest of the time. Because of the political influence they command, such teachers cannot be disciplined. Often, powerful teacher-politicians block modernization of the syllabus because that will entail them to renew their teaching preparations. At the University of Delhi, its highest body, the

Executive Council, has a quaint system of "zero hour." For several hours leaders of teachers unions hold forth on trivial issues of administration, such as grants of medical leave, providing little time for discussions on academic policy. The system effectively sidelines sincere and competent teachers and leaves the university at the mercy of teacher-politicians who are so powerful that no government dares to control them. Virtually all universities in India are in a similar state of academic paralysis. That is how syllabi at most universities do not change for decades at a time.

Quality of Industry

At Western universities, there is a watchful but fruitful interaction between universities and industry. It is common for industries to provide substantial research grants for in-depth studies on matters of practical interest. Such interaction is often, though not always, mutually beneficial. It makes teachers compete among themselves for grants and forces them to take interest in the practical problems of interest to industry. It limits the tendency of pedantic scholars to get bogged down on "how many angels can dance on the head of a pin" kind of inquiry. No doubt, taken to excess, industrial support does harm pure academic pursuits. Yet, in general, universities derive much benefit, financially and intellectually, by interacting with industry.

Universities cannot repair machines, rectify production breakdowns, or even design machinery; university-industry interaction is fruitful only when it relates to basic studies. In turn, only industries that operate at the cutting edge of innovation encounter basic problems. Unfortunately, Indian industrialists rarely innovate; they do not generate technology on their own but depend on foreign manufacturers for production know-how. Once their product becomes obsolete, they buy new machine tools and expertise from foreign manufacturers. Hence, their skills are devoted to operating machines, not designing them—let alone inventing them. For that reason, Indian industrialists expect Indian laboratories to provide machines for manufacturing, not ideas for better manufacturing. Universities are not conversant with the process of technology transfer from the laboratory to the market. For that reason, Indian universities are unable to interact with the world of work and get blamed for being "ivory towers."

Any research university, in any country, needs to stress advanced technology. Many sincere people in India have taken Mahatma Gandhi's ideas literally on technology issues. This philosophy views labor-displacing machinery as evil and hand tools as the best. From this perspective, because India's poor lack skills, the machinery used should also be the simplest possible. People committed to these beliefs do not accept that sophisticated machines can be handled by semiskilled operators. In fact, modern technology is rejected as satanic. Even though advocates of traditional tools are in the minority, they do impede the nation's attempts to modernize.

Since the 1990s, social activists have been causing considerable alarm about the harmful effects of technology on the environment. They constitute a powerful lobby. One group delayed the construction of the Narmada Dam by several years, leading to cost escalation of over US$2 billion. No major engineering project in the country—whether it is irrigation, hydropower, or industry—exists that is not resisted vigorously. By threatening to commit suicide if their views are not accepted and mobilizing large crowds in support, activists are able to halt technology projects rather than remedy their deficiencies. The damage they cause is often fatal, leading to many useful projects being abandoned altogether.

Technology imports have become a major source of financing for political parties and for corrupt politicians. Hence, at the very top, there are many who are opposed to India advancing in science and technology.

Furthermore, India's success in software services has been a mixed boon. A false impression has been created that, unlike China, India can short-circuit the historical process of development and skip the manufacturing stage and jump across directly to the services-dominated stage that the United Kingdom and the United States have reached. As a result, India is not investing in manufacturing technology the way Western nations did and as China is doing even now. For all these reasons, in the field of science and technology, Indian universities are handicapped compared to those in developed countries.

ESTABLISHING A WORLD-CLASS RESEARCH UNIVERSITY

Attracting Faculty

How to recruit world-class faculty at Indian salary levels is the basic issue. In a way, teachers in India are quite well paid. While professors in the United States earn barely 2 to 3 times the average per capita income, in India professors are paid 20 times the country's average per capita income. At prestigious institutions, the faculty also obtain several perquisites, including a quality of housing that even the very rich cannot hope to enjoy. However, the actual salaries range from US$10 to 12,000 (450,000–

550,000 rupees) a year—not enough to afford luxuries like exotic holidays or even necessities like homes large enough to keep book collections after retirement. Further, teachers in India do not command funds for travel and research equipment as do teachers in the West. Moreover, they also lack the quality of administrative support that teachers in the West take for granted. On the contrary, administrative staff in India act like the police, forever checking, obstructing, and investigating what teachers do.

Israel has one solution to offer. Unable to attract notable professors full-time, it has encouraged joint appointments with US universities. In India, there is no longer any legal impediment to such appointments (only for professors of Indian origin). A potential research university could try this approach and induce outstanding persons to lend a portion of their time and reputation.

In the United States, the National Science Foundation selects Presidential Young Investigators and offers them awards. India has similar awards but they are far less attractive. Further, the United States draws talent from all over the world. Without attracting talent from all over the world the way the United States does now, and the United Kingdom used to do, India will not be able to establish world-class universities. Like the United States, India should consider offering US$1 million-plus grants, spread over five to six years, to bright young academics (irrespective of nationality) on the condition that they teach at an Indian institution

An Indian institution could consider inviting a few Nobel Laureates to give short courses and guide research scholars (long distance) with the help of research assistants located in India and getting million-dollar grants from alumni or even from industries—some of which have already begun making considerable contributions to the IITs. In the age of the Internet, this arrangement could be as positive as having the international scholars next door. If, furthermore, the administration were to become supportive rather than inquisitorial, such an institution could become an impressive research university with a relatively moderate financial outlay.

Admitting the Right Students

Admissions determined by national tests taken by hundreds of thousands of potential students have made the selection process mechanical. Students who can afford to receive training in taking such tests enjoy a significant advantage. Thus, India's professional colleges (including the IITs) have shut their doors to a vast pool of talent among the poorer sections of society and are missing out on true scholars not interested in rote learning.

Indian universities cannot avoid the distortions of the government's reservation policy until they learn to identify talent among the poor. In this connection, the United Kingdom's experience after it abolished grammar schools is illuminating. Until the late 1960s, Britain had the eleven-plus system by which, at age 11, via a secondary school entrance examination children were "streamed" (tracked) academically: gifted ones went to grammar schools, the more practical to vocational schools, and the rest (the majority) to secondary modern schools. The streaming of bright students into grammar schools was abandoned in the 1960s since it was felt that adversely affected children from poor families would not be able to compete with upper-class students at the tender age of 11. An article in the *Economist* expressed concerns about this structural change:

> The abolition of grammar schools is probably one reason why recent figures suggest that social mobility in Britain has slowed: Many of the best state-funded schools chose to go private as a result, so the gap between rich and poor people's education widened. . . . Of the 100 schools that get the top A level grades now, only two are comprehensives: they rank 96th and 99th. Compared with children who grew up in the 1960s and 1970s, those who grew up in the 1980s had less chance of being more successful than their parents. . . . The answer is not to tweak the system when people are 18, but to provide them with better education earlier on. The government needs to re-create something like the grammar schools, to let down for the next generation the ladder up which this generation of top people climbed. (*Economist* 2002)

This policy debate in the United Kingdom constitutes an important lesson for India. "Catching them young and nurturing them well" is a better strategy than neglecting children when they are young and giving them the special privilege of reservation too late. If India learns this lesson, research universities will benefit from multilevel selections. The first selection occurs, unavoidably, through parental motivation—how well they inculcate an interest in schooling when their children are young and to which schools they send their children. From the UK experience, academically oriented children should be tracked at a reasonably young age, possibly at the end of the primary school stage. Just as American universities shortlist applicants from India on the basis of the reputation of the colleges they come from, an Indian research university could give preference to students from well-reputed schools, which would make those schools an additional level of selection. While the university entrance examination would continue, it could be treated only as an extra shortlisting criterion (and as a window for students from lower-ranked schools) and not as the final deciding factor it is today. Based on these multiple selection stages, a research university may interview two to three candidates for each vacancy and test their aptitudes. In short, the research university may admit students the way universities in developed countries do.

Financing Quality Education

Quality education is expensive and the returns are often invisible or slow to arrive. At the same time, the cost of education should be low enough that it never deters a competent student from attending a university. That problematic reality is the dilemma of university finance. A university is like a rose garden, with thorns in the form of vocal scholars who take to task the government of the day with the slightest excuse. Unlike a jungle, and like rose gardens, universities require constant nurture. Farsighted vision is needed, as well as a high level of aesthetic sense, to appreciate universities' value. However, at the first whiff of financial distress, governments tend to decrease the support they give to higher education. Thus, drastic cuts have been imposed on allotments to higher education in India and even in the wealthy United Kingdom and United States. To make matters more difficult, few faculty take any interest in this "mundane" issue of money.

Good governments treat universities as public goods and patronize them well. Unfortunately, the World Bank declared higher education as a "non-merit good" and persuaded governments in India to virtually abandon higher education (World Bank 1986). Though the central government is still generous toward the IITs and the IISc, it has started slowly eroding their autonomy with the help of submissive faculty. As the following history of the IITs shows, it is wise not to embrace the government too closely.

When the first IIT was established at Kharagpur, the annual cost per student was 1,460 rupees (110 pounds, in those days) at the Imperial College, London and 1,520 rupees (US$320) at the Massachusetts Institute of Technology (MIT). On that basis, 1,500 rupees a year was deemed a reasonable cost for the new IIT. It was decided that one-third of that cost would be met from fees, one-third from government grants, and the remaining one-third from industrial consultancy. The government also agreed to meet any deficit the IIT might suffer before it could develop consultancy projects. That scheme never materialized: thus, IIT Kharagpur started with the laudable ambition of matching what the Imperial College or MIT spent on education. However, since no correction was made for inflation, when prices shot up the government resisted increasing fees and raising grants to meet world standards. As Indian industry was wedded to imported technology, industry support likewise failed to materialize. IITs became entirely dependent on the government.

When the government faced an acute financial crisis in the 1990s, it decided to freeze its grants to the IITs but agreed to provide matching grants for whatever sums the IITs could earn on their own. The IITs succeeded much beyond expectations in generating private funds. Alarmed at the burden of providing matching grants (and at the prospect of the IITs declaring independence), the government unilaterally scrapped the contract for matching grants and returned to the previous method of "deficit financing." It also issued an edict that the IITs not accept any endowments directly and that such funds should be paid first to the government, which would then decide what should be done with such funds. Naturally, that created a furor. The government has now agreed to return all such bequests to the intended IIT. However, the rule remains that the government has primary control over all bequests; the IITs are not free to accept them directly. Further, the endowments the IITs can accumulate is a small fraction of what top-class research universities have. Some Indian Institutes of Management have tried to get completely independent of government support. That too has been refused. There is a lesson to be learned here: once the government tastes power over a university, it will not let that go. In recent years, India has had two governments with widely differing, even conflicting, ideologies. But they share some characteristics: they are authoritarian; they are not in sympathy with the idea of academic freedom; and they will not let a thousand flowers bloom. Hence, in India, a research university should be wary of accepting state patronage.

Autonomy

By and large, the central government in India respects university autonomy but the state governments are less committed. Yet even the central government at times interferes in the selection of heads of institutions, often with unhappy results. A college or university excessively dependent on the government is likely to be considered a "state institution," with its autonomy subject to the discretion of the government. Even if it receives no grants, it will come under state control if it awards degrees. For that reason, the recently started Indian School of Business neither accepts grants nor awards degrees. IISc also did not award degrees for several decades, and the Indian Institutes of Management do not do so even now.

The Indian School of Business is an extreme case; management institutions can recover their entire costs by charging high fees. That option is neither feasible nor desirable for a comprehensive university. As whoever pays the piper calls the tune, it is best that the university is as free as possible of financial support from the government. Even then, as the fate of many Hindu temples has shown, there is no guarantee that the government will not take over. A strong socialist streak exists in government (and in academia, too). Hence, Indian universities have to maintain constant vigilance to ensure freedom.

In the United States, several private universities enjoy greater success and prestige than state universities. Hence, private funding may be considered best for a research university in India as well. Unfortunately, private funding has its own drawbacks as Derek Bok, former president of Harvard University, explains in the form of a colorful dream:

> The first "dream" began at a dinner in New York where I met the alumnus, an extravagantly successful investment banker. After listening to my troubles raising the money to meet Harvard's never-ending needs, he persuaded me to take the gigantic loan. . . . The next and happiest "dream" saw Harvard enter a wildly successful period. . . . All too soon, however, my euphoria ended. From that night on, each successive "dream" brought forth a more difficult, more controversial scheme to earn the money needed to meet the escalating payments required by the loan. . . . Undaunted, I quickly changed course and offered interested companies exclusive rights to license the discoveries in our best life-science departments, a gambit that worked for a time but not well enough . . . . He returned the following night with one final proposal to spare me the public disgrace of having to default on the loan. All I had to do, he said, was to agree to set aside the last one hundred places in every entering Harvard College class and auction them off to the highest bidders. (Bok 2003, viii–ix)

This imaginary dream describes in minute detail how commercialization can bring disaster to a university. The moral is that though private funding is useful or even necessary, for their own good universities should be cautious not to get into a trap. In particular, they should not go into debt; nor should they seek bargains from houses of business or politicians. On worldly matters, when it comes to bargaining, universities are not as adept as businesspersons and politicians are.

Concern about private funding becomes particularly acute when it comes from multinational corporations. Several multinationals are actively supporting graduate programs in India (but practically no Indian ones).

However, can India attract donors the way American universities do? Experience has shown that most endowments are given by individuals for sentimental reasons (which has already started happening in India with IIT alumni making impressive donations) and not by companies based on commercial interest. The question remains whether such endowments should be encouraged.

Interaction with the World of Work

No research university can work in isolation and far removed from the country's economic forces. Technology education, in particular, depends on the standards of local industry. Even if its graduates are sought worldwide, the field of technology has to depend on local industry for ideas and, like vegetables, it must *always* stay fresh to remain profitable. If Indian manufacturers had been committed to improving their technology continuously, they would have felt a need for a research university or at least a world-class teaching university in technology. Instead, Indian industrialists flog every expertise purchase to death, leading to a longtime gap between technology renewals. Consequently, the technology gap becomes too wide to be bridged. Hence, Indian industry has no option but to import technology once again. Thus, Indian industry needs only maintenance engineers and no designers or innovators. In recent years, the situation has changed somewhat; many sectors like the automobile and pharmaceutical industries have started to upgrade their technology regularly and to develop their own designs instead of buying them. With this change in the culture of industry, India needs research universities for the first time. Of late, the IITs have received considerable financial support from industry but mostly from foreign firms, not as yet from Indian ones. There are indications that Indian industry will, in the future, provide useful support to university education.

Land as a Financial Resource

In India, once a rural area is developed, the value of land increases a hundredfold or even more. While in the vicinity of a university land speculators can profit from this rise in property values, a university may reap that benefit instead. Often builders are happy to provide some free construction in return for the option to market the remaining part. Thus, a research university could acquire two to three times more land than it needs for academic buildings (and for housing the staff) and lease the surplus property in exchange for buildings for its own use.

In recent years, many research universities have benefited greatly, both financially and academically, by establishing technology parks. For instance, the Research Triangle Park in North Carolina is spread over 7,000 acres and employs 50,000 workers, 99.4 percent of whom are engaged in research and development. Such parks are likely to become an essential adjunct for all research universities. The National Manufacturing Competitiveness Council has recently accepted my recommendation in support of establishing substantial technology parks in India. By establishing research and development divisions, industry and the university can share laboratory facilities and exchange experts as well. Commercial rent paid by such industries will be a useful financial resource for the university.

Using revenue from real estate to run universities is not a new strategy. At its inception, the Indian Institute of Science was endowed by the Tatas (a philanthropic family) with large chunks of property in Bombay. Unfortunately, because of rent control, those properties fetch not even one percent of the market rate. Hence, any real estate given as endowment should be free of such political interference.

Tuition Fees

The cost of education at prestigious private universities like Harvard is about the same as their country's per capita income. Although Harvard is privately managed, it has such a large endowment that—some people claim—the tuition is significantly less than the actual cost of instruction per student. In contrast, almost all private professional colleges in India are de facto for-profit institutions run by local politicians and others. Their tuition fees can exceed per capita income tenfold, making their promoters millionaires overnight.

In India, relative to per capita income, the costs per student are bound to be much higher, both because of relatively high salaries and because equipment has to be acquired at world prices. Hence, relative to paying capacity, Indian tuition fees also tend to be much higher than rates in the United States. Hence, private universities in India have much greater difficulty in keeping fees at affordable levels. In professional programs (possibly in all programs at an actual research university), it is possible to attract enough rich students to subsidize poor and more meritorious students. Whether such subsidies are desirable or not is a matter of bitter controversy.

Throughout the world it is accepted that talented athletes can be admitted even with limited academic ability. In India, it is considered a moral principle to admit backward-class students even if their academic performance is poor. Yet any proposal to admit rich and even better students for payment of high fees is condemned as immoral.[6]

At some US universities, tuition rates are linked to students' ability to pay and sometimes to academic performance. In India, the same fees are charged for both millionaires and paupers. Regarding these policies, there appears to be a lot that India can learn from the US system. Several Indian academics have proposed that college tuition fees should be linked to what the individual students paid at school. Then, automatically, rich students who go to private schools will pay more and poor students who go to subsidized state schools will pay much less. However, that proposal has not been accepted—reason can rarely overcome ideology.

Three Alternatives

Assuming that India has the will to establish a research university, there are three possible developments.

Upgrading select institutions. Raising existing institutions to the level of research university offers the advantage of low cost, establishes physical and administrative infrastructure, and provides experienced core faculty. The disadvantages include overloaded infrastructure, rigidified administration that may or may not be suited to support competitive research, and political control that may or may not support quality education. Established institutions will also have a number of faculty members who are too conservative and unreceptive to academic innovations. They may also feel threatened by the induction of more competent young academics from outside who may demand international salaries. Invariably, the existing infrastructure is run-down, and the existing faculty are below world-class standards and will resist the recruitment of highly qualified international staff.

Establishing a new university. India has adopted this approach for new initiatives. That is how IITs arose as independent entities rather than as institutions embedded within existing universities. A new institution has the advantage that selected and well-pruned faculty can be inducted without embarrassment and at international salary levels. Innovative academic and administrative processes may be introduced without having to face opposition from entrenched vested interests. The disadvantage is that many well-reputed faculty may not agree to shift from their existing institutions. Infrastructure (both academic and social) will take quite some time to develop fully. After all the effort and expenses, the new institution may not be any better than the old ones.

Creating a non-degree-awarding institution in the private sector. The Indian Institute of Science began with a special injunction from Jamshedji Tata not to tie students to any examination system. Five years after its founding in 2001, the Indian School of Business emerged in a similar manner in Hyderabad. It is entirely privately funded, accepts no grants from the government, and awards no degrees. Thus, the institution has freed itself of all government control. It can and does pay salaries high enough to attract reputed faculty from around the world. It has introduced new standards in management education the same way IISc did for science education a hundred years ago. However, only the very rich can afford to study at the Indian School of Business. The question remains whether such institutions may attract endowments and scholarships to the same extent as US private universities do and thus make tuition fees affordable for all qualified students.

All three alternatives will have both supporters and detractors, but it will require more extensive analysis to conclude which option will suit India best.

In brief, India's higher education system is like the proverbial curate's egg—what is good is very good; what is bad is very bad. These discrepancies exist because the country's power elite—politicians, administrators, and academics—have little pride in performance.

NOTES

Author's Note: In preparing this essay I had the good fortune to obtain critical comments on an earlier draft from a number of top academics in the country. Not surprisingly, there was considerable diversity of opinion among them. I am thankful to K. L. Chopra, B. Deb, B. L. Deekhatulu, U. B. Desai, G. Govil, K. Joshi, L. S. Kothari, S. C. Lakhotia, S. K. Pal, T. J. Pandian, G. Padmanabhan, K. R. Parthasarathy, S. Prasad, V. Rajamani, V. Rajaraman, B. Ramachandra Rao, S. Ranganathan, P. V. S. Rao, M. M. Sharma, S. P. Sukhatme, Suma Chitnis, B. Yegnannarayana, and M. S. Valiathan. Dutta Roy has been particularly helpful in more ways than one, and my wife Jaya patiently went through several drafts. I have tried to accommodate their criticisms as well as possible, but the final responsibility is entirely my own. Thanks also to Philip Altbach, without whose encouragement I would not have attempted to undertake this chapter at all.

1. As there is another chapter on India in this book (by N. Jayaram, a social scientist), this chapter concentrates on university education in the physical sciences, particularly technology.
2. So high is the international reputation of IIT scholars that, in April 2005, the

US House of Representatives commended the contributions made to the US economy by Indian Americans, and particularly by IIT graduates.

3. I have recently become the chairman of the board of governors at this institution.

4. This pessimism will be contested. Unfortunately, for 50 years, Indian academics have been insensitive to threats of slow decay. They are like frogs that let themselves be cooked to death when the water is heated gradually. It is not an accident that no significant studies have been conducted into why once-great universities like Calcutta and Allahabad, which produced a number of Fellows of the Royal Society and even a Nobel Prize winner, decayed steadily. Further, Indian academics do not have, as the case of the dismissal of 11 directors of the National Institute of Technology demonstrates, the stomach to take on politicians who seek to destroy them. IIT faculty have not realized that the same fate can visit them as well.

5. A government college in Rajasthan has been graduating students in history for some years without even one teacher on the faculty. In physics, it had just one teacher. Such lapses are prevalent all over the country.

6. Once I was invited to advise a top politician on educational policy. Not accustomed to moving in such exalted circles, I sought the advice of Arun Shourie, a journalist and cabinet minister in the previous administration. He advised me to go with the remark "It is better to educate our rulers than to suffer the consequences of their ignorance." Likewise, it is better to educate wealthy citizens rather than suffer the consequences of their ignorance—particularly when they are considered fit enough to be admitted to universities like Harvard and Oxford.

REFERENCES

Altbach, Philip G. 2005. Higher education in India. *Hindu*, April 12.

Bok, D. 2003. *Universities in the market place: The commercialization of higher education.* Princeton, NJ: Princeton University Press.

Chidambaram, R. 2005. Measures of progress in science and technology. *Current Science* 88 (6): 856–60.

Economist. 2002. How Britain's elite has changed. December 5.

Hindu. 2005. CAG points out irregularities in IITs. May 21.

Indiresan, P. V., and N. C. Nigam. 1993. The Indian Institutes of Technology: Excellence in peril. In *Higher education reform in India: Experience and perspectives*, ed. S. Chitnis and P. G. Altbach, 334–64. New Delhi: Sage Publications.

Institute of Development Studies. 1987. *Why do students learn? A six country study of student motivation*, IDS Research Reports Rr-17, Institute of Development Studies, University of Sussex, Brighton, UK.

Ministry of Human Resource Development. 2003. Revitalizing technical education: Report of the review committee of the All India Council of Technical Education.

National Assessment and Accreditation Council. 2003. *State-wise analysis of accreditation reports—Tamil Nadu,* January.

Tilak, J. B. G. 2004. Quality of higher education. NAAC Decennial Lectures, National Assessment and Accreditation Council, August.

United Nations Educational, Scientific and Cultural Organization (UNESCO). 1999. *Statistical yearbook*. Paris: UNESCO.

University Grants Commission. 2004. *University Grants Commission annual report, 2004*. New Delhi: University Grants Commission.

World Bank. 1986. *Financing education in developing countries*. Washington, DC: World Bank.

6
The Making of a World-Class University at the Periphery

Seoul National University

Ki-Seok Kim & Sunghee Nam

In response to the globalizing economy, many developing countries have been paying serious attention to building world-class universities. Creating a world-class university is challenging on many fronts, especially in a peripheral country like Korea. As Philip Altbach (2003) points out, the patterns, ideas, and values of a world-class university in the Western tradition reflect high academic standards. It is increasingly difficult for a middle-income country to become a competitive player at this elevated level of competition, because the fiscal demands of playing on the world stage of science and scholarship are growing dramatically.

Despite these challenges, there have been noticeable achievements in building a competitive university in many developing nations, particularly in Asian countries. Singapore's attempt to establish the "Boston of the East" and South Korea's Brain Korea 21 (BK 21) program are cases in point (Altbach 2000). China launched the 211 Project in 1994 with an ambitious goal of building 100 select universities by the early 21st century, and the 985 Project in 1998 with an impressive budget of US$3.4 billion invested in 33 key universities to create world-class universities. While Altbach (2000) maintains that these attempts produced mixed results, it is premature to come to any conclusive evaluation.

Korean universities have seriously committed themselves to producing internationally competitive human resources. A central strategy was to focus on doctoral programs and to build them up to the world-class level.

According to various measures and standards, Seoul National University (SNU), a flagship university in Korea, seems to have reached the world-class level. In 2005, the *Times Higher Education Supplement*, a British newspaper, ranked SNU as the 45th among the world's top 100 science universities (THES 2005). After the institution's short history of 60 years and 30 years of full-fledged doctoral programs, SNU's accomplishments are extraordinary. What were the driving forces behind the remarkable achievements of SNU?

This chapter examines the process of transforming SNU into a world-class university in Korea. The analysis focuses on the internal reforms implemented at SNU during the past 10 years and the effectiveness of these policies in building a world-class university. SNU is an important case study that bears vital theoretical and practical implications for other Korean universities, as well as for universities in other middle-income countries.

ECONOMIC RESTRUCTURING AND HIGHER EDUCATION REFORM

The speed and extent of economic development that Korea has achieved since the early 1970s have been well documented. By 1996, South Korea—with a $10,000 per capita national income—had become a major competitor in the world market. By the late 1990s, however, the Korean economy faced serious economic hardships, mainly due to the foreign exchange crisis. The unemployment rate jumped up from 2.6 percent in 1997 to 7.9 percent in 1998. This economic crisis uncovered the limitations of a material-oriented manufacturing economy, and the Korean government proposed a shift to a knowledge-based economy as one of its major policy goals. The Ministry of Education formulated a series of educational reform policies to prepare for a knowledge-based society. In this context, building world-class research universities that will play a central role in Korean economic development has become a national priority.

A major strategy for world-class research universities was BK 21, which is a major higher educational reform project to cultivate the creative and high-quality human resources necessary for a knowledge-based society. To accomplish this goal, the Korean government decided to invest about US$1.2 billion in universities over the seven years between 1999 and 2005. In contrast to other previous educational reform policies, this project focuses on graduate programs. The graduate students at the selected schools are the direct beneficiaries of the project. Research funds do not go directly to the faculty in the form of grants. Instead, three-quarters of the whole budget is used to provide a supportive educational environment for graduate students in the form of stipends, financial support for overseas study, and research infrastructure.

The budget allocated for BK 21 was unprecedented. However, the available funding for policy-related reform programs was still relatively limited. For example, in 2004, the Ministry of Education allocated 13 percent of its budget (about US$28 billion) for higher education. This amount is about 0.43 percent of the Korean gross domestic product (GDP), which in comparison to other Organization for Economic Cooperation and Development (OECD)-member countries is less than half of the average percentage (0.9) of GDP spent on higher education. The actual amount spent on policy-related reform programs is only 1.3 trillion won (US$1.3 billion), which is less than 40 percent of the total budget. In the same year, the ministry spent 858.2 billion won (US$8.6 million) on R&D at universities. Of the budget allocated for R&D, 31 percent was given to research universities with graduate programs, 46 percent to four-year teaching universities, and the rest to support vocational colleges and schools. About 140 billion won (US$140 million) from the budget allocated for R&D was spent on BK 21, and 123.7 billion won (US$123.7 million) was spent on pure sciences and the humanities. Besides the Ministry of Education, other government agencies provided financial support for R&D for universities. In 2003, about 2 trillion won (US$2 billion) was spent on R&D at universities—76 percent came from the government, 14 percent was donated by private parties, and 9 percent was supplied by universities themselves. The largest portion went to the field of engineering. The second and the third largest amounts of research funds were given to the fields of natural sciences and pharmacy, respectively. The most competitive university received the largest amount of financial support for its R&D. The top 10 universities received 46 percent of research funds and the top 20 universities 63 percent. Two-thirds of research funds were given to public universities.

Although the funds available for the actual reform policies were limited, BK 21 has had an enormous impact on Korean universities as a whole. Particularly, its emphasis on the graduate programs and graduate students and the scale of the project have provided Korean flagship universities, particularly SNU, with an unprecedented chance of obtaining a world-class university in the periphery.

TRANSITION TO UNIVERSAL ACCESS

As Martin Trow (1970, 2001) has repeatedly pointed out, higher education in today's society has gone beyond the stages of elite education and mass education and has entered the stage of universal education. The stages of development of higher education in the United States is a case in point.

Since the mid-1980s, higher education in Korea has expanded in a rather unique way. The speed of transition has been impressive. In about three decades, Korean higher education has advanced to an extent that took half a century in the United States (Trow 1961) As of 2000, Korean high school graduates were 5 percent more likely to obtain higher education in one form or another than their counterparts in the United States. In the same year, Korean enrollment rates at four-year colleges stood at 38 percent, and the enrollment rates at various higher educational institutions reached 81 percent. This trend continued in 2005. It appears not only that tertiary education has become universal but that even graduate education is becoming increasingly massified in Korea. Between 1995 and 2000, the number of graduate students doubled to 230,000 and is continuing to increase. Unlike the US time frame, in Korea the rapid transition of higher education to a mass system occurred almost immediately after or alongside the swift transition to universal secondary education. These unprecedented, accelerated transitions, with a few adjustments, have brought about a so-called examination hell or severe bottleneck in advancing from secondary to tertiary education.

The Korean higher education system has been challenged by several issues due to its rapid transition. Most universities have experienced rapid expansion or, rather, "explosion"—without adequately changing their missions, functions, and structures. Instead, most universities offer similar programs and majors without functional differentiation. All universities in Korea consider SNU as the "defining institution," using Steedman's term (1987), and attempt to adopt the SNU model. In other words, what David Riesman in the 1950s called a "meandering procession" in the United States (Altbach 2003), in which most of academe seeks to emulate the top schools, was also happening in Korea. Most universities in Korea are aspiring to become flagship universities like SNU, a Korean Harvard or a Korean "Todai" (Cutts 1999).

The rapid transition of higher education also caused a serious funding issue. The expansion of higher education in Korea exceeded the government's ability to support the system financially, which resulted in a greater financial responsibility on the part of parents and students. It is worth noting that the rapid transition of higher education in Korea was set into motion by the zeal and willingness of parents to finance their children's higher education rather than by the central planning of the government. As a matter of fact, 83 percent of the national budget for higher education comes from family funds (Kim et al. 2005), a phenomenon unseen even in Japan or America, where the private sector is far more dominant than the public sector.

Private education has always played a key role in Korean higher education. While privatization of education in Korea began long before the open-door era, the modern form of private education appeared with the arrival of Western missionaries in Korea (Lee 2004) and continued during the colonial period (1910–1945). From 1948, when the independent Korean Republic was founded, privatization was further intensified as the country experienced rapid educational expansion without the central government's financial commitment or capacity. Currently, more than 80 percent of college students attend private schools. In Korea—unlike in the United States, where private universities were founded and sponsored by private donations—private universities are sponsored and financially sustained mainly by student tuition.

UNIQUE ASPECTS OF KOREAN UNIVERSITIES

There are several unique characteristics of Korean universities that evolved during the course of their historical development. In the traditional Korean society, the ruling elites were the main benefactors of the educational system. A number of academic circles (or what Korean scholars sometimes call "gates")[1] were formed with prominent scholars of Buddhism and Confucianism as central figures. Indigenous scholastic traditions were cultivated and maintained through academic discussions and extensive manuscripts and correspondence. Unlike in Europe, a formal educational institution like *universitas*, identified by Durkheim (1938) in his historical sociology of the medieval University of Paris, did not serve as the institutional basis of intellectual life and scholarly activities in Korea. During the Chosun Dynasty (1392–1910), there was a system with formal governmental educational institutions that could be readily found in China (Min 2004). However, intellectuals in Korea participated in academic activities through informal channels of communication between mentors and their disciples. As Western scholasticism flourished in medieval universities, Korean Confucianism underwent a renaissance among the competing scholastic groups based on loosely connected mentor-disciple relations, rather than at any formal institutions founded by central or local governments. Interestingly, these traditions and practices are found even in today's academic environment in Korea and serve as a powerful and effective driving force for the success of academic achievement. It was in opposition to this Korean cultural heritage that Western ideas of the university were introduced and implemented by American Protestant missionaries (Lee 2004) first and Japanese colonizers later.

During the colonial era (1910–1945), Japan imposed its own idea of the university, which was adopted from Germany based on the Humboldt model (Fallon 1980). This Japanese version of a research university was transplanted to Korea in the 1920s, when Keijo Imperial University was founded (Altbach 1998). The current system of higher education in Korea was established during the US occupation (1945–1948). In 1946, a Columbia University graduate who worked as deputy director at the Bureau of Education under the military government introduced an American idea of the university with a whole system of modern public education. However, graduates of Japanese colonial universities and colleges made persistent efforts to maintain the colonial legacy of the Japanese-German idea of "the university," as a "faculty republic" (Fallon 1980; Musselin 2001).

SNU was founded in this context of severe power struggles between advocates of the two conflicting ideas of the university under the same banners of decolonialization and democratic reforms (K.-S. Kim 1996). In other words, the SNU at its inception and throughout its subsequent development has reflected the "twisted roots" of Western university patterns (Altbach 1998) or, in more specific, internal (faculty autonomy) and external (boards of directors) governance. SNU integrated the Seoul Imperial University and other professional colleges with the American university system of departments as key units of the school and a Carnegie course credit system for student grading and measurement. The American model was further reinforced by the educational background of the faculty. Since most professors at Korean universities, especially those at SNU, earned doctoral degrees from universities in the United States, their idea of the university is the one from their alma mater. Thus, it is not surprising to find that the American pattern has served as a benchmark in recent efforts to restructure Korean higher education. In short, the current structures and operational environment of Korean universities, including SNU, reflect various systems and models, including the traditional mentor-disciple (gate) relationship, a German model of a research university adopted and altered by Japan, and an American system of tertiary education. That is, like other Asian universities, the Korean ones are indeed "hybrids" (Altbach 1998). Furthermore, the effect of three conflicting ideas of the university may explain the enormous difficulties in producing a working consensus among professors on how to reform their own universities and colleges—let alone on how to attain a world-class-university status.

The differentiation of Korean universities can be depicted as in accordance with either reputation or areas of specialty. SNU and the Korea Advanced Institute of Science and Technology (KAIST), both of which are public institutions, and Pohang University of Science and Technology (POSTECH), a private university, are the most prominent Korean research universities. In addition to these three, Korea University and Yonsei University, both of which are private schools, comprise leading flagship universities. In a ranking by the *Times Higher Education Supplement*, SNU, KAIST, and Korea University found themselves placed among the 200 best universities in the world for the first time. The next tier consists of four-year comprehensive universities in the metropolitan area of Seoul. The following group is composed of provincial public and private universities. The last group in the differentiation based on reputations includes two- and three-year junior colleges and vocational schools. Differentiation in accordance with areas of specialty relates to their prestige and desirability in the job market. The fields of medicine (including traditional Chinese medicine), law, business, pharmacy, and education comprise the top tier.

In Korea the differentiation of institutions is determined by the level of student applicants' academic qualifications and graduates' employment. For example, specialty-based differentiation is consistent with the applicants' test scores on college entrance examinations (which are equivalent to the Scholastic Aptitude Test in the United States). The ranking of colleges is determined by the proportion of graduates placed in high-ranking jobs—for example, as prestigious civil servants (e.g., judges, attorneys, diplomats, civic officials, and teachers); medical doctors and pharmacists; and employees in large companies, such as Samsung, LG, and SK. The academic backgrounds of high-ranking government officials, judges, journalists, and CEOs of large corporations reflect the ranking order of colleges in Korea.

A typical path taken by a successful student is to be a top-caliber student in high school, to be admitted to a high-ranking college (such as SNU), to pass a qualifying examination, and eventually to become a medical doctor, judge, or attorney. A similar pattern is found in Japan as well (Cutts 1999). Unfortunately, this sequence of events turns the educational experience in high school, as well as in college, into rote memorization of formal knowledge rather than higher-order thinking and creativity, because students must focus on college entrance examinations while in high school and while in college must prepare for various examinations that lead to prestigious jobs. Even children in elementary school start to attend a private academy (*juku* in Japan) with an ultimate goal of entering a top-ranking college in the future. After entering college, instead of concentrating on the college curriculum, students are concerned with the job market and start preparing for various qualifying examinations for future careers. Even students majoring in engineering and natural sciences are spending three to four years during college to prepare for civil service examinations to obtain careers in law and public service. It appears that education in Korea, rather than reducing the level of social and economic inequality, perpetuates, reinforces, and even justifies inequality in the social and economic system.

INSTITUTIONAL UPGRADING EFFORTS

SNU

The current system of doctoral programs at SNU was implemented in 1976 as part of the university's upgrading after it moved to a new campus and embraced all the separate colleges except for the medical one. Obsolete was the "old form" of the doctoral program in which a degree could be earned based solely on a thesis. It was a common practice originating from the colonial Japanese university—explaining the term *old form*. The "new form" required graduate coursework and a qualifying examination before the writing of a doctoral thesis in accordance with the standards of American research universities. As mentioned above, while Japanese colonial universities were influential at SNU's inception, its structure and operation since then has been modeled after the American universities.

It is important to note that institutional efforts toward building a world-class university began long before the launching of the BK 21 in 1999. Altbach (2003) points out several important conditions that a world-class university requires, including excellence in research by top-quality scholars, institutional autonomy, academic freedom, adequate facilities for academic work, and long-term public funding. The main strategy for elevating SNU to the world-class level was to pursue excellence in research, the first of five conditions identified by Altbach. As a major benefactor of the seven-year program of major public funding, SNU was provided with extraordinary resources to pursue its long-cherished goal, with the commitment of the faculty, to become a world-class university.

To promote quality research among faculty, publications in internationally acclaimed scholarly journals were made mandatory for the consideration of new hires as well as the tenure-review process, which, since 2000, has been delayed to the stage of promotion to full professor from associate professor. Since 1994 the research records of top-ranking US schools served as a benchmark to evaluate the progress in terms of annual academic achievements and productivity in Korea. Internal evaluation of the progress was conducted at the university, college, department, and research group levels (K. Kim et al. 2004; K.-S. Kim 2005; K.-w. Kim et al. 2005) A self-diagnosis appears to be the only reasonable way to achieve the goal, for there is no "perfect" solution to turn a flagship university in the periphery into a world-class university (Altbach 2003). SNU bolstered the graduate program by providing graduate students with generous stipends and research assistantships. The postdoctoral program was expanded to support young scholars.

Global connection and cooperation are also critical elements for creating a world-class university. SNU promoted the global connection by regularly inviting internationally known, accomplished scholars in various fields for short-term and long-term appointments. International cooperation was pursued by implementing a joint-degree program with foreign universities and other scholarly exchange programs. SNU has academic exchange programs with about 90 universities from 27 countries all over the world. There were only 100 foreign students in 1995 but more than 700 in 2005. The number of foreign professors doubled since 2000, reaching 58 in 2005. SNU supported graduate students for their overseas studies and participation in international conferences. These overseas experiences were particularly significant and important, in that they gave junior scholars self-confidence in their competitive status in the international arena. Additionally, there was a considerable infrastructural support, including an electronic library with easy access to various academic databases, high-technology computer laboratories, and housing facilities for international scholars and students.

These series of changes and reform policies had impressive results. Senior officials at SNU started to pay attention to the number of scientific papers published in America and in other advanced countries. It is a well-known fact among scientists that the Institute of Scientific Information (ISI) in the United States maintains a database on annually published scientific articles in the Science Citation Index (SCI). Reform-minded school administrators and government officials as well assume that the number of published articles in the SCI serves as a quantitative indicator of a university's productivity. According to the tally of the number of published articles in SCI, the world ranking of SNU stood at 75th in 1999 but has dramatically increased since then year after year, finally reaching 34th in 2003 (K. Kim et al. 2004). Even though this quantitative index is a controversial one, the consistently improving rankings gives senior officers a sense of the success of SNU's own upgrading efforts.

A major issue with using the SCI index is the overreliance on quantity rather than on ways of measuring quality. Since 2004, SNU no longer uses the SCI index as a critical mechanism but has begun to use an index of the citation numbers for each published paper. There are other aspects that the SCI index cannot cover but that are equally significant for developing world-class research. Too much emphasis on the outputs or products would harm the spirit or moral of schools as an academic community.

The measurement of productivity levels by the number of published scientific articles provides insufficient information, however, for it only captures the gross productivity, not the real net productivity. The real productivity actually depends on the level of financial investment devoted to the school under consideration. Harvard University, the University of Tokyo, and the University of California, Los Angeles are the top three universities with regard to the number of published articles in 2004. As a matter of fact, Harvard University produces three times as many articles as SNU (9,421 versus 3,116). However, looking at the financial resources invested in each institution produces a somewhat different ranking order. Table 6.1 compares the real productivity levels of these top three universities with those of SNU in terms of quantitative indexing, annual budgets, and research funds[2] (Office of Research Affairs 2006). SNU's budget is only about one-quarter that of Harvard University. The amount of funds spent on research at Harvard University is more than twice as high as that at SNU.

As shown in table 6.1, in spite of the relative lack of financial resources available at SNU, the productivity rates per units of investment at SNU are not far behind those at other top-tier universities. For 10 billion won (US$10 million) of the operating budget, SNU and Harvard produced about 5 and 3 articles, respectively. Every 10 billion won of research funding resulted in 12 articles at SNU and 15 at Harvard. When measurements move from gross to real productivity, adjusted for the levels of R&D expenditure, some potential international competitiveness in research is achieved at SNU.

Table 6.1 University Publications and R&D Expenditures at SNU and the Top Three World-Class Research Universities, 2004

Variables	Harvard	Tokyo[c]	UCLA	SNU
Publications[a] (ranks)	9,421 (1)	6,631 (2)	5,232 (3)	3,116 (31)
Operating budget				
Total Costs (TBW)[b]	2,857	1,732	3,651	647
Publications per TBM[b]	3.3	3.8	1.4	4.8
Research funding				
Total funds (TBW)[b]	648	426	611	270
Publications per TBW[b]	14.5	15.6	8.6	11.5

Source: Office of Research Affairs (2006, 10).
Note: Exchange rates: US$1 = 1,100 Korean won; 1¥ = 9 Korean won.
[a]SCI-indexed articles.
[b]TBW = 10 billion Korean won, approximately US$10 million.
[c]University of Tokyo data from 2003.

However, making a world-class university requires qualitative rather than just quantitative advancement. Principal investigators of the BK 21 groups began searching for a qualitative index to reveal the level of research competence at SNU. Kuy-won Kim and his colleagues (2005) produced an internal evaluation of SNU's international competitiveness in terms of the level of research competence in the field of science and technology. The report analyzed both the quantity and quality of research articles published in SCI-indexed journals within six different fields: mathematics, physics, biological science, chemical engineering, mechanics and aerospace engineering, and pharmacy. As indicators of the quality of research papers, investigators counted the number of citations of published paper based on the ISI Web of Science Database. Tallying the citations for each scholarly contributor is a time-consuming and tedious, as well as error-laden, job. Not surprisingly, the estimated margin of error is said to be about 10 percent (K.-w. Kim et al. 2005). To make a specific comparison with US counterparts, two groups of US universities were identified based on the annual rankings for selected fields reported by the *U.S. News and World Report*. The "top university" referred to an American university that ranked among the top three in a particular field, and "high-ranking" referred to the top 20 to 30 US universities.

The report included a comparison of the quantity of articles published. SNU produced 75 percent of the totals of top universities in the United States in 1994 and 151 percent in 2004 (K.-w. Kim et al. 2005). According to the report's quality index based on citation numbers during 1994/95,

SNU showed 35 percent of the top-university citations and 53 percent of high-ranking universities' numbers. Since then, there has been a significant and steady improvement, and in 2005 SNU reached 74 percent of the US top-university rate. In comparison with the group of high-ranking universities, SNU's figure exceeded theirs by 37 percent in 2002–2003. Judging by the quality of published journal articles, SNU's graduate program in science and engineering is equivalent to the 20th institution among high-ranking universities in the United States.

This internal review, however, provoked heated debates and controversies with deep skepticism about the estimates, simply because of where SNU was ranked in comparison with American research universities. However, the *Time's Higher Education Supplement's* international survey in 2005 of the world's top 100 science universities is consistent with SNU's internal review.[3]

The SNU's ranking would no doubt fall if other indicators were taken into account regarding world-class universities, such as the professor-student ratio and the number of foreign students and visiting or hired foreign scholars. While the American model may have served as a benchmark, it should be noted that SNU has made an effort to develop an academic model that is both globally competitive and culturally relevant.

The Chronicle of Higher Education (July 23, 2005) introduced "Asia's New High-Tech Tigers" in Korea—KAIST and POSTECH, as well as SNU (Brender 2004). Among these, KAIST has taken a somewhat different approach than SNU in its building of a world-class university.

Korea Advanced Institute of Science and Technology

KAIST, a public research university, has taken an unusual approach to upgrade its educational system to a world-class level. The effort to restructure KAIST has brought about impressive results. Between 2001 and 2003, each faculty member at KAIST published an average of 11.12 articles in SCI-indexed journals. Comparable figures in the United States are as follows: Massachusetts Institute of Technology (MIT) (6.64), Stanford (6.47), and the California Institute of Technology (15.08). KAIST has adopted a rather innovative academic system. College students are admitted without taking entrance examinations. The school does not have a standard system of departments or degree structure. It allows students to graduate as soon as they complete the minimum credit requirements. The college classes are intricately connected to the graduate program, and the credits are transferable between the two levels. Advanced research classes are available to college students. All students reside in dormitories. Graduate students are selected and admitted on the basis of their qualifications as submitted in their application packages, without entrance examinations or interviews. The master's degree program course credits are transferable to the doctoral program. One of the requirements for the doctoral degree is to publish a research article in a distinguished journal.

KAIST invited Robert B. Laughlin, an American Nobel Prize winner to be a president of the university. At the time of his inauguration, Laughlin expressed a critical assessment of KAIST. He believed that the school in its current status did not have a competitive edge in the global community. However, he envisioned KAIST becoming comparable with MIT in the United States. To accomplish this goal, he first suggested eliminating nonessential courses based on student evaluations.[4] Second, he promised to reward top-notch professors enough to succeed in recruiting them from prominent universities in other countries. He planned to dismiss unqualified professors and to recruit 15 percent of the faculty from among overseas scholars. He expressed his intention of lowering the school's dependency on the government and increasing international competitiveness. Laughlin's idea of privatization was confronted by strong opposition from the faculty. The conflict between the American president and the Korean faculty stems from a fundamental disagreement on the vision and direction of KAIST. It is premature to assess the effectiveness of Laughlin's restructuring vision and policies concerning KAIST. If his ideas and policies bring about the intended results, this development will have great significance for the educational restructuring process in Korea. In other words, the American private university would serve as an ideal model for the future of Korean universities.

In addition to the three tigers, Korea University and Yonsei University are leading flagship universities that have taken serious and effective steps in building world-class academic institutions. It appears that private universities enjoy more autonomy and organizational flexibility in their restructuring process than do public institutions. This seems to allow reform policies to become more efficient. The sudden rise of KAIST in the 2005 *Times Higher Education Supplement* ranking shows that is the case.

CONCLUSION

The remarkable accomplishments in terms of excellence in research shows that SNU appears to have reached the world-class level. It demonstrates that a flagship university in the periphery can become a world-class university. There are many factors that may have led to these impressive achievements.

The first supportive factor is the fundamental strength of the Korean secondary education system. Students enter SNU with high-quality preparation. According to the international survey published by the OECD, Korean students in secondary education ranked among the top three countries in terms of problem-solving and mathematical skills (OECD 2004a, 2004b). Thus, it is not surprising that SNU, which admits top-notch students, has the potential of becoming a world-class university.

The second factor is the quality of undergraduate education received by the students while at SNU. In the *Chronicle of Higher Education* it was reported that SNU was second only to the University of California, Berkeley in producing more undergraduate students who later earned doctorates from American universities between 1999 and 2003 (Gravois 2005). The undergraduate programs of SNU seem to serve as the second-best "university college," an outstanding source of undergraduates who went on for advanced study in the United States (Jenks and Riesman 1968, 20–27).

The third factor supporting the creation of world-class universities involves the Korean intellectual tradition of a strong and committed relationship between a mentor and a disciple that serves as a potent academic force for graduate programs. It is fascinating to see the Korean traditional cultural pattern playing a useful role as a crucial resource for globalizing its modern educational institutes.

One of the reasons for Altbach's (2000, 2003) pessimism about the possibility of a middle-income country establishing a world-class university is the issue of institutional autonomy, which is particularly critical for academic creativity and freedom. He questions whether the ambitious Korean BK 21 Project would be effective, given the lack of institutional autonomy in Korea. Since central governments in many middle-income countries are attempting to build world-class universities to promote economic growth, it is challenging for academic institutions to maintain a meaningful level of autonomy. In fact, it has been difficult for SNU to remain autonomous as a public institution, especially because it was a main recipient of public financial resources. To receive adequate funding, SNU has had to compromise its autonomy, which made it difficult to maintain consistent policies. Given their insufficient financial resources, even private universities in Korea face this dilemma—although to a lesser extent.

There is another unique Korean dynamic that has affected SNU's autonomy. In the Korean educational arena, the private sector plays an important role. The educational zeal of parents has been the strength and driving force behind the swift transition to universal higher education in Korea. The highly competitive college entrance examination system has always been a major source of conflict among parents, teachers, the government, and the universities. The policy concerning the college entrance examination system has become a political bargaining chip between the government and the private sector, which in turn has threatened the autonomy of universities. SNU, the flagship university and the dream of all Korean students, has paid a heavy price for its academic prestige. For SNU, all policies in general, and admissions policies in particular, were under strict scrutiny by politicians as well as the public, resulting in the loss of institutional independence. It is not a university like SNU but, rather, the central government that set critical limit on admissions policies. Among the "four essential freedoms" of a university, SNU lacks the freedom to determine "who may be admitted to study" (Bok 1980, 81). In the current political milieu of emphasizing social equity in Korea, the coming of a credential-based society and intensifying pecking order among universities are hotly debated political issues. There have even been radical proposals, such as one in which SNU would be completely closed down to defuse and resolve the intensifying competition.

The achievements of SNU are indeed remarkable and should serve as a model and encouragement to other middle-income countries with similar aspirations and determinations. On the other hand, lessons can be learned by reflecting on the SNU's experiences. First, the focus of higher education reform policies should be on comprehensive and fundamental change. Although quantitative measures have been taken, they should not be the sole approach to making a world-class academic institution.

The delicate balancing act between institutional autonomy and the role of the central government is critical for building a world-class research university in middle-income countries. While the government should provide financial and institutional support, as Altbach argues, institutional autonomy is a critical aspect of the intellectual environment that promotes academic freedom and innovation.

Lastly, scientific knowledge is not immune to political and ideological forces. A challenge that will require ongoing attention is the task of enabling a university in a middle-income country to find a niche in the global intellectual community while maintaining a commitment to the country's unique traditional heritage without compromising the institution's international competitive edge. Participation in the global community of world-class universities as a competitive partner requires enormous determination, tremendous effort, and a plethora of resources. Even while taking as a benchmark the models developed and refined in the core industrial countries, middle-income countries should not abandon their own intellectual traditions. These countries need to be relevant in the global intellectual community while being mindful not to become victims of the intellectual neocolonialism of the 21st century.

NOTES

1. The term *gate* originated from and was widely used in the Buddhist academic traditions and practices from thousands of years ago. The Buddha himself is, for example, the gate to the Buddhist way for his many thousands of disciples and greater number of faithful followers. Likewise, Confucius himself is also the gate to the Confucius way for his legendary 3,000 disciples from all over China. For Buddha and Confucius, a gate signifies the highest degree of intellectual excellence combined with the same degree of moral integrity of a prominent mentor. Entering a certain gate means positioning oneself as a lifetime disciple of the mentor. Korean scholars often call someone a "student working under a certain gate" to classify a serious and committed disciple of a particular prominent scholar. Here "under" means making the student a humble disciple. Heated debates among competing gates reinforce their own intellectual standings among scholars with and without civil service jobs. Sometimes a group evolves into a political party, especially when national security is in danger. These circles constitute loosely connected mentor-disciple relations but have neither an institutional base as in European universities nor an organizational base as in medieval guilds among artisans. These relations, however, have been the center of excellence in research in keeping with the Confucian way and teaching of the power elites during the Kingdom of Chosun.

2. For data on Harvard, see the school's 2004 *Analysis of Financial Results*. For data on the University of Tokyo, see the school's statement of 2003 (www.u-tokyo.ac.jp/fin)01/06_01j.html); its total research funds included a research subsidiary from the Japanese Ministry of Education, Culture, Sports, Science, and Technology, in addition to external funds from private groups, enterprises, and other sources. For data on UCLA, see the Campus Facts in Brief 2004–2005 (www.universityofcalifornia.edu/annualreport /2005/).

3. According to the *Times Higher Education Supplement*, SNU with the score of 38.3 is located between Johns Hopkins University with 39 and the University of California, San Diego, with 36.7. If we only count American research universities—leaving out European, Japanese, and Chinese among the top 100 universities—Johns Hopkins University is 16th and the University of California, San-Diego, is 17th. If these rankings are valid, we hardly reject SNU's self-diagnosis of its standing among its benchmarking counterparts in America.

4. "Nonessential" courses are those that are seen as redundant, too narrow, or specifically in the field of engineering and, thus, incompatible with a series of courses that Laughlin wanted to introduce (e.g., arts, literature) and preparatory courses for law, medical, and business management schools. "Student evaluations" are surveys of satisfaction for each of all the courses—popular votes, of sorts.

REFERENCES

Altbach, P. G. 1998. Twisted roots: The Western impact on Asian higher education. In *Comparative higher education: Knowledge, the university and development*, ed. P. G. Altbach, 55–80. Hong Kong: Comparative Education Research Centre, University of Hong Kong Press.

———. 2000. Asia economic aspirations: Some problems. *International Higher Education*, no. 19:7 8.

———. 2003. The costs and benefits of world-class universities. *International Higher Education*, no. 33:5 8.

Bok, D. C. 1980. The federal government and the university. *Public Interest* 58 (Winter): 80–101.

Brender, A. 2004. Asia's new high-tech tiger: South Korea's ambitious, and expensive, effort to bolster university research is paying off. *Chronicle of Higher Education* 50 (46): A34.

Cutts, E. L. 1999. *An empire of schools: Japan's universities and the molding of a national power elite*. Armonk, NY: M. E. Sharpe.

Durkheim, E. 1938. The birth of the university. Trans. P. Collins. In *The evolution of educational thoughts*, 75–87. London: RKP.

Fallon, D. 1980. W. v. Humboldt and the idea of the university: Berlin, 1809–1810. In *The German university: A heroic ideal in conflict with the modern world*, 28–31. Boulder, CO: Colorado Associated University Press.

Gravois, J. 2005. Number of doctorates edges up slightly. *Chronicle of Higher Education* 51 (18): A34.

Jenks, C. S., and D. Riesman. 1968. *The academic revolution*. Garden City, NY: Doubleday.

Kim, Ki-Seok. 1996. The formation of a divided higher education system in Korea after liberation, 1945–1948: The rise of Seoul National University and Kim Il-Sung University. *Sadae Nonchong* (a College of Education bulletin) 53:85–110.

———. 2001. Can Korea build a world-class university? On the practicality of Korea's ambitious aspirations. The First International Forum on Education Reform: Experiences of Selected Countries, Bangkok, Thailand: Office of National Education Commission.

———. 2004. Some progress of BK 21 projects at Seoul National University. Paper presented at the Beijing Forum, Peking University.

———. 2005. How to get a world-class university in Korea: The case of self-strengthening program of SNU, 1994–2005. *Research Note* (Educational Research Institute, Seoul National University), no. 24:1–36.

Kim, Ku, et al. 2004. An evaluative study on the accomplishments of the BK 21 in SNU. *Research Bulletin* (Seoul National University), 1–104.

Kim, Kuy-won, et al. 2005. An assessment of research competence in science and engineering. *Research Bulletin* (Seoul National University), 1–45.

Lee. S. H. 2004. Korean higher education: History and future challenges. In *Asian universities: Historical perspectives and contemporary challenges*, ed. P. G. Altbach and T. Umakoshi, 145–74. Baltimore: Johns Hopkins University Press.

Min, W. 2004. Chinese higher education: The legacy of the past and the context of the future. In *Asian universities: Historical perspectives and contemporary chal-*

lenges, ed. P. G. Altbach and T. Umakoshi, 53–84. Baltimore: Johns Hopkins University Press.

Musselin, C. 2001. The "Faculty Republic." In *The long march of French universities*, 23–29. New York: RoutledgeFalmer.

OECD. *See* Organization for Economic Cooperation and Development.

Office of Research Affairs. 2006. *Research activities at Seoul National University: 2005/2006*. Seoul: Office of Research Affairs, Seoul National University.

Organization for Economic Cooperation and Development (OECD). 2004a. *Learning for tomorrow's world*. Paris: OECD.

———. 2004b. *Problem solving for tomorrow's world*. Paris: OECD.

Steedman, H. 1987. Defining institutions. In *The rise of the modern education system*, ed. D. Muller, F. Ringer, and B. Simon, 11–134. Cambridge: Cambridge University Press.

Times Higher Education Supplement (*THES*). 2005. World university rankings. http://www.thes.co.uk/statistics/international_comparisons/2005/top_100_science.aspx.

Trow, M. 1961. The second transformation of American secondary education. *International Journal of Comparative Sociology* 2:144–65.

———. 1970. Reflections on the transition from mass to universal higher education. *Daedalus* 99 (1): 1–42.

———. 2001. From mass higher education to universal access: The American advantage. In *In defense of American higher education*, ed. P. G. Altbach, P. J. Gumport, and D. B. Johnstone, 110 45. Baltimore: Johns Hopkins University Press.

PART II

Latin America

7

Brazil's Leading University

Original Ideals and Contemporary Goals

Simon Schwartzman

The creation of the Latin American nation-states in the early 19th century was accompanied by a commitment to establish institutions of higher learning, which could bring to each new country the values of modernity and rationality that were also shaping the construction of the modern nation-states in Europe, particularly in France. Some countries carried out this task more successfully than others. In some places the old colonial Catholic universities, established in the 16th and 17th centuries, were transformed and incorporated into the new academic and educational setting (Halperín Donghi 1962; Schwartzman 1991a, 1996; Serrano 1994). This period is the origin of the national "flagship universities" in the region—the Universidad de Chile, Universidad de Buenos Aires, Universidad Nacional Mayor de San Marcos in Peru, Universidad Nacional Autónoma de Mexico, Universidad de la República in Uruguay, and others.

In the early 21st century, the prevailing concept of a flagship university is strongly associated with scientific research and technology. Latin American flagship universities, however, were slow to incorporate the research component, and today research still has to compete with other values and motivations in the debates over the priorities of the universities.

This chapter examines the case of the Universidade de São Paulo (USP), which is Brazil's leading academic institution in research and graduate education. It was also the first university in the country, created in the 1930s—about 100 years after its sister institutions in other countries in the region. USP is not a national university, but an institution created by the political elite of the State of São Paulo, Brazil's richest economic region—

in clear competition with the federal government, which was working at the same time for the establishment of a national university in Rio de Janeiro, the Universidade do Brasil (Schwartzman, Bomeny, and Costa 2000). Today, Brazil has about 4 million students attending federal, state, private, and municipal universities and higher education institutions, 70 percent of which are private institutions.[1] Many states have their own universities, financed with public money (the constitution forbids charging tuition at public institutions), but the São Paulo state system occupies a special place. Besides USP, the state of São Paulo has two other, newer, public universities, the Universidade de Campinas and the Universidade Estadual Paulista "Júlio de Mesquita Filho." Together, these institutions are responsible for about one-third of all doctoral degrees awarded annually in Brazil. No US institution awards as many PhDs as USP, except if the degrees at all the campuses of the University of California are combined (see table 7.1).

Table 7.1 The Top 10 Doctorate-Granting Universities in Brazil and the United States, 2003

Institution	Doctoral Degrees
Universidade de São Paulo	2,180
University of California, Berkeley	767
Universidade de Campinas	747
Nova Southeastern University, Florida	675
University of Texas, Austin	674
Universidade do Estado de São Paulo	663
University of Wisconsin–Madison	643
Universidade Federal do Rio de Janeiro	653
University of Michigan, Ann Arbor	618
University of Minnesota, Twin Cities	565
University of Illinois at Urbana-Champaign	614

Source: For US institutions, National Science Foundation, Survey of earned doctorates (2003, table 3); for Brazilian institutions, Universidade de São Paulo (2004).

The USP's impressive achievements are even more significant because of the high quality of most of its doctoral degrees, thanks to the strict system of peer-review assessment implemented by the Brazilian Ministry of Education (discussed below). Nevertheless, USP is relatively unknown internationally and is not well positioned in the several recently published international rankings of universities. This could be attributed, in part, to the general ignorance that exists internationally about Brazil. However, the lack of international standing is linked to the absence of an explicit effort by the institution and public authorities to prepare it to take on the role of a leading, world-class research university in the current sense. This chapter reveals some of the current predicaments facing Brazilian higher education as a whole.

USP—BRAZIL'S FIRST UNIVERSITY

In Latin America, Brazilian higher education is a special case, both because of its narrow coverage of the age cohort and the high quality of some of its best professional schools, graduate education, and research programs. It is also special because of the belated founding of its institutions. Other countries in the region have universities dating back to the 16th or at least the 19th century, while the first Brazilian universities are from the 1930s and 1940s. Thus, Brazilian higher education remained for a long time untouched by the "university reform" movement that started in Cordoba, Argentina, in 1918 and swept across many countries in the region—Argentina, Peru, Uruguay, Venezuela, and Mexico—leading to a peculiar pattern of university autonomy and politicization, as well as poor academic standards.

The first Brazilian university legislation, enacted in 1931, granted the future institutions the authority to issue "university privileges," including the right of diploma holders to practice in the learned professions. The legislation paid due respect to the usual notions of culture, research, and institutional autonomy. However, the main concern was to control the standards and size of the professions, and for that reason the universities were placed under tight ministerial oversight. The assumption was that the one "model university" in the country's capital should set the pattern for all others.

As it happened, the 1930s were also a period of intense ideological disputes and political conflict, and for a while it looked as if the national government would put the Catholic Church in charge of the main institution within the Universidade do Brasil, the Faculty of Philosophy, Sciences, and Letters (Faculdade de Filosofia, Ciências e Letras) (Schwartzman 1991b; Schwartzman, Bomeny, and Costa 2000). This faculty was supposed to be the core unit within the university, to develop research and high-level teaching in science and the humanities, prepare teachers for secondary schools, and infuse scientific competence in the old professional faculties that were brought in when the university was established. For different reasons, this agreement with the Church did not work, and in the 1940s the Catholic Church decided to create its first private university, also in Rio de Janeiro.

In fact, the first and most successful university of the 1930s turned out to be not the national university in Rio de Janeiro but the University of the State of São Paulo, known today as USP, established in 1934. For several decades, the state of São Paulo had been the most important pillar of economic growth in the country, first as the leading region of coffee plantations and exports, later as a dynamic industrial center making use of the entrepreneurial skills of large numbers of European immigrants as well as of Brazilians coming from other regions. The São Paulo elites succeeded in helping to bring down the centralized monarchy that had ruled the country until the late 19th century and creating a decentralized republic that redistributed power among the leading states. In the 1930s, however, these elites failed in their attempt to stop a new centralization drive and in 1932 led a frustrated armed rebellion (known as the "Liberal Revolution") against the government of Getúlio Vargas. This combination of wealth and political frustration goes a long way in explaining the original ambitions of the USP, as well as its early success.

A leading personality in the creation of USP was Júlio de Mesquita Filho, whose family owned (and still does) the newspaper *O Estado de São Paulo,* a respected and traditional publication dating from the 19th century. He believed that for São Paulo to recover and maintain its preeminence in the country it would be necessary to create a new elite, educated both in the modern sciences and in the most advanced business and management practices. The project received the support of the state governor and led to the creation of two new institutions—the new university and an independent school of sociology and political science. In both cases, professors were brought in from abroad to teach and to develop their research interests. The School of Sociology and Political Science (originally the Escola Livre de Sociologia e Política de São Paulo), staffed mostly by Americans, remained obscure in spite of some significant achievements in sociology itself and still exists (Limongi 2001). USP, as did the university in Rio de Janeiro, brought together several preexisting institutions in the state (including the old faculties of law, medicine, and engineering, and the Escola Superior de Agricultura Luiz de Queiroz, all established in the late 19th century) and created a new institution for science and the humanities, the Faculdade de Filosofia, under the 1931 legislation. USP became the first academic institution in Brazil to carry out research (except for faculties of medicine that conducted some medical research), and it is still the major public university in the country. This is how Mesquita Filho, writing in 1937, described his motivations:

> Defeated by the strength of arms, we knew perfectly well that only through science and continuous effort could we recuperate the hegemony we had enjoyed for several decades in the federation. *Paulistas* to the bones, we had inherited from our ancestors, the *bandeirantes*, the taste for ambitious projects and the patience needed for large undertakings. What larger monument than a university could we build for those who had accepted the supreme sacrifice to defend us against the vandalism that had just desecrated the work of our elders, from the *bandeiras* to independence, from the Regency to the Republic? . . . We came out of the 1932 revolution with the feeling that destiny had placed São Paulo in the same spot as Germany after Jena, Japan after its bombardment by the American navy, or France after Sedan. The history of those countries pointed to the remedies to our evils. We had experienced the terrible adventures caused, on one hand, by the ignorance and incompetence of those who before 1930 had decided on the destiny of our state and our nation and, on the other hand, by the emptiness and pretentiousness of the [1930] October revolution. Four years of close contacts with leading figures of both factions convinced us that Brazil's problem was above all a question of culture. Hence the foundation of our university and later the Faculdade de Filosofia, Ciências e Letras.[2] (Mesquita Filho 1969, 164; Schwartzman 1991b, 129)

The key decision in those years was that all the professors in the new Faculty of Philosophy should be from abroad. Thanks to the economic and political uncertainties in Europe in those years and the wealth available for the project from São Paulo's government, it was possible to send a recruiting mission to Europe and to attract young professors from Italy, Germany, and France. One of them was Claude Lévi-Strauss, who used the opportunity to visit the Bororo Indians and collect materials for his writing years thereafter, without leaving much imprint in Brazil.[3] Others, less well known, had a much more enduring influence: the anthropologist Roger Bastide, who formed a whole generation of renowned Brazilian social scientists, including Florestan Fernandes, Fernando Henrique Cardoso, and Octávio Ianni; Gleb Wathagin, a White Russian living in Italy, who worked on particle physics and established a strong group of disciples; Gustav Brieger, who brought modern genetics to the Luiz de Queiróz School of Agriculture; and Heinrich Reinboldt and Heinrich Hauptman, who introduced the German tradition of chemistry research.

Paulo Duarte, a journalist and writer who in the early 1930s joined

Mesquita and participated in the decisions on how the university should be organized and who should be hired, stressed in an interview many years later that there was an explicit effort to recruit only natural scientists and mathematicians from the fascist countries, Germany and Italy, reserving the places in the social sciences and humanities for France. Interestingly, England, although mentioned, seemed to be out of their conceptual map; the United States was out of question; and economics did not exist as a meaningful subject. Duarte explained the goal of drawing upon the best academics "not just from one advanced country but also from all advanced countries":

> Thus, Italy was to provide professors of mathematics, geology, physics, paleontology, and statistics; Germany would provide those in zoology, chemistry, and botany; England could help in another branch of natural history and perhaps psychology; and for France would be reserved the chairs of pure thought: sociology, history, philosophy, ethnology, geography, and perhaps physics. It was not always possible to meet this plan. (Schwartzman 1991b, 130)

From the start, USP was a world-oriented institution, staffed by European academics and attended in large part by the children of European immigrants, who constituted a sizable part of the population of São Paulo. In the early years, the new university's goal was not just to develop professional competence and applied knowledge for the economy to grow, which it did in any case, but also to bring civilization to Brazil through "pure science" and "pure thought."

The adoption of the French model (both Mesquita and Duarte had studied in Paris) meant that the professors who came to USP were perceived not just as scientists and specialists but as intellectuals, founders of a new cosmopolitan intelligentsia—with their words and deeds always in the spotlight, thanks, among other things, to the permanent coverage by Julio de Mesquita's influential newspaper. Except, perhaps, for the French, foreign professors never assumed this role, but some of their disciples did—not only in the social sciences but also in the natural sciences and particularly physics. The building of the old Faculdade de Filosofia on Rua Maria Antônia, in downtown São Paulo, became the symbol of the unity of the Brazilian intelligentsia, beyond disciplinary barriers. For physicists, the big challenge was to bring the benefits of atomic energy to Brazil, and they provided intellectual and technical support to the policies of atomic self-sufficiency developed by the Brazilian governments since the 1950s, with the ups and downs associated with the cold war. The social scientists adopted the French-type, Marxist-oriented approach, which seemed to provide the answers for the country's economic and social predicaments and to point the way toward solutions. They wrote in the newspapers published for the wider public and got involved in party politics. Many natural and social scientists joined the Communist Party at some point and remained associated with the traditional left.

USP IN THE CONTEXT OF BRAZILIAN HIGHER EDUCATION

Brazilian higher education has expanded rapidly in recent decades, with a total enrollment in 2004 of about 4 million students, one million of whom were at public institutions. The federal government is responsible for a network of 44 universities and 39 smaller centers for technological education—at least one in each state and several in a few states such as Minas Gerais and Rio de Janeiro (INEP 2003). Some of these institutions—like the universities of Rio de Janeiro, Minas Gerais, and Rio Grande do Sul—are considered good and others less so; there are always large variations in quality at every institution among different fields of study. At these institutions, student selection is carried out through written examinations, most classes are attended during the day, and there is no tuition. Besides, several states have their own public institutions, most of them providing evening courses for working students who could not get admitted to federal institutions and cannot afford to study during the day. Most private higher education is also geared toward students who are able to afford a modest tuition; and there is a growing segment of expensive private higher education institutions catering to upper-class students—in fields like management, economics, and dentistry—who want more than what the public institutions can provide.

Higher education in the São Paulo state has several peculiarities. Besides USP, São Paulo has two other state universities: the Universidade de Campinas, about half the size of USP, established in the 1960s as a high-technology institution, with a larger proportion of graduate students than any other university in the country; and the Universidade do Estado de São Paulo, which developed from a network of local institutions in the state's municipalities, geared toward professional and undergraduate education. Since São Paulo is Brazil's richest state and had its own universities, the federal government never invested much in higher education there and today has only two small institutions in the area, one specialized in medicine (the Universidade Federal de São Paulo, formerly the Escola Paulista de Medicina) and another in engineering (the Universidade Federal de São

Carlos). Put together, all the five public institutions in São Paulo do not enroll more than 10 percent of the students in the state, leaving room for a large and vigorous private higher education sector.

THE UNIVERSIDADE DE SÃO PAULO TODAY

After World War II, as Brazil's economy continued to grow, USP also expanded, moving from old downtown buildings to a modern campus, establishing branches in other cities in the state, and consolidating several of its main research and graduate programs. In 1968, a new national higher education reform ended the old university chair system and introduced the American model of graduate education. Soon, the natural sciences left the old Faculdade de Filosofia, creating their own institutes and academic departments.

Today, USP is a large complex of more than 50 departments, institutes, and faculties, enrolling 25,000 doctoral and master's students in more than 200 degree programs. About 5,500 students are admitted each year in its 43 first-degree professional programs, selected from about 75,000 applicants. It is not the largest institution in terms of the number of students (exceeded by a few private universities)[4] but has the largest budget—1.5 billion reais (US$1.272 billion)[5] from the state treasury in 2003; substantial research grants and other resources obtained for research, technical assistance, and extension work;[6] and the most extensive graduate and research programs and activities. Graduate programs in Brazil are permanently assessed by the Ministry of Education in terms of their research, academic standards, and productivity. Of the 1,189 graduate programs assessed up to 2003, 62 were seen as meeting international standards; of those, 20 (or a third), are at USP: 10 in the natural sciences, 5 in the social sciences and humanities, and the others in engineering, agrarian sciences, health, literature, and multidisciplinary degrees. Of the about 8,000 doctoral degrees awarded in Brazil in 2003, 2,000 were earned at USP. Some USP institutes and departments are highly prestigious at the professional or undergraduate level (regarding the number of applicants per place) and of good quality (regarding the national assessment of programs); some are prestigious but not good; and a few are clearly below standard. Thus, more than 20 prospective students apply per place in administration, architecture, civil engineering, journalism, pharmacy, and psychology; and the best-rated programs are those in accounting, administration, agronomy, economics, engineering (civil, mechanical, and chemical), law, literature, mathematics, medicine, and veterinary sciences.

This is, then, USP's position in Brazil's higher education system: a large institution, with about 65,000 students, responsible for the education of a large portion of Brazil's PhDs and academic research—including some of the leading professional faculties in areas such as medicine, engineering, and law, as well as Brazil's largest medical complex. This university is fully supported with a fixed fraction of the state's revenues and is able to tap into the resources of Brazil's largest science research supporting agency, São Paulo's Fundação de Amparo à Pesquisa (FAPESP), and a large body of about 5,000 academics, most of them holders of doctoral degrees and 78 percent working full-time.[7]

Table 7.2 Profiles of the Universidade de São Paulo (USP) and the University of California, 2004

Characteristics	USP	University of California
Enrollments (undergraduate)	44,696	159,486
Graduating students (undergraduate)	5,515	37,125
Enrollments (graduate)	24,312	44,317
MA-level dissertations	3,366	7,359
Doctoral dissertations	2,164	2,764
Docents	4,953	9,093
Yearly budget (thousands)	US$1,530,475	US$9,933,455
Dollar PPP budget* (thousands)	US$1,290,842	US$9,933,455
Expenditure per student	US$18.71	US$48.74
Expenditure per docent	US$260.62	US$1,092.43

Source: Prepared originally by Carlos Alberto Brito Cruz. The source for Universidade de São Paulo is USP, Anuário Estatístico, 2004.http://sistemas.usp.br/anuario/; the source for the University of California is http://budget.ucop.edu/rbudget/200304/contents.pdf. Data for UC refer only to "Budget for current operations" and does not include "extramurally funded operations."

* Dollar PPP refers to the purchasing power parity between currencies, which is supposed to be more accurate than market exchange rates. The exchange rate was about 3 reais per dollar in 2003.

International comparisons show that Brazil spends several times more per student in public higher education than any other country in the region and the equivalent of many countries in Western Europe. These estimates vary according to whether resources for retirement benefits and the maintenance of university hospitals are included (which is usually the case in Brazil) and whether revenues from research grants, technical assistance, and contract and extension work are included (which is usually not the case). Another factor involves how the conversion between the Brazilian currency and dollars is carried out. Data for 2002 suggest that USP spent about US$19,000 (54,000 Brazilian reais) per student, in contrast to US$12,000 (30,000 reais) in the federal system. Although high by many standards, these figures are well below the expenditures of the University of California (see table 7.2).

In spite of these impressive credentials and relatively high cost, USP fulfills less than about 5 percent of the demand for higher education in the state and a tiny proportion of the country's demand. What role should this institution play in the future? Are the aspirations and ideals of its founding fathers still valid? Should it aspire to constitute a leading, world-class university, or should it shed its elitist bias and extend its reach, providing greater access to more people, perhaps at lower costs? Should it demand more public resources, to increase enrollments? Or, should it remain relatively small and stress its role as an elite, standards-bearing institution? Or is the USP losing its hedge and forsaking its original purpose and ambition?

Do the Old Ideals Prevail?

One could argue that the notions of "pure philosophy" and "high culture" in the minds of the university's founding fathers 60 years ago have proved to be little more than ideological constructs. Now disinterested, pure science was replaced by the quest for practical results. In practice, from the beginning, the professional faculty that were assembled when the university was founded resisted the academics in the new Faculty of Philosophy who were brought over from Europe (they used to be scorned as "the philosophers"). The faculty in the professional fields continued their traditional task of providing skilled and prestigious liberal professionals for an expanding urban and industrial economy.

Did the university succeed in creating a "new elite" for the country, recovering the national preeminence the state of São Paulo lost during the 1930s, in keeping with the ambitions of the old Latin American flagship institutions? Up to a certain point, the USP can be seen as having met these expectations. Fernando Henrique Cardoso, Brazil's president between 1995 and 2002, was a direct product of the Universidade de São Paulo and probably the best example of the French-style intelligentsia the university hoped to create. His successor, Luis Ignacio Lula da Silva, is a metalworker with little formal education who was born in the poor northeast but has always been surrounded by intellectuals and militants educated at USP. The largest Brazilian companies and most of the country's more influential newspapers and magazines are based in São Paulo, and it is likely their top managers also earned their degrees from USP.

Still, the preeminence of USP alumni in Brazilian society could be just a consequence of the economic weight of the state of São Paulo, not the result of the special characteristics of its main university. It is interesting, in this regard, to look at USP in combination with its younger sister, the Universidade de Campinas, which was established with the clear intent of becoming a modern research university, the leading place for the incorporation of high technology, and part of an ambitious project of economic and technological development led by the Brazilian military government in the 1960s and 1970s. One of its more important initiatives was the creation of a department of solid-state physics, led by Sérgio Porto, Rogério Cerqueira Leite, José Ellis Ripper, and other Brazilian scientists trained in the United States and working at Bell and other preeminent US laboratories and research centers and later attracted back to the country with the promise of strong support for their projects. Another initiative was the creation of the Department of Economics, staffed by economists trained in the nationalist tradition of the United Nations Economic Commission for Latin America—including Maria da Conceição Tavares, Antônio de Barros Castro, and Carlos Lessa.

It can be argued that for this new generation of physicists and economists the modern research university was indistinguishable from the more traditional political intelligentsia and thus academics were following the same path as USP. Instead of atomic energy, the main projects for physicists were self-sufficiency in the computer sciences and the production of new materials. For economists, industrialization and economic planning replaced the Marxist sociological analysis that dominated the work of USP intellectuals.

Technological self-reliance was part of a broader policy of import substitutions that provided Brazil with many years of sustained economic growth. However, Brazil never became self-sufficient in atomic energy or computer sciences (Schwartzman 1988), and its economy was never ruled according to the principles of central planning or the precepts of the United Nations Economic Commission for Latin America. The more ambitious projects for technological self-sufficiency undertaken by both the physicists of the older generation at USP and of the new generation at the Universidade de Campinas ultimately failed—not because their science was bad but because it was not extensive enough. Soon after World War II, the quest for self-sufficiency in atomic energy became embroiled over issues of national security and the cold war, and scientists lost their influence in the field to the military and the utility companies (Adler 1987). Years later, the ambitious project for self-sufficiency in computers and semiconductors was overwhelmed by the sheer speed of technological change in this area, an international trend that Brazilian firms and research centers could not achieve, in spite of a closed market that protected them for a few years (Botelho and Smith 1985).

As the technological and business frontier advanced, the scientists in these fields had trouble getting enough demand and resources to continue their work. In some cases, they were able to establish long-standing relationships with military projects and state-owned corporations in the areas of atomic energy, space research, electricity, telecommunications, transportation, and environment. In the 1990s, as most Brazilian public corporations were privatized and the nationalist ambitions of the military lost ground, these partnerships also suffered. In other cases, important private spin-offs were created under the leadership of former academics who left the universities for the business sector. Several scientists from these universities developed important careers as public personalities, managers of large public corporations, and ministers and vice ministers in the areas of energy, science, technology, and economic decision making. These individual success stories often meant, however, that the universities lost some of their brightest minds, and their academic departments suffered.

In the social sciences, it is also possible to argue that the growing influence of some of the best-known sociologists from USP and the Universidade de Campinas as writers, intellectuals, and politicians was not matched by a corresponding improvement of their academic work. USP was slow in incorporating the Anglo-Saxon traditions of empirical sociology that became dominant worldwide since the 1960s and for many years did not differentiate among sociology, political science, and anthropology in its organization. In the meantime, economics at USP remained close to administration and business, in isolation from the other social sciences, and did not lead to an intellectual drive to shape the country's economic policy,[8] as sought later on by the economists from Campinas. There, the economists tried to play a direct role in shaping the country's industrial and technological policies and were always active in politics and policymaking. In the 1980s, the first civilian government after 20 years of military rule created a Ministry for Science and Technology, which was supposed to continue the policy of technological self-reliance of the previous years and was led by an economist from Campinas, Luciano Coutinho, in his role as vice minister. Other economists from that university became well known for their participation in the debates on economic policy and occupied important government posts at different points in time.[9] However, none of them remained at the university, and today the Department of Economics in Campinas is not rated by CAPES (Coordenação de Aperfeiçoamento do Ensino Superior [Office for the Improvement of Higher Learning]) as among the country's best. So, in many ways, both USP and Universidade de Campinas succeeded in projecting themselves as institutions with a strong national impact, and became references for other higher education institutions. But it is fair to say that these individual success stories were the exception, not the rule, and seldom led to consistent and long-lasting improvement in the academic and research quality of the departments from which they originated.

From Intellectual Leadership to Social Inclusion

It is possible to conclude, from these brief stories, that intellectual influence and academic excellence differ and perhaps do not even go along well together. Today, there is little or no space left for intellectuals trying to play the role of national intelligentsia; in the social sciences, the ideological flag moved away to a large extent from sociology, political science, and economics, where it occupied the central stage, to restricted niches in areas such as geography, education, and literature.[10] The best academic departments and institutes are not those that tried to play the roles of the intelligentsia but those that built their competence by keeping in touch with the international community and developing pragmatic links with the surrounding society.

The election of Luis Ignácio Lula da Silva as Brazil's president in 2002 marked an important shift in the perceptions about national priorities. Until then, the dominant notion was that Brazil was an "underdeveloped" or "developing" country, a condition that needed to be overcome through the incorporation of advanced technologies, the modernization of the economy, and the rationalization of public bureaucracies. This view was shared by political, military, and civilian elites and led to unexpected alliances between left and right, particularly in high-technology areas such as atomic energy and information technology policies, based on a common belief in the powers of planning and the importance of modern science and technology. The Fernando Henrique Cardoso period, from 1995 to 2002, was perhaps the last of a sequence of "modernizing" governments dating back from the 1930s and was successful in bringing inflation under control after many years of fiscal irresponsibility and in opening up the country to the international economy. This, however, was not enough to make the economy grow again or to deal with the problems of poverty, inequality, and growing demands for political participation that came to dominate the political agenda.[11]

The election of Lula as president was the turning point. The slogan of the presidential candidate, that Cardoso had "forgotten the social," was brilliantly conveyed through a skillful and highly professional marketing campaign. With the new government, money would be spent on social issues, not on interest payments to bankers; management of public agencies and implementation of social policies would be handed over to unions and social movements, not to bureaucrats; and the economy would grow through the increase of the purchasing power of a newly empowered and subsidized population, not through special privileges granted to national and international capitalists.

Electoral victory did not translate easily into policy implementation. The new government tried, simultaneously, to implement an orthodox economic policy, based on high interest rates, budget restraint, and innovative social initiatives—such as the "hunger zero" program, based on subsidies given to poor families. As of September 2005, the economic policies seemed to be working well enough to keep exports high and inflation down, but most social programs are in disarray and the government is immersed in a wide-range, paralyzing political bribery scandal.

For higher education, the government prepared controversial new legislation that is still to be submitted for congressional approval. The main points are a significant increase in resources for federal universities, increased restrictions and control of private higher education, a greater presence of "organized society" in the oversight of public and private institutions, coupled with more institutional autonomy, and affirmative action, with the introduction of quotas for blacks and students coming from public school in public universities.[12] Without waiting for approval, the government launched a program called "Universities for All," which exchanged fiscal benefits for the admittance of about 100,000 low-income and minority students at private institutions; and several public universities started to implement quota policies for blacks and students coming from public secondary schools. Also, together with the promise of additional money, federal universities are being pressed to increase enrollments by opening up more evening courses for poorer and older students. The ideas that universities should strive for quality and that student admissions should be based on merit were never challenged as such, but the new emphasis is clearly on the side of social inclusion rather than academic excellence.

USP was not immune to this trend and has tried to find a middle ground. Its main initiative was to open a new campus in one of the poorest quarters of the city of São Paulo, the Zona Leste (east zone). Starting in 2005, the new campus is admitting about a thousand students a year, in programs like environment management, information systems, management of public policies, marketing, technology of the textile and clothing industries, teaching in natural sciences, leisure and tourism, sciences of physical activities, gerontology, and obstetrics.

These are mostly vocational-type programs, and the assumption is that admissions, to be done through competitive examinations, would require less previous education than the more traditional careers. The newspaper *O Estado de São Paulo* published a long editorial on the new campus, which was reproduced later on the Web site of the São Paulo government:

> While in the University City [USP's main campus], in the southern part of São Paulo, only 10% of the students are black, in the new campus the mean is above 21%. Besides, only 29% of the students in the traditional units of USP come from public schools, but in the new campus the figure is 47%. In other words, half of the students came from families who could not afford to send their children to private schools. . . .
>
> The most important thing is that the students in the Zona Leste campus did not enter USP through some kind of privilege, as happens in universities that are implementing the quota system. On the contrary, since there is no racial filter, the new USP students are the ones who got the highest marks in a rigorous and competitive exam. "Before that, they used to see USP as something very far away, in all senses," said Sônia Penin, USP's vice-rector for undergraduate studies.
>
> The decision to preserve meritocracy is the main difference between the model adopted by the São Paulo government and the quota policies of the Federal Government. The quotas, insofar as they allow less-qualified students to enter the university instead of other more-qualified students, replace competency with other criteria, like race and school origin. Those who benefit from these policies are admitted, but many of them are unable to follow the programs, and end up flunking their exams or being treated as second-class students by their teachers. ("A USP na Zona Leste" 2005)

Public Universities and the "Privatization" of Higher Education

The other component of the higher education policies proposed by the federal government, with strong support from teachers unions and student associations, is the opposition against what is perceived as a trend toward the privatization of higher education. With 70 percent of enrollments already in private institutions, there is a real issue of the role of public and private higher education in the country and of the regulatory framework that should exist to stimulate quality, make sure that philanthropic institutions are authentic, and limit the excesses of profit making. Another issue, however, is whether the existing public institutions, like USP, are also being privatized in some sense of the word.

From the point of view of unions, this is a real threat, associated with at least four issues: the charging of tuition at public institutions; the status of teachers and university employees as civil servants; the introduction of external assessment leading to competition among the institutions for prestige, recognition, and resources; and the ability of the universities to raise and manage money independently. According to their view, a fully public institution should be free for the students, provide job stability to its staff, and does not have to worry about going out and competing for resources.

The right for tuition-free public universities is written down in the 1988 Brazilian constitution, and no government dared to suggest changing that provision. The same constitution granted lifelong job stability to all employees, teachers, and staff at public universities, and the same principle is adopted at state institutions like USP. None of the assessment systems tried by the different governments, except perhaps the assessment of graduate education by CAPES, has linked achievement with resources.

The only break with this fully public model was the creation, by public universities, of foundations established as private entities to manage resources unencumbered by the rigidities and formalities of the civil service. Initially, these foundations were created with the support of other public agencies outside the Ministry of Education, to receive and manage research and contract grants given to specific departments and projects, bypassing the central bureaucracies. In other cases, they were created by the university's central authorities, to provide them with flexibility to manage extrabudgetary resources. There are many institutions of this kind; USP has 32 foundations established by its different departments and institutes, besides one created by the rector's office.

Universities, departments, and institutes can obtain important benefits if they are able to raise resources through research grants, contract work, and extension courses. The foundations can buy equipment; pay the salaries of visiting professors and short-term staff; provide fellowships to students; complement the salaries of professors and employees; and meet the general and extraordinary expenses when the regular budget is not sufficient. They can also facilitate the links and interchanges between universities and the external world, reducing the institutions' isolation. The negative side is that, if universities are not properly administered, they can easily develop interests that benefit a small group of academics, at the expense of research, scholarship, and the broader goals of education. Another consequence is the creation of rich and poor departments and institutions within the same universities, in terms of both their resources and the income of their staff.

In 2004, the private foundations at USP came under strong attack from the teachers and employees unions and student associations. This is how a journalist from *Folha de São Paulo* described the situation:

> One of the most controversial alternative ways of raising resources are the MBA programs offered by FIA, the Fundação Instituto de Administração, and Fipecafi, the Fundação Instituto de Pesquisas Contábeis. Atuariais e Financeiras [Institute of Administration Foundation and Institute of Accounting, Actuarial, and Financial Research Foundation] both linked to the Faculdade de Economia e Administração [Faculty of Economics and Administration]. The courses cost between 18 and 20 thousand reais,[13] and most of them provide a certificate that is recognized by USP. Part of the resources are transferred to USP, but most remains with the foundations. Last year, FIA received 63 million and handed 3 million to the university. The remaining 60 million were used to pay its 450 employees and about 55 professors from the accounting departments that teach at FIA. The main discussion is whether it is legitimate to use the name of the university in private activities and if there is a conflict between the activities of the professor in the University and in the Foundation, where his earnings can be higher than the regular salary. (Trevisan 2004)

For the faculty union (Associação de Docentes da Universidade de São Paulo), this is a scandal:

> The use of the USP trademark, of its facilities, and the tax exemption granted to the private foundations are enough to characterize the support of private interests with public money. To this, one should add all the millionaire contracts with the public sector, surprising by the variety of areas involved and services provided. Differently from what the managers of these foundations say, regarding the consulting projects, research, and courses they provide, most of the money goes not to the university but to the pockets of the foundation's partners and to the foundation's overhead, used to start up other private deals. (Associaçao de Docentes 2001)

Roberto Macedo—now a columnist of *O Estado de São Paulo*, but formerly director of FEA (the Faculty of Economy and Administration), which runs one of the largest foundations at the university—was one of the voices defending the foundations. It is not true, he said, that their money does not benefit the university, since most of it is used to complement the salaries of the professors, according to well-established procedures. The foundations are important not just for the money they bring in but also for the quality of their work and the enhancements they provide for the university. "Many of the best talents of USP work in the foundations, and their entrepreneurship is indispensable for the growth and consolidation of institutions. It will be a big disaster if their initiative is curtailed. Without them, USP would be waiting forever for additional resources from a Godot who never arrives" (Macedo 2004).

A final aspect of privatization has to do with internationalization. Brazil has an important tradition of sending its best students to study abroad, particularly to the United States, France, and England, and there is a permanent flow of academics traveling back and forth between Brazil and these and other countries. In 2003, USP received as visiting professors 297 Americans, 91 Germans, 82 Portuguese, 63 Mexicans, 42 Italians, and 36 Japanese, among others. However, the percentage of foreign graduate students is just about 3 percent—about 180 of the about 5,500 graduate students. The number of foreign students among the 45,000 undergraduates is unknown. No established procedures exist for foreign students to apply to the undergraduate programs without going through the regular written exams in Portuguese. Admittance to graduate programs is more flexible, but the university does not have an active policy of bringing in foreign students and providing them with support. It is unlikely that Brazil would attract many students from Asia, the United States, or Western Europe, but USP could be attractive to students coming from other Latin American countries and an excellent choice for students and scholars interested in interchange programs from all over the world. One factor that kept the international dimension of the university from developing is that a large influx of foreign students would not bring any direct benefits since the university cannot charge tuition. Such a move would also require significant changes in the way the university operates, affecting admission procedures, the use of foreign languages in classes, exams, and dissertations, investments and support for housing, and so forth.

More broadly, Brazilian universities, including USP, remain local, inward-looking institutions. It would not be difficult to draw up a long list including professors at the best universities who were educated abroad, foreign academics who come to work or visit on a regular basis, and articles published by Brazilian professors in the international literature. In this context, the universities remain linked to the international scientific community. However, for most of these scholars, studying abroad signified a step in their local careers, and their reference remains their local institutions. This was shown clearly in the 1993 Carnegie Foundation international survey of the academic profession, in which Brazilians were seen to be much more attached to their institution than scholars in other countries.[14] This is coherent with the fact that academics working at public institutions in Brazil have civil servant status, are stable in their jobs, and usually cannot move from one institution to another except upon retirement. An important correlate of this localism is inbreeding, which is particularly strong at the São Paulo universities. The Carnegie Foundation survey showed that fully 90 percent of the academics with doctoral degrees and higher at São Paulo universities had obtained their higher degrees from Brazilian institutions (presumably USP itself), against 63.3 percent for those in federal universities. This was not an effect of age differences, since the average age in the two groups was about the same (48 years) but is related to the fact that São Paulo has the oldest and best doctoral programs in the country, limiting the need (and the benefits) for its academics of going abroad for their higher degrees. In 2003, a similar survey showed that, in a national sample of academics, 41 percent of those from the Universidade de Minas Gerais and 25 percent of those from the Universidade do Rio de Janeiro had obtained their doctoral degrees abroad, against only 15 percent of those from USP.[15]

This local culture, combined with the fact that Portuguese is also a local language and Spanish is less widely known and understood in Brazil than is usually thought, makes the country less accessible to the trend of internationalization of higher education under way in other countries. Foreign institutions find it difficult to get established in Brazil, and Brazilians tend to view them with mistrust. The new higher education legislation proposed by the Brazilian government limits the participation of foreigners at proprietary private higher institutions in the country by 25 percent of controlling assets, and this is justified as a move to resist the invasion of and destruction of Brazilian culture through the international flow of educational services that is being proposed to the World Trade Organization under the General Agreement on Trade in Services.

CONCLUSION

In a recent article, Philip Altbach observed that, in the world today, "everyone wants a world-class university. No country feels it can do without one" (Altbach 2003, 5). In Brazil, however, there is no general feeling that the country needs a world-class university, and USP, the university that could aspire to this role, prefers to see itself as a local institution. Considering its size, the qualifications of its staff, the research being produced, and the assets and the resources it mobilizes, USP could already be considered to be among the leading universities in the world. However, given the way it recruits its students, the small number of foreign students and scholars, and the almost exclusive use of the Portuguese language,[16] it is a local institution. More than that, it remains a provincial institution, strongly identified with the state of São Paulo, with less of a national presence than it could probably have.[17]

The importance of world-class universities does not relate only to the need to participate and compete internationally in the areas of advanced science and technology. It is not true, as it is often claimed, that the new "knowledge economy" requires that everybody should have a higher education degree and become a specialist in some kind of advanced technology. Everywhere, employment expands mostly in the services sector, and ample working space and opportunities exist for persons with general education who can read and write, know more than one language, and are able to understand and to move around in the social context in which they live.

The exclusive emphasis on research is an exaggeration. World-class universities should develop science and technology, but they also need to educate persons, endowing them with culture, general education, and the ability to understand what is happening in their countries and the world. These universities need to educate diplomats, civil servants, politicians, journalists, historians, and writers. They should work as bridges between the country and the larger world and provide standards of intellectual excellence to other institutions.

Finally, world-class universities represent the only intelligent way of dealing with higher education globalization trends, a broad process that includes the creation of branches of prestigious, world-class universities in other countries and the expansion of a growing knowledge industry led by big companies through the use of new technologies of distance learning or the spreading of local franchises. It is difficult to imagine that this trend could be stopped by closing the country to foreign influences, forbidding the entrance of foreign institutions, or controlling the access of students to distance education. In general, the regulatory powers of public authorities can only be applied to programs providing formal degrees associated with professional licensing and market privileges of some kind. Increasingly, however, markets are looking for other kinds of certification through extension programs such as the MBAs offered by the FIA and other foundations at USP or non-university institutions such as Fundação Getúlio Vargas, which could also be easily provided by foreign institutions. There is no way to stop the flow of informal knowledge through the Internet. Nowhere, not even in more homogeneous societies like Germany or the Scandinavian countries, could *all* the universities try to play this international role. However, some universities can reach that level and could be stimulated to develop and grow in quality, competence, and international outlook.

In his overview, Altbach looks at this drive for world-class universities with skepticism, and we come back to his doubts later on. First, however, we should look at the characteristics such universities need, according to him, to earn this title.

First, world-class research, internationally recognized—for this standing, it is necessary to have excellent professors, good working conditions, and competitive salaries. Good working conditions include job stability for the best qualified and salaries high enough to compete with those of the private sector or other universities in the country and abroad.

Second, freedom of research, teaching, and expression—professors, researchers, and students should be free to choose research topics and to express their findings and interpretations without limitations or constraints. This freedom should extend beyond the specialties of each professor or researcher, including the freedom to take stands on broader issues of social and cultural importance of concern to society as a whole.

Third, academic autonomy—the universities, through their best-qualified academics, should have the freedom to establish their main areas of teaching and research and the mechanisms to select staff, admit students, and set the criteria for the provision of degrees and certificates.

Fourth, infrastructure—good universities need up-to-date laboratories, libraries, and computer facilities, access to national and international databanks, and good working environments for academics and students (offices, lecture halls, an efficient administrative staff, and permanent maintenance of buildings and open spaces).

Last but not least, money—high-quality universities are expensive, costs are constantly rising, it is impossible to replace high-quality, personalized teaching with technologies, and not all departments and institutions are equally able to get external resources on their own. World-class universities, to exist, need substantial and permanent public support.

The first characteristics listed by Altbach were present in the creation of USP 70 years ago and were adopted thereafter, at least on paper, by all Brazilian higher education legislation. The traits derive from the work on universities by Cardinal Newman, Abraham Flexner, and the admirers of the old Humboldt University. These ideals still exist in broad terms but do not account for the dramatic transformation higher education has undergone since these classic writings.[18]

In Brazil, as in many other countries, these values were undermined when confronted with the demands, values, and perceptions of education authorities, professional corporations, and the generalized demand for higher education credentials. At its worst, research became a game based on points measured by publications, which are converted into grades, promotions, and resources. Little attention is focused on the relevance of what is actually being researched and published. Job assurance for academics turned into rigidity and immobility, and the hiring of new academics developed into bureaucratic rituals that are not immune from manipulation by small cliques. Public financing for the universities seems to have reached its ceiling, and resources are distributed according to past history or the political clout of the universities, without due consideration of needs and the quality of teaching and research. Autonomy turned many institutions into mini-republics governed by the majority votes of its students and academic and administrative staff, without much regard for the hierarchy of knowledge and competence and the broader goals of the institutions. Not all institutions have such an internal configuration, and there are many places where academic values and culture prevail, but these trends are well known and particularly strong in institutions created by political and administrative fiat, without a strong academic community at its core. Given these trends, is it still possible to try to come back to the old ideals of Newman and Flexner, as the core values of the new, world-class universities?

I do not interpret Altbach's article as a plea to a return to the past. The best universities today do seem to be traditional institutions that have retained their culture of autonomy and standards of quality in the recruitment of their staff and students. However, in order to keep the old values, these traditional universities had to go through deep transformations and modernization. The solution, and the challenge, is to combine these two things: the best academic traditions and the required transformations and adaptations to modern times.

There are three other characteristics that should be added to Altbach's list: cosmopolitanism, diversity, and modern management. World-class universities should assemble professors from the country and abroad and a large number of foreign students. With them, they can create an environment in which local assumptions and experiences are permanently compared and contrasted with those of other countries, not only regarding specific contents of research and programs but largely the tacit assumptions and ways of life familiar to those who have had the experience of living with different cultures. The use of English as a second language is essential. Some countries, particularly in Asia and Africa, decided to adopt English as the working language of their main universities. European countries such as the Netherlands, Sweden, and increasingly Germany and France, are offering courses in English and admit students working in English, particularly in graduate programs. In Brazil, besides the adoption of English, it would be necessary to adopt Spanish as an alternate language option.

Diversity has to do with social inclusion but involves more than that asset. World-class universities should be open to persons from different cultural and social origins and backgrounds and allow for the emergence and strengthening of a more diversified leadership. This can be done through admissions and hiring policies that take social and cultural diversity into consideration, and the creation of alternative programs to enrich the university experience for all participants. This is difficult to do in Brazil, given the general assumption that student admissions and the hiring of academic staff should be done through formal procedures and written tests. These formalities are perceived as "objective" procedures, meant to limit the use of particularistic and self-serving practices that could prevail in more informal, "subjective" methods. These assumptions are an important obstacle for the implementation of affirmative action in higher education institutions, since the introduction of racial quotas leads to clear violations of the principle of objectivity, which should be immune from racial, ethnic, regional, and religious considerations.

The next crucial issues include autonomy, management, and financing. University autonomy today is different from the ideals of the 1918 Cordoba university reform movement in Latin America that embodied political autonomy coupled with slow, collegial decision-making procedures. This kind of autonomy is convenient for leaving things as they are and inconvenient for making decisions that can affect established interests. Latin Americans still talk with pride about their tradition of university autonomy but usually do not understand that this political arrangement may underlie the academic weakness of most of their institutions. A modern university should be autonomous enough to open and close departments, hire and dismiss teachers and researchers, and direct resources to meet new challenges without having to ask for government permission or to negotiate each decision with all their students, staff, and employees.

To exert this autonomy, universities need a new type of management. University rectors cannot remain as paper shufflers or presidents of endless meetings of university councils. It is necessary to establish priorities, assess costs and benefits, develop long-term financial plans, and manage assets. Instead of routine competition for academic posts, it is necessary to develop active human resource policies—searching for talent, attracting the best with good offers of salaries and working conditions, and administering the departure of those who are considered below standards or inappropriate for the institution. Instead of routine and formal procedures for student admissions, institutions need to develop active policies for searching for and attracting students within the country and abroad. It is necessary to choose the fields on which to concentrate research resources and take decisions about traditional sectors that have become obsolete and lost their edge.

It is not easy to reconcile this management style, typical of business corporations, with the traditional values and cultures of academic life. The ideal situation arises when institutional leadership is carried out by persons with strong academic and intellectual credentials and recognition. This, fortunately, is not an impossible combination, given the fact that successful scientists and academics are often persons with strong managerial and entrepreneurial talent and experience.[19]

Management issues relate to the question of the organization of the universities along professional and disciplinary lines. Originally, Brazilian universities, following the Napoleonic model, were organized along the lines of professional schools (in fact, professional schools preceded the universities and in many cases were never fully integrated into them). Later, with the 1968 university reform, universities started to be organized around departments and institutes, defined along disciplinary lines. One negative effect of this transformation was that many programs, particularly in areas with scant professional traditions, turned into a sequence of unconnected programs offered by different departments, without unified management and leadership. Moreover, today research is not restricted by disciplinary or professional boundaries, and the universities have found it difficult to open spaces and provide support for this new type of trans- or multidisciplinary work.

The downside of the organization of universities into departments and institutes has led many to believe that the departments should be abolished—a difficult position to sustain since it does not seem to make sense to return to the traditional combination of the chair system and of professional faculties, or schools. In practice, different institutional arrangements can work well, or they may fail. The main issue is how to endow the universities with strong and relatively autonomous decision-making and management centers to lead the different activities in teaching, research, and extension work, keeping them in tune with the institutions' overall management and institutional goals.

Concerning research, academic freedom should be combined with clear policies of priorities and focus. Teachers and researchers cannot be stopped from saying what they think, in class or outside it, and from undertaking the research they believe to be most important. This freedom, however, needs to be combined with proper peer review and with the understanding that research is an expensive and potentially profitable activity and may also lead to ethical problems. Issues of intellectual property and ethical behavior, particularly in the social and medical areas, must also be addressed and cannot be left totally to the discretion of the individual researcher or department heads. Finally, recognition that the boundaries between basic and applied research are mostly gone, if they ever existed, leads to both complex issues and new opportunities, associated with interaction between universities, governments, and business interests that universities must learn to face and administer.

For all things considered, nothing can be achieved without significant levels of money. World-class universities cannot exist without public support, but even that is not enough. It is necessary to charge for services, carry out donation campaigns, charge tuition, and set a professional policy of long-term investments. Incentive policies will be needed to stimulate good results. If the money comes earmarked in the budget for specific purposes or if the savings in one area at one point cannot be used later in another area, then there will be no incentives to manage resources efficiently. There is a clear incompatibility between the management requisites of a world-class university and the rules and regulations of public service, which in Brazil as in most countries tend to be characterized by detailed budgets, rigid procurement procedures, and formalized rituals for hiring staff and admitting students. These challenges do not mean that world-class institutions cannot be in the public sector. However, they need a new kind of working contract with the public sector, based on global budgets, long-term investments, autonomy to establish their own policies for personnel and admissions, and greater flexibility in the management of resources.

There are clear limits on what a university can do to achieve world status. Costs are high, and not all countries and regions can or should make the necessary investments. Revenues from services, research grants, tuition, and other "soft" sources cannot fully compensate for a lack of significant public support. Worldwide, besides in Europe and the United States, serious efforts are under way in China, Korea, India, and Singapore to enter this select club. The United Kingdom is concentrating its research resources at leading universities, such as Cambridge and Oxford, to maintain their international competitiveness. Germany, with a much more egalitarian tradition, is also starting to confront the issue. Even the best universities in the world cannot be excellent in all fields. Harvard, the first in all rankings, is not considered strong in engineering, and Princeton does not have a medical school.

However, even the most global universities exist within countries, from which they receive most of their resources and recruit most of their students and staff. There are subjects, issues, research topics, and professional profiles that are typical of specific regions and countries and need to be respected. World-class universities need to have strong roots in their societies, and it is only from these roots that they can branch out to other cultures and societies. Lastly, not all universities and higher education institutions should aspire to the same goals and follow the same models. In the large universe of higher education institutions that exist today, there is ample space for different roles and vocations, and to be a world-class institution is one option among others.

On its 70th anniversary, USP needs to decide whether it wants to return to its original ideals and become a leading, world-class university, making the necessary adjustments and changes, or remain one among many other higher education institutions in Brazil, teaching and doing research with competence but not aiming at more than that. This cannot be a simple decision to be taken by a university rector or a group, since it would require the commitment of the state government and the support of the broader academic, professional, and business communities. Such a project will call for identifying more clearly the role of a leading university in the contemporary world. The current role cannot be the nurturing of an old-fashioned intelligentsia, professional education for the elites, or the provision of mass higher education but entails a much more complex and daily integration and interchange with the worlds of high technology, business, and public policy and a much more cosmopolitan outlook. Brazil needs world-class universities, and USP, with the support of the state's resources and tradition of leadership, is one of the few institutions in the country with the intellectual, material, and political resources to accept, confront, and win this challenge.

NOTES

Author's Note: I am grateful for comments, corrections, criticism, and additional information from Elizabeth Balbachevsky, Universidade de São Paulo; Edson Nunes, Universidade Cândido Mendes; Mariza Peirano, Universidade de Brasília; and, particularly, Carlos Henrique Brito Cruz, former rector of the Universidade de Campinas and current scientific director of São Paulo's state research foundation, FAPESP.

1. See Chapter 8 for an overview of higher education in Brazil today. See also Schwartzman (1992, 2004).

2. *Bandeiras*—literally, flags—was the name given to the explorers who, since the 16th century, went from the old captaincy of São Vicente, now São Paulo, to faraway regions in the unknown continent of South America in search of gold and slaves, opening new territories, creating settlements, and expanding the frontiers of what is Brazil today. The myth of the *Bandeirantes*, or flag carriers, became a symbol of São Paulo's entrepreneurship (Moog 1964; Morse 1965).

3. For Lévi-Strauss's unflattering recollections of the USP in those years, see Lévi-Strauss (1997).

4. The total enrollment in first degree programs in 2003 was 44,000, compared with about 100,000 for the Universidade Estácio de Sá in Rio de Janeiro and 92,000 for the Universidade Paulista in São Paulo, both private, mostly teaching institutions (Brasil Ministério da Educação 2004).

5. US dollars are in PPP. PPP refers to the purchasing power parity between currencies, which is supposed to be more accurate than market exchange rates.

6. The three São Paulo universities are entitled to a fixed percentage of 9.57 percent of the state main tax revenues (Imposto de Circulação de Mercadorias), according to rules established by the state legislature: 5.029 percent for USP, 2.196 percent for Universidade de Campinas, and 2.345 percent for the third university, Universidade Estadual Paulista. In addition, there are resources from medical authorities for university hospitals, and research money from both the state and the federal governments. In 2003, the medical complex of Hospital das Clínicas of the University of São Paulo had a budget of about 500 million reais (US$423 million), with most of the resources coming from the Health Ministry (Hospital das Clínicas da Universidade de São Paulo 2003). Besides, researchers at USP are able to tap into the resources of Brazil's largest science research supporting agency, São Paulo's Fundação de Amparo à Pesquisa.

7. In 2003, at USP there were 3,873 academics working full-time, out of a total of 4,953. The largest proportions of part-time academics are in the professional schools of medicine, dentistry, law, and agrarian sciences (Universidade de São Paulo 2004, table 2.11).

8. An exception was Antônio Delfim Netto, a professor of economics at USP and currently a congressman, who was Brazil's economics minister between 1967 and 1985, the years of the "economic miracle" and of deep transformations in the economy. Delfim Netto was easily the most effective Brazilian economist in the 20th century. Still, it is difficult to identify a "Delfim Netto school of economic thought" at the USP, as we do with the social scientists at USP or later with the economists at the

University of Campinas.

9. Barros Castro was president of Brazil's largest public investment bank, the National Bank for Economic and Social Development in the mid-1990s (and the bank's planning director in 2005), and Lessa occupied the same post 10 years later, in a very different political context. Conceição Tavares became a member of Parliament, an influential intellectual of the Workers' Party, and for a while led the opposition to the conservative economic policies of Luis Ignácio Lula da Silva's government.

10. The case of the Centro Brasileiro de Análise e Planejamento, established by Fernando Henrique Cardoso and his colleagues after his return from political exile in the 1970s, is emblematic: as Cardoso's political presence in the country as a leading politician increased, the intellectual significance of his center declined (Sorj 2001).

11. It is not true, as is sometimes said, that the social conditions in Brazil deteriorated during the Cardoso period, as a consequence of fiscal and economic adjustments. It is true, however, that the economy remained mostly stagnant, as it had been since the early 1980s (Schwartzman 2000).

12. The expression "organized society" is part of the new jargon used by members of the PT (Partido dos Trabalhadores [Workers Party]) party to refer to trade unions, social movements, and other grassroots organizations. For a critical view of the government's higher education reform proposal, as well as the first version of the reform proposal, see Castro and Schwartzman (2005).

13. The market exchange rate was about 3 reais per dollar in 2003; the surcharging power parity was estimated to be 1.18.

14. In the survey, 76 percent of the Brazilian academics considered their institutional affiliation to be "very important," the highest of the 13 countries in the study, compared with 65 percent in Chile, 56 percent in Mexico, 36 percent in the United States, 19 percent in Sweden, and 8 percent in Germany, among others (Boyer, Altbach, and Whitelaw 1994, 80).

15. I am grateful to Elizabeth Balbachevsky for sharing this information from the 2003 Brazilian National Survey on the Academic Profession, sponsored by the Ford Foundation.

16. The university bylaws require that all dissertations should be written in Portuguese, with possible exceptions in foreign literature (I am indebted to Elizabeth Balbachevsky for confirming this information).

17. In the ranking produced by the Institute of Higher Education of Shanghai Jiao Tong University, the best-placed Latin American universities are the Universidad Nacional Autónoma de México (UNAM) and the USP, both tied at the 153th ranking place; neither USP nor UNAM appears in the ranking produced by the *Times Higher Education Supplement*, although they are obviously better than several institutions listed there, in many dimensions (Institute of Higher Education 2004).

18. For a contemporary overview, see the "knowledge" chapter 1 in Clark (1983, 11–26).

19. Bruno Latour has elaborated this point in several places. See, for instance, the introductory chapter of *Science in Action* (Latour 1987).

REFERENCES

Adler, E. 1987. *The power of ideology: The quest for technological autonomy in Argentina and Brazil*. Berkeley: University of California Press.

Altbach, P. G. 2003. The costs and benefits of world-class universities. *International Higher Education*, no. 33:5–8.

Associaçao de Docentes da Universidade de São Paulo (ADUSP). 2001. Dossiê Fundações. *Revista ADUSP*, March. www.adusp.org.br/revista/22 /Default.htm.

A USP na Zona Leste. 2005. *O Estado de São Paulo*, March 12. www.saopaulo.sp.gov.br/sis/leimprensa.asp?id=62045.

Botelho, A. J., and P. H. Smith. 1985. *The computer question in Brazil: High technology in a developing society*. Boston: Massachusetts Institute of Technology, Center for International Studies.

Boyer, E. L., P. G. Altbach, and M. J. Whitelaw. 1994. *The academic profession: An international perspective*. Princeton, NJ: Carnegie Foundation for the Advancement of Teaching.

Brasil Ministério da Educacão. 2004. Censo da Educação Superior 2004—Resumo Técnico, Tabelas Anexo. www.inep.gov.br/download/superior/censo/2004 ResumoTecnico2003_ANEXO.pdf (accessed June 30, 2005).

Castro, C. d. M., and S. Schwartzman. 2005. *Reforma da Educação Superior—Uma Visão Crítica*. Brasília: FUNADESP.

Clark, B. R. 1983. *The higher education system: Academic organization in cross-national perspective*. Berkeley: University of California Press.

Halperín Donghi, T. 1962. *Historia de la Universidad de Buenos Aires*. Buenos Aires: Editorial Universitaria de Buenos Aires.

Hospital das Clínicas da Universidade de São Paulo. 2003. Relatório Anual de Atividades. www.hcnet.usp.br/publi cacoes/index.htm (accessed June 30, 2005).

INEP. 2003. Censo do Ensino Superior. www.inep gov br/superior /censosuperior/.

Institute of Higher Education, Shanghai Jiao Tong University. 2004. Academic ranking of world universities. http://ed.sjtu.edu.cn/ranking.htm.

Latour, B. 1987. *Science in action: How to follow scientists and engineers through society.* Cambridge, MA: Harvard University Press.

Lévi-Strauss, C. 1997. *Tristes tropiques*. New York: Modern Library.

Limongi, F. 2001. A Escola Livre de Sociologia e Política de São Paulo. In *História das ciências sociais no Brasil*, ed. S. Miceli, vol. 1 (2a edição revista e corrigida ed.), 257–76). São Paulo: Sumaré.

Macedo, R. 2004. Fundações fortalecem a USP. *O Estado de São Paulo*, April 29. www.universiabrasil.com.br/html/noticiaggejh.html.

Mesquita Filho, J. d. 1969. *Política e cultura*. São Paulo: Livraria Martins.

Moog, C. V. 1964. *Bandeirantes and pioneers*. New York: G. Braziller.

Morse, R. M. 1965. *The bandeirantes: The historical role of the Brazilian pathfinders*. New York: Knopf.

National Science Foundation. 2003. Survey of earned doctorates. www.nsf.gov/statistics/srvydoctorates/.

Schwartzman, S. 1988. High technology vs. self reliance: Brazil enters the computer age. In *Brazil's economic and political future*, ed. J. M. Chacel, P. S. Falk, and D. V. Fleischer, 67–82. Boulder, CO: Westview Press.

———. 1991a. Changing roles of new knowledge: Research institutions and societal transformations in Brazil. In *Social sciences and modern states: National experiences and theoretical crossroads*, ed. P. Wagner, C. H. Weiss, B. Wittrock, and H. Wollman, 230–60. Cambridge: Cambridge University Press.

———. 1991b. *A space for science: The development of the scientific community in Brazil.* University Park: Pennsylvania State University Press.

———. 1992. *The future of higher education in Brazil.* Washington, DC: Woodrow Wilson International Center for Scholars.

———. 1996. *América Latina: Universidades en transición.* Washington, DC: Organization of American States.

———. 2000. Brasil, the social agenda. *Daedalus (Proceedings of the American Academy of Arts and Sciences)* 129 (2): 29–53.

———. 2004. Equity, quality and relevance in higher education in Brazil. *Anais da Academia Brasileira de Ciências* 26 (1): 173–88.

Schwartzman, S., H. M. B. Bomeny, and V. M. R. Costa. 2000. *Tempos de Capanema.* 2nd ed. São Paulo, Rio de Janeiro: Paz e Terra, Editora da Fundação Getúlio Vargas.

Serrano, S. 1994. *Universidad y Nación: Chile en el siglo XIX.* Santiago de Chile: Editorial Universitaria.

Sorj, B. 2001. *A construção intelectual do Brasil contemporâneo da resistência à ditadura ao governo FHC.* Rio de Janeiro: Jorge Zahar Editor.

Trevisan, C. 2004. USP discute onde obter verbas para manter e ampliar pesquisas. *Folha de São Paulo*, January 23. www1.folha.uol.com.br/folha /educacao/ult305u14843.shtml.

Universidade de São Paulo. 2004. USP—Anuário Estatístico. http://sistemas.usp.br/anuario/.

8
Brazilian Research Universities

João E. Steiner

Research and graduate education universities constitute the top of the education system pyramid. Most countries with a high degree of economic and social development have robust and diversified educational systems. In the age of the "knowledge society," no country can do without a significant sector of research-oriented institutions.

Experts say that biological diversity is the basis of wealth—a sort of fundamental law of evolution. With regard to educational institutions, could institutional diversity equally represent a source of wealth? The case of the United States, which boasts of having the planet's most diversified and successful system, seems to corroborate this prospect. Individual and institutional potentialities flourish whenever there is diversity and freedom of organization. In most developed and developing countries, the system of higher learning is complex and diverse. In Brazil, the system's institutional diversity expanded in the 1990s and now performs a plurality of functions in academic and professional development (Martins 2000). Legally speaking, the system comprises universities, university centers, and affiliated colleges and schools—public, private nonprofit (community, religious, foundation-sponsored, etc.), or private for-profit. Not all universities are research universities, and not all research universities are involved in research with the same intensity (Lobo 2004). How, then, does one best characterize systemic diversity?

Assessments and evaluations are an essential part of academic activity. The evaluation of students is a universal practice. Although institutional evaluation is less common, a robust educational system must be transparent to its users and to society. With regard to graduate education in Brazil, the Ministry of Education's CAPES (Coordenação de Aperfeiçoamento do

Ensino Superior [Office for the Improvement of Higher Learning])[1] has been doing some strategic work to evaluate programs over the years.

ORIGINS

Higher learning in Brazil was created in the early 19th century. After D. João VI, the Portuguese king, fled from Europe to Brazil in 1808, the country's first medical programs were established—one in Salvador and two in Rio de Janeiro. In 1810, the Royal Military Academy was founded (currently the School of Engineering of the Federal University of Rio de Janeiro). The law schools of São Paulo (in the city's downtown São Francisco square) and Olinda (in the state of Pernambuco) were established in 1827. In the final years of the Second Empire (1840–1889) and in the early Republican era (1889–1900), several professional schools were created, encompassing the fields of medicine, engineering, agriculture, and law.

During the early 20th century the creation of professional schools was accelerated. Soon, some of these schools merged, forming the first universities: the Federal University of Paraná in 1912, the Pontifical Catholic University of Rio Grande do Sul in 1924, and the Universidade Federal de Minas Gerais (UFMG) in 1927. However, these schools all focused on disseminating culture or providing professional training; entirely absent was the concept of teaching-related research, which at the time was already common in the Humboldtian universities of Europe and the United States, where teaching, learning, and research were closely associated. Brazilian politics was then dominated by conservative agrarian oligarchies, a state of affairs known as *Café com Leite*[2] politics. The 1930 revolution swept Getúlio Vargas into power, broke up the *Café com Leite* regime, and led to the appointment of the first minister of education and health, Francisco Campos, who carried out conservative reforms in the country's higher learning system patterned after the already outmoded pre-Humboldtian universities.

By the late 1950s, Brazil had nine federal, two state, and eight religious universities. In the 1960s there were two surges in the creation of universities—institutions that are now research universities—during a troubled time in Brazilian politics. The first phase occurred between 1960 and 1962—a period of regime changes and an intensification of student unrest goaded by the so-called crisis of the surplus students.[3] The second surge took place during the university reforms of 1968, coinciding with the rise of international student movements and a toughening up of the military government in Brazil.

After this second spurt, the ability of the federal government to create other universities withered. Corporate-like universities began to appear in the early 1970s, a situation that continued until the end of the military regime. In 1985, when the country was redemocratized, private universities began to appear in earnest.

Since the mid-1980s, Brazil's higher learning system has enjoyed substantial growth and witnessed great diversification. Nevertheless, the country still lacks a way of classifying institutions such as the Carnegie Foundation's system (Lobo 2004).[4] In the absence of such metrics, this chapter uses the Carnegie criteria to rank the institutions of graduate and research-oriented higher education. While following this approach is not ideal for depicting the country's reality, it does provide a direct comparison with the American system. The criteria for graduate programs are more objective than the ones used for research institutions, inasmuch as there is no homogeneous database covering the actual production in all fields of knowledge. For instance, Brazilian research in the area of the natural sciences is almost entirely published in English, whereas in the humanities publications are mainly in Portuguese, making it difficult to establish a standardized means of measuring research.

How does one characterize institutional diversity? The Carnegie Foundation developed a system that enables all US higher education institutions to be classified. It was first developed in 1971, under the leadership of the educator Clark Kerr, and the first version was published in 1973 (updated in 1976, 1987, 1994, and 2000). The 2000 version defines three categories: doctoral/research universities (extensive and intensive); master's universities and colleges (also divided in two groups, I and II); and baccalaureate institutions.[5] The doctoral/research universities are classified as extensive if they grant at least 50 PhDs per year in at least 15 programs; intensive research/doctoral universities grant at least 15 PhDs per year or 10 PhDs in at least 3 programs. In 2005 the Carnegie Foundation released a new and more complex classification system, but the analysis of this modification is beyond the scope of this chapter.

A COMPARISON BETWEEN BRAZIL AND THE UNITED STATES

The US system of higher learning is currently one of the most admired in the world. American research universities, in particular, are a solid model of a good university. Nevertheless, the American graduate education system is not a paradigm for Brazil. Yet a statistical comparison between both countries is in order, since data based on the same classification criteria are available. This type of benchmarking is always useful to provide a better understanding of the similarities and differences between the two systems and, in consequence, of the reality of Brazilian universities.

The United States has 872 universities offering graduate programs in the four categories mentioned in table 8.1. These universities are almost evenly split between the public and private nonprofit categories, while for-profit universities account for only one percent of American higher learning institutions. In Brazil, on the other hand, out of a total of 93 surveyed universities offering graduate programs, 53 are public, 24 are private—community-based, religious, or "philanthropic"—and 15 are corporate-like private institutions. The United States has approximately 10 times more research universities than Brazil. This is also the rough proportion between the gross national product (GNP) of the two countries—a parallel that goes beyond a mere statistical detail but has a deeper meaning since in the knowledge and information age higher education is intimately associated with a country's economic performance.

Table 8.1 Doctorate/Research, Master's/Baccalaureate Institutions, in Brazil and the United States

Institutions	Public	Nonprofit	Private	Total
Brazil (2003)				
Doctoral/research	32	7	0	39
Master's	21	18	15	54
Baccalaureate	142	292	1,120	1,554
Total	195	317	1,135	1,647
United States (2000)				
Doctoral/ research	166	93	2	261
Master's	272	331	8	611
Baccalaureate	1,183	1,251	607	3,041
Total	1,621	1,675	617	3,913

Source: Instituto Nacional de Estudos e Pesquisas Anísio Teixeira, Ministério da Educação (INEP, www.inep.gov.br); and the Carnegie Foundation.

Note: In Brazil, nonpublic universities can be described as in two groups: nonprofit universities have religious or "philanthropic" origins; private universities are corporate-like institutions and aim for profit. However, although there is a significant difference in their academic performance, the divide between the two groups is not clear.

As shown in table 8.1, at the top of the pyramid, public universities dominate the doctoral/research system in both the United States (166) and Brazil (32), whereas the share of private for-profit universities is negligible in both countries: none exist in Brazil and no more than two in the United States. However, the similarities end here. The master's universities are overwhelmingly private nonprofit in the United States. In spite of their strong presence in Brazil, this type of university has less impact than in the United States. However, the major difference between both systems is the presence of for-profit private institutions, which are almost nonexistent in the United States but constitute a recent and rapidly growing phenomenon in Brazil—even if in terms of graduate education their scope is limited to the master's universities. Significantly, at the baccalaureate level, Brazil has two times more private institutions than the United States.

With regard to Brazil's research universities, one is struck by the presence of religious institutions. Paradigmatic among the extensive doctoral/research universities are the three Pontifical Catholic Universities in São Paulo, Rio de Janeiro, and Rio Grande do Sul. Among the intensive universities are the Pontifical Catholic University of Campinas, the Jesuit Universidade do Vale do Rio dos Sinos, and the Methodist Universidade Metodista de São Paulo. Among the master's universities, eight have Catholic origins, one Methodist, one Presbyterian, and one Lutheran.

Taking American and Brazilian universities as a whole (Brito Cruz 2005), of the top 10 doctorate-granting institutions, 4 are Brazilian (Universidade de São Paulo, Universidade Estadual de Campinas, Universidade Estadual Júlio de Mesquita Filho, and Universidade Federal do Rio de Janeiro) and 6 are American (University of California, Berkeley; Nova Southeastern University; University of Texas, Austin; University of Wisconsin–Madison; University of Illinois, Urbana-Champaign; and University of Michigan). The University of São Paulo in 2003 granted more doctorates (2,180) than the 3 top-ranking American universities combined.

A comparison between the relative and absolute numbers of doctorate recipients in various fields of knowledge in 2003 reveals some surprises. One often hears that in Brazil the doctoral degree holders in areas of basic research far outnumber those in applied research. However, contrary to this urban legend, the percentage of engineering doctorates in Brazil (13 percent) is identical to the US figure (see table 8.2). In basic science, the percentage is less in Brazil (13 percent in the biological sciences, 11 percent in the exact and earth sciences) than in the United States (14 percent and 15 percent, respectively). Most surprising, though, is that the absolute number of doctorates in some areas of applied science in Brazil (1,026 in agrarian sciences, 1,549 in health sciences) is similar to the US numbers (1,042 and 1,633, respectively); this means that, in relative terms, their numbers are five times larger in Brazil than in the United States.

When only US citizens are taken into account, the number of doctorates earned is even more surprising. In areas of applied science, the absolute numbers of US citizens are similar or even less than those of Brazilians. Only 7 percent of citizens in the United States earned engineering doctorates, a mere 4 percent obtained doctorates in the area of health sciences, and 2 percent in agrarian sciences (see table 8.2). These figures imply a clear risk of brain drain in fields of applied science, a potentially damaging situation for countries like Brazil.

Table 8.2 Doctorates Granted by Field in Brazil and the United States, 2003

Fields	Brazil	US Totals	US Citizens
Agrarian sciences	1,024 (13%)	1,042 (3%)	481 (2%)
Biological sciences	1,028 (13%)	5,694 (14%)	3,782 (14%)
Health sciences	1,549 (19%)	1,633 (3%)	1,166 (4%)
Exact and earth sciences	913 (11%)	5,963 (15%)	3,143 (12%)
Engineering	1,023 (13%)	5,265 (13%)	1,898 (7%)
Social sciences	736 (9%)	6,763 (17%)	4,947 (19%)
Humanities/education	1,821 (22%)	14,350 (35%)	10,996 (42%)
Total	8,094 (100%)	40,710 (100%)	26,413 (100%)

Source: CAPES (Brazil) and Survey of Earned Doctorates (United States).

REGIONAL DISTRIBUTION

The regional distribution of Brazilian doctoral/research universities is highly uneven. There are three major regions with distinct characteristics and HDI (human development index) rates:

The *South/Southeast*, with an HDI between 0.79 and 0.82, takes the lead, with 15 extensive and 14 intensive doctoral/research universities. These 2 regions have 101 million inhabitants, comprising 56 percent of the Brazilian population.

The *Northeast*, with an HDI between 0.65 and 0.70, has 2 extensive doctoral/research universities (the federal universities of Pernambuco and Bahia) and 5 intensive ones. This region has 68 million inhabitants, or 38 percent of the Brazilian population.

The *Amazonia*, with an HDI between 0.70 and 0.72, has only one intensive research university (Universidade Federal do Pará). The population of this region is approximately 20 million.

Some regions have different patterns of institutions. In the state of São Paulo, for instance, the university system is dominated by the three large state universities, and the private sector shows a strong presence of religious universities. However, one should note the sizable deficit of federal universities (there are only two, inadequate given the size of the population) and the complete absence of a nonreligious municipal or other community-based (*comunitário*) university sector, which explains the explosive growth of private universities. The same absence of such community-based universities can be found in the states of Rio de Janeiro and Minas Gerais, where there is a strong presence of federal universities and, in the case of Minas Gerais, an incipient state system of higher education. The southern region, which also has a strong presence of federal universities and an incipient system of state universities, is characterized by the presence of a robust system of community-based universities, notably in the states of Rio Grande do Sul and Santa Catarina. Finally, in the northeast all seven research universities are federal.

RESEARCH UNIVERSITIES: GRADUATE STUDIES AND QUALITY

Since 1976, CAPES has carried out periodic assessments of all graduate programs in Brazil. Until 1997, each program was graded from A to E, according to criteria established by each area's committee. From 1998 onward, CAPES adopted a 1 to 7 grading scale, whereby programs that score 6 and 7 are deemed world class. To ensure the validation of these metrics, CAPES organizes periodic evaluations of all programs with high-level international committees.

CAPES attributes a grade for each master's and doctoral program (master's programs that do not offer doctoral degrees can achieve a maximum score of 5). This chapter extrapolates CAPES practices and assigns an average grade for each institution. The quality of each university's graduate offerings is measured based on the weighted average of all its graduate programs, assigning the CAPES grade for each program and using the number of doctorate recipients per year as the weight.

The overall Brazilian weighted average of CAPES grades wavers around 5.0 (between 4.9 and 5.1) for doctoral programs, although there are significant variations from area to area, and not all fields of knowledge exhibit the same quality. In the health sciences, for instance, the average is 4.2, whereas in the exact and earth sciences it is 5.7. Some universities remain systematically below this average in their programs, while others have sustained systematically an above-average standing. One may conclude that, in terms of both institutions and disciplines, Brazil has many so-called islands of excellence.

Six of Brazil's doctoral/research universities are specialized, having one or two dominant major fields: four are specialized in agrarian sciences (Universidade Federal de Viçosa, Universidade Federal de Lavras, Universidade Federal Rural do R. de Janeiro, and Universidade Federal Rural de Pernambuco), one in medicine (Universidade Federal de S. Paulo), and one in the social sciences and humanities (Pontifícia Universidade Católica de São Paulo).

It is common knowledge that Brazilian public universities tend to offer high-level education and that the quality of private universities is often questionable. At least with regard to graduate studies, these views can be tested. The average CAPES grades for public, community, and private master's and doctoral universities show a correlation between each type of university. Extensive doctoral/research universities obtain the best grades, followed by intensive master's I and master's II universities, which received the worst grades. Surprisingly, because it goes against the grain of conventional wisdom, no significant correlation was found, regarding quality levels, with the administrative nature of the institution. For a given type of institution, the score averages are basically the same in public and in private nonprofit (religious and "philanthropic" [*filantropico*]) universities.

The presence or absence of doctoral programs, as well as the extent of graduate education, seems to correlate more closely with the average score than the administrative nature of the institution. The master's degree scores are consistently low for universities that do not offer doctoral programs, regardless of the nature of the institution. For universities that offer doctoral programs, the average scores relate to the size of the graduate activities for both master's and doctoral programs, the scores being higher for larger institutions. Corporate-like private universities do not offer doctoral programs, with few exceptions. As a consequence, these institutions have poor scores, as do public universities with similar graduate programs.[6]

RANKING UNIVERSITIES AROUND THE WORLD

In 2004, two world-class surveys were carried out in an attempt to classify the universities of the world, one by the Shanghai Jiao Tong University[7] and the other by the British *Times Higher Education Supplement*.[8] The Jiao Tong University survey was based on the following criteria (and weights): alumni who received a Nobel Prize or the Fields Medal (10 percent); professors who received these awards (20 percent); highly cited researchers (20 percent); articles published in *Nature* or *Science* (20 percent); articles listed in the Science Citation Index and in the Social Science Citation Index (20 percent); and the sum of the indicators above divided by the size of the staff (10 percent).

The *Times Higher Education Supplement* survey was based on the review of 1,300 specialists in 88 countries, with a 50 percent weight. In addition, the research considered the cosmopolitan nature of faculty (5 percent) and students (5 percent), the faculty-per-student ratio (20 percent), and the number of citations per faculty member (20 percent).

Clearly, both surveys have many flaws. However, so far no one has discovered how to carry out this type of survey in a way that does not attract criticism. One of the major restrictions on such studies is that they are often biased by their anglophone viewpoint. The standard measurements mainly take into account publications in the English language, but a large part of Brazilian scientific research is published in Portuguese (especially in the humanities and social sciences) and thus is not included in international statistics. To obtain a useful indication of the current productivity of Brazilian researchers, one should check the database of the Scientific Electronic Library Online (Scielo).[9] This virtual library now contains almost 150 Brazilian journals, with an impressive total of 2 million accesses per month. Yet only a small fraction of these journals are indexed in databases of the Institute of Scientific Information; of the 10 most-accessed titles in Scielo, 9 are printed in Portuguese.

Still, even if the aforementioned caveats as well as others are taken into account, the fact is that from an international perspective no world-class universities exist in Brazil. The Shanghai Jiao Tong University survey identities the top-ranking Brazilian university as the University of São Paulo, but it occupies the bottom rungs of the 200 best institutions in the world (Universidade Estadual de Campinas [UNICAMP], Universidade Federal do Rio de Janeiro [UFRJ], and Universidade Estadual Júlio de Mesquita Filho [UNESP] are included among the top 500 universities). In the *Times Higher Education Supplement* survey, however, which lists the 200 best universities in the world, no Brazilian institutions are mentioned.

In the research universities milieu, one often hears the expression "world-class universities." A world-class university has been described as needing to

> develop science and technology, but also culture, general learning, knowledge and the ability to understand what happens in one's country and in the world.

> It must prepare a broad diversity of professionals, such as professors, diplomats, high public officials, politicians, journalists, historians, etc. It must act as a bridge of contact and communication between the country and the world, and be a standard of quality for other institutions. (S. Schwartzman 2005)

So does Brazil have world-class universities? Based on the above descriptions, the country's doctoral/research universities possess, to some degree, all the listed features, but no Brazilian university was included among the world's 150 best universities in the two aforementioned surveys.

The CAPES assessments did not indicate that any university in Brazil has an overall average grade of 6 or more, which according to CAPES standards would place it at the international level, at least in terms of graduate programs. In a few major fields, however, some universities have attained this level—in agrarian sciences (UFMG), in the exact and earth sciences (Universidade de São Paulo, UNICAMP, UFMG, and Universidade Federal de São Carlos [UFScar]), in the human sciences (Universidade Federal Fluminense), in engineering (UNICAMP and UFSCar), and in linguistics, literature, and arts (UNICAMP).

RANKINGS AND PRESTIGE

Rankings of college programs and universities are routinely published in Brazil. Popular magazines such as *Playboy* and *Guia do Estudante* (Student Guide), and large-circulation newspapers like *Folha de São Paulo* and *Estado de São Paulo* periodically carry out and publish such surveys. Research universities (albeit called otherwise) are frequently mentioned as the best. It is important to note that in the academic milieu a program's prestige depends on its scores in the CAPES evaluations. Grades 6 and 7 (which CAPES formally considers as the international level) are often mentioned as evidence of high levels and prestige. For a university, the relevant indicator is the number of programs that receive grade 6 or 7, and even in publications and surveys made for popular consumption, this is an important reference.

The annual *Guia do Estudante*, which enjoys great prestige among students preparing to take college admissions exams, also evaluates Brazilian undergraduate programs. Each program receives a certain number of stars, from one to five. The publication only mentions "starred" programs—that is, programs that earned three, four, or five stars. According to the *Guia do Estudante*, 185 institutions had starred programs in 2004, the most prestigious being those with the greatest share of three- to five-star programs.

Using these criteria, the 2004 edition listed the top 10 universities, which incidentally are the same institutions that are also the first on the list of extensive doctoral/research universities in the Carnegie classification. It is important to point out that the Carnegie criteria are quantitative and refer to doctoral programs, whereas the criteria of the *Guia do Estudante* are qualitative and pertain to undergraduate programs.

In spite of the popular notion that people who graduate from "good public universities" are better equipped than graduates from other schools, it is unlikely that data exist on their employability and salaries. However, it is known that a worker's average income is strongly dependent on the number of years of study, including undergraduate and graduate education (see S. Schwartzman 2004).

RESEARCH INSTITUTES

Academic research and teaching are not only conducted at universities. In Brazil, research institutes also are quite active. The Instituto Tecnológico de Aeronáutica, for instance, is famous for graduating high-quality aeronautic engineers over the past 55 years. As a consequence, a major aeronautic industry has been established—the fourth largest in the world. Another important institute that does not have teaching activities is Empresa Brasileira de Pesquisa Agropecuáriua, in the field of agrarian sciences. This institute, which has about 40 departments scattered all over the country, has been instrumental in the development of the strong Brazilian agribusiness. The institutes FIOCRUZ (Fundação Instituto Osvaldo Cruz) and Instituto Butantan have played a major research role in the health sciences, including the production of vaccines. A few dozen other institutes linked to various federal ministries or state-level departments have played important roles in academic research.

THE ACADEMIC PROFESSION

The academic profession varies significantly in the different groups of universities. Public universities have mostly full-time teachers and professors, while private institutions have mostly part-time staff. As an example, the University of São Paulo currently has about 5,000 faculty—77 percent full-time and 94 percent with PhDs. Such a pattern exists at most of the best federal universities. Surprisingly, some of the not-so-good public universities also have mostly full-time faculty, while the percentage of faculty with PhDs is significantly lower. At private universities, in contrast, faculty are mostly part-time and fewer are graduate degree holders. The higher education system in Brazil is still expanding quite a bit, as a consequence of the demographic demand from the graduates of the high school system.

THE CURRENT SCENARIO

Demographic and Political Pressures

The increasing demand for higher learning is exerting powerful pressures on the system. In recent years, elementary education has been universalized, while secondary education has expanded threefold, generating growing demographic pressures with political consequences that force public universities to increase their enrollments (not necessarily accompanied by a corresponding expansion of infrastructure and personnel). The fact that the public sector is not satisfying this demand led to an increase of private initiatives, not always with adequate supervision and evaluation by the government and causing serious problems concerning educational quality.

Admissions and Affirmative Action

Admission to public universities is extremely competitive, not only because the institutions are free but also because of their greater academic prestige. This prestige derives from the fact that most of the country's research is carried out at such institutions, as confirmed by the statistics that 91 percent of all doctorates are granted by them.

Consequently, the Brazilian middle class keeps its children in private high schools so that they might have a better chance of performing well in college admissions exams. Families with fewer resources have to educate their children in lower-quality public secondary schools, diminishing their chances of attending college free of charge and forcing them to enroll in tuition-charging private colleges.

In Brazil, it is traditional for each university to organize its own admissions exam, defining who will be admitted. In recent years, some universities have included academic achievement in high school as part of this process. In tandem, some public institutions have also recently established a racial quota system, an initiative that has proven to be quite controversial.

Autonomy

The Brazilian 1988 constitution ensures the autonomy of universities. However, the process was never regulated at the federal level. Autonomy indicates the power of self-normalization (Ranieri 2005), and this provision conflicts with external demands for social accountability.

For federal universities, autonomy has long been requested, although its exact meaning, scope, and limitations are not clear (Durham 2005). Thus, autonomy has emerged as a central issue of university reform that the Ministry of Education proposed in 2005. The basic idea is to extend to the federal system the autonomy given to the state universities of São Paulo in 1989 (this is basically budgetary autonomy). However, given the national political crisis that emerged in mid-2005, it is unlikely that this reform will pass in the Congress in the foreseeable future.

Institutional and Research Financing

The basic needs of Brazilian public universities (for personnel, infrastructure, and services) are funded by the government, and research financing (for projects, scholarships, and infrastructure) comes from specific federal and state agencies.

Federal universities are funded by the Ministry of Culture and Education. State universities are financed by their respective state governments and private universities by student tuition. According to J. Schwartzman (2005), the institutional budget of the private university system is approximately 12 billion (Brazilian) reais (US$6 billion) per year; of federal universities, 6 billion reais (US$3 billion); and of state universities, 3 billion reais (US$1.5 billion).

Research in Brazil, on the other hand, is funded in an entirely different manner. At the federal level, the main financing agency for researchers is the CNPq (Conselho Nacional de Desenvolvimento Científico e Tecnológico [National Council for Scientific and Technological Development]), an office of the Ministry of Science and Technology that maintains a vigorous program of graduate scholarships for master's degrees and doctorates, in addition to a program of scientific innovation. CAPES, an agency of the Ministry of Culture and Education, also provides scholarships for master's degrees and doctorates. FINEP (Financiadora de Estudos e Projetos [Financing Agency for Studies and Projects]) helps to fund institutions, having been strengthened with the creation of the so-called Fundos Setoriais (federal funding from discrete private sources).

At the state level, several supporting foundations have been established. The pioneer and paradigmatic agency is FAPESP (Fundação de Apoio à Pesquisa do Estado de São Paulo [Foundation for Research Support of the State of São Paulo]), which boasts a tradition of efficiency in providing support for individual research projects and a fine program of master's degree and doctorate scholarships, in addition to programs for scientific innovation and postdoctoral studies. Inspired by its success, similar foundations were created in other states—including Rio de Janeiro, Minas Gerais, Pernambuco, Rio Grande do Sul, Amazonas, and recently Santa Catarina—although they all face various instabilities and irregular funding. In recent years (since 1997), FAPESP launched one program to provide institutional support and another to provide support for small, technology-based companies.

The Legal Framework and Institutional Assessments

Given the growing difficulties faced by public universities in fulfilling the demand for expanding enrollments, private institutions are becoming ever more numerous and important. However, this expansion has not been accompanied by the requisite quality control or even quality assessment. A legal framework is required, to make the system more transparent for users and for society as a whole.

Leadership

The process of appointing university presidents is a frequent source of controversy. Some groups lobby for indirect procedures and others for direct elections. The latter often include the more articulate segments of the student body, as well as actions of unionized faculty and staff. As a rule, the best international practices are either unknown or ignored (Marcovitch 2005).

The militant activities of unionized faculty and employees, as well as the organized activism of students, have led to frequent strikes at public universities, causing an accelerated erosion of their image in Brazilian public opinion.

There also seems to be a declining institutional commitment on the part of academic leaders, who seem more concerned with their (legitimate) research activities and other professional interests. Managerial hindrances, excessive bureaucracy, and the wear and tear of political and ideological confrontation, among other issues, seem to constitute the causes of such disinterest.

CONCLUSION

The institutional diversity of research, graduate, and undergraduate institutions has increased in Brazil since the 1980s. Based on criteria from the Carnegie Foundation to classify institutions of higher learning, Brazil had 39 doctoral/research universities, 54 master's universities, and 1,554 baccalaureate institutions in 2003.

The ratio between graduate universities and gross domestic product (GDP) is approximately the same in Brazil and the United States. Brazilian doctoral/research universities, like their American counterparts, are chiefly public institutions. Local universities in Brazil have predominantly religious origins. As has been discussed in this chapter, the regional distribution of Brazil's research universities is highly uneven. The undergraduate programs of Brazilian universities are irregularly evaluated, but graduate programs have been assessed systematically and rigorously by CAPES since the 1970s, by means of highly credible peer-review procedures.

Contrary to common wisdom, Brazil produces a larger percentage of doctorates in applied areas than the United States. In fields like agrarian sciences and health sciences, the absolute numbers are similar. This implies a clear risk of future brain drain in these fields of knowledge, which would be potentially damaging for countries like Brazil.

As mentioned, according to both international and national evaluations, Brazil lacks an acknowledged world-class university, while some universities have reached international levels in various major fields. Taking into account only the average CAPES scores, Brazil's largest universities that come closest to being world-class institutions are UNICAMP and UFMG, although USP is generally recognized as the leading university in the country. A public university is financed by the government that created it, as required by the federal constitution, whereas a private university is funded by its tuition revenues. Both the public and private sectors suffer from funding problems.

Discussions involving the fortunes of research universities in Brazil are centered on the federal government's proposal for university reform and include, among other issues, the following topics: demographic and political pressures to increase enrollment opportunities in public universities, together with affirmative action for social and racial inclusion; institutional autonomy, associated with more effective means of institutional and research financing; a legal framework and the evaluation of private institutions; and the establishment of institutional leadership.

NOTES

1. See the CAPES Web site: www.capes.gov.br.

2. *Café com Leite* (coffee and cream) refers to the oligarchies of the coffee growers of São Paulo alternating power with the oligarchies of dairy farmers of Minas Gerais.

3. This crisis involved students who had been officially approved by means of university admissions exams but were unable to enroll due to the lack of space in the classes.

4. See the Carnegie Foundation Web site: www.carnegiefoundation.org.

5. A description of the Carnegie Foundation classification criteria can be found at the Web site: www.carnegiefoundation.org.

6. A more detailed analysis of the quality and institutional diversity of Brazilian universities involved in graduate programs can be found in Steiner (2005).

7. Shanghai Jiao Tong University Web site: http://www.sjtu.edu.cn/www/english/.

8. *Times Higher Education Supplement* Web site: www.thes.co.uk/.

9. Scielo (Scientific Electronic Library Online): www.scielo.org.br.

REFERENCES

Brito Cruz, C. H. 2005. Pesquisa e Universidade. In *Os Desafios do Ensino Superior no Brasil.* São Paulo: Instituto de Estudos Avançados da USP. www.iea.usp.br/ensinosuperior/.

Durham, E. R. 2005. A Autonomia Universitária: Extensão e Limites. *Desafios do Ensino Superior no Brasil.* São Paulo: Instituto de Estudos Avançados da USP. www.iea.usp.br/ensinosuperior/.

Lobo, R. L. S. 2004. As Universidades de Pesquisa. *Folha de São Paulo*, September 20, 3.

Marcovitch, J. 2005. Eleições na Universidade. In *Os Desafios do Ensino Superior no Brasil.* São Paulo: Instituto de Estudos Avançados da USP. www.iea.usp.br/ensinosuperior/.

Martins, C. B. 2000. O Ensino Superior Brasileiro nos Anos 90. *São Paulo em Perspectiva* 14 (1): 41–60.

Ranieri, N. 2005. Aspectos Jurídicos da Autonomia Universitária no Brasil. In *Os Desafios do Ensino Superior no Brasil.* São Paulo: Instituto de Estudos Avançados da USP. www.iea.usp.br/ensinosuperior/.

Schwartzman, J. 2005. O Financiamento das Instituições de Ensino Superior no Brasil. In *Os Desafios do Ensino Superior no Brasil.* São Paulo: Instituto de Estudos Avançados da USP. www.iea.usp.br/ensinosuperior/.

Schwartzman, S. 2004. Equity, quality and relevance in higher education in Brazil. *Anais da Academia Brasileira de Ciências* 76 (1): 173–88.

———. 2005. A Universidade de São Paulo e a questão universitária no Brasil. In *Os Desafios do Ensino Superior no Brasil.* São Paulo: Instituto de Estudos Avançados da USP. www.iea.usp.br/ensinosuperior/.

Steiner, J. E. 2005. Qualidade e diversidade institucional na pós-graduação brasileira. *Estudos Avançados* 54:341–65.

9

La Máxima Casa de Estudios

Universidad Nacional Autónoma de México as a State-Building University

Imanol Ordorika & Brian Pusser

Visitors to Mexico and international scholars alike frequently notice that the Universidad Nacional Autónoma de México (UNAM) is commonly called the *máxima casa de estudios*[1] by a large majority of Mexicans (Rhoads and Durdella 2005). This title expresses the people's deep appreciation of Mexico's most prominent university. Admiration for the Universidad de la Nación[2] or Mexico's alma mater is deeply embedded in Mexican society and runs across different classes and social groups.

UNAM is one example of a distinctive institutional type that we identify as state-building universities. UNAM—and other such universities, including the Universidad de Buenos Aires, the Universidad Nacional de Cordoba, the Universidade de Sao Paulo, and the Universidad Central de Venezuela—are dominant teaching and research-oriented universities. They have also been central in building the material conditions for the expansion and consolidation, as well as the intellectual and social legitimacy, of their respective states. While scholars of international higher education have endeavored to understand universities on the periphery in light of models of higher education at the center of global economic and political power, insufficient attention has been paid to the role of state-building activities in defining prominent universities on the periphery (Ordorika forthcoming).

To conceptualize these universities, we have focused essentially on Latin American institutions and more particularly on the Mexican case of UNAM. However, there are a number of other institutions around the world for which a similar case could be made. These institutions are in most cases located in nations on the periphery of world economic and political power. While the state-building university shares many of the attributes of flagship universities in the United States and abroad, its distinctive and historically contingent role in the formation of states on the periphery marks the state-building university as a unique institution. However, under the political economic pressures of neoliberalism and globalization, UNAM, like other state-building universities, has been hard pressed to maintain its dominance and centrality in state projects. In this chapter, we examine the current state of these universities, the pressure they face to emulate the flagship model, and their future prospects. We also consider the likelihood that these institutions might transform themselves into something closer to flagship universities, and we offer some speculations on the meaning of such a shift for postsecondary education in nations on the periphery. Because we see UNAM as a fundamental example of the origin, emergence, and contemporary crisis of a state-building university, we present its case in some detail.

THE CASE OF UNAM

The history of UNAM goes back to the Real y Pontificia Universidad de México, established in 1553. After undergoing a number of transformations over the centuries, the university was reconstituted in 1910. It has taken the better part of a century for the national university in Mexico to develop fully the attributes of a state-building university. At various points in its long history, UNAM has played a major role in the creation of such essential state institutions as public health ministries and the Mexican judicial system. The national university has also played a key role in the design of innumerable government bodies and offices and in educating and credentialing the civil servants who dominate those offices. UNAM has served since its founding as the training ground for Mexico's political and economic elites as well as for a significant portion of the nation's professionals (Ordorika 2003b).

Perhaps most important, at many key moments in Mexican history, UNAM has served as a focal point for the contest over the creation and recreation of a national culture that placed such postsecondary functions as critical inquiry, knowledge production, social mobility, and political consciousness at its center. This role was particularly relevant during the late 1940s and the 1950s in a period that has been labeled the "Golden Era" of this university. The strength and clarity of purpose of UNAM during this period were deeply connected to its centrality in state-development projects. With the demise of these projects and the precarious state of the Mexican economy since the late 1970s, UNAM has faced critical challenges. Institutional identity has been eroded and the university's capacity to respond to multiple demands has been called into question.

UNAM is not alone. The crisis of legitimacy that UNAM faces has emerged over the past 20 years in a context in which public institutions across the world, in every sphere of society, have been challenged. The crisis of legitimacy faced by state-building universities is fundamentally the crisis of public-sector institutions under siege from neoliberal restructuring and privatization projects (Marginson 1997; Levin 2001). In Mexico, as is the case with other nations on the periphery, the number of private higher education institutions and their enrollments have expanded, often with state support. In concert with the shifting postsecondary context, the discourse of institutional legitimacy has also changed. In the wider political economy, private organizations and practices have been depicted as more successful and efficient than their public counterparts, while public universities have become the object of close scrutiny and intense critiques. The intensity of the contest between the historical legitimacy of state-building universities and the contemporary push for market-based and privatized institutions reflects both the rising tide of neoliberal challenges and the continuing symbolic and functional importance of the public sector.

The enduring legitimacy of state-building universities is understandable, as these institutions are a powerful representation of the communal knowledge and power of the intellect in the state.

THE CONCEPT OF THE STATE-BUILDING UNIVERSITY

The concept of the state-building university is rooted in a broad understanding of the state as the web of relations between individuals and among social groups in a given societal arrangement shaped by historical traditions, culture, economic development, and political processes. The state is organized in institutions or apparatuses that express these social relations. These social relations are also essentially unequal and imply the domination of some groups over others. Both the government and universities are institutions of the state (Ordorika 2001, 2003b).

State-building universities are defined by their assumption of central roles in building nation-states. They have been key players in the development, expansion, and maintenance of the state as an integral entity as well as other state institutions (i.e., the executive, legislative, and judicial branches of government), and particularly in the national project of building and extending postsecondary education. Their role as state-building institutions has been both historically contingent and key to shaping the character of national institutions and national postsecondary capacities.

State-building universities share many of the attributes of flagship universities, yet they are distinctive in important ways. First, state-building universities often embody the aspirations of the emerging society, with powerful linkages to historical and contemporary social and intellectual movements, in ways that are increasingly distinct from the emerging missions of flagships. Second, state-building universities stand as the reification of a particular form of national sovereignty, as sites of the preservation of collective autonomy through intellectual development and social contest. Third, the state-building university embodies the creation myth of the national intellectual, social, and political projects, the legacy and promise of scholarly purpose and national advancement. The presence of the state-building university reifies the symbolic national saga of national pride, opportunity, and development through higher education. It is an institution that nurtures the intellectual and personal aspirations of the nation and its people, its social movements, revolutions, and restorations. To describe these complex and often contradictory institutions, which are understood at the same time as temples of learning, crucibles of social justice, seedbeds of knowledge generation, and hotbeds of social protest, tests the limits of language. State-building universities exist not only *in* the hearts and minds of the people, they are *of* their hearts and minds. The institution is an anchor and a point of departure, both a statement of *nacion* and a manifestation of *el pueblo*.[3]

The purpose of this chapter is to delineate the conditions that have enabled state-building universities to emerge in nations on the periphery and to consider the degree to which this vision of the university can be preserved in a rapidly globalizing world. We believe UNAM, in its transformation into the *máxima casa de estudios,* and in its relationship with the Mexican state, the political system, and the broader society, offers a useful case for understanding the future of state-building universities on the periphery. It is also a helpful example of the distinction between the state-building universities and the flagships.

FLAGSHIP UNIVERSITIES

Can we talk about a Mexican flagship? The answer is a qualified "no."

Although state-building universities have been a distinct form that reached particular prominence during a developmentalist era, internal and external pressures are driving state-building universities to emulate flagship universities. To understand this assertion, and the pressures for adaptation faced by state-building universities, it is useful to explore the notion of the flagship university in its original context.

The term *flagship university* has three different though deeply interconnected connotations in the English-speaking world. First, it is used in a simple way as a strictly descriptive term. Second, it is a concept that characterizes a particular type of higher education institution that developed in the United States and subsequently appeared in a few other parts of the world. Finally, the term has been used in a prescriptive way to symbolize a model of an institution that prominent universities in every country face demands to emulate.

A Descriptive Term

References to flagship universities immediately imply an allusion to the leader, the most prominent or the finest among a broader group of state or national higher education institutions. The term *flagship* is derived from naval warfare and in its more contemporary usage refers to leading or prominent institutions in competitive arenas (e.g., the flagship of the department store chain). In these uses it entails an understanding that can be common to different nations, states, regions, and realities. Flagship universities constitute, almost universally within the English-speaking world, postsecondary institutions that constitute the pinnacle of a state or national higher education system, those that excel among others. This understanding usually depicts the largest, oldest, most traditional, and most highly regarded institutions within a larger set of colleges or universities. The flagship has long implied the dominant public institutions in a postsecondary system. Contemporary analyses often include private universities. While this may be analytically appropriate for flagships, it is at odds with the historical development of the flagship concept and serves as a useful starting point for understanding the distinction between flagships and state-building universities.

The Historical Concept

In the United States, the flagship concept is fundamentally connected to the historical development of the land grant universities founded in the

United States in the late 19th and early 20th centuries (Berdahl 1998).

The flagship concept is complex and, like the public universities it characterizes, its meaning has evolved historically. According to various authors (Rudolph 1965; Flexner 1994; Kerr 2001), the contemporary "American model" of higher education is the product of a fusion between two distinct higher education traditions: on the one hand, the German-based graduate schools that provided research and high-level professional education (essentially in medicine and law); and on the other hand, the British tradition of the liberal arts college, with its strong emphasis on the humanities. The emerging hybrid form developed in the United States at private institutions like Johns Hopkins, Harvard, and Cornell.

The success of these institutions had a strong influence on the land grant colleges created under the Morrill acts of 1862 and 1890 (Kerr 2001). Over time, such powerful public state colleges as Michigan, Minnesota, and Wisconsin evolved toward the research university model (Rudolph 1965). In this way, public land grants became flagships and then what Kerr termed, "multiversities," on the way to becoming some of the world's most influential postsecondary institutions. Berdahl offers three key reasons for the evolution of the flagship concept. The first is the expansion of enrollments in postsecondary education in the United States after World War II. That expansion led to the creation of branch campuses of the original state universities, branches that lacked the resources and prestige of the original campuses. Second, in the 1960s, as the college-going population continued to increase and more campuses were opened, state postsecondary systems were created—as was the case, for example, with the University of California system under the California Master Plan (Douglass 2000). Another key reason for the creation of systems was to ensure political and economic support for the original campuses as the number of public institutions within a state expanded. In this manner the original dominant public and land grant universities within each state emerged at the head of powerful systems of public universities with widespread popular and political support (Berdahl 1998).

The evolution of the flagship universities in the United States is linked to strong state support and commitment toward the emergence, expansion, and maintenance of public higher education institutions in the states. Historically this commitment has been expressed in state and federal support for undergraduate teaching, graduate and professional education, and scientific research (Kerr 2001). Over the past decade, flagships in the United States have rapidly raised undergraduate, graduate, and professional tuition in order to continue to compete for institutional prestige and influence (Geiger 2004). These tuition increases, in combination with rapidly increasing college costs, have strained relations between flagships and the state legislatures that have long supported them. These conflicts are not new phenomena.

Over the past two decades, the prestige competition has engendered significant contest over access and affordability in the flagships. In the 19th century, negative popular perceptions about the elite nature of emerging higher education institutions were in some places so strong that the creation of new public institutions was intensely contested. This was the case, for example, in the struggle over the foundation of the University of California (Douglass 2000). In spite of these conflicts, throughout the land grant movement new state universities that would combine elite teaching, training, and research were created across the United States.

There is a paradox embedded in the mission of the flagship university today. On the one hand, the flagship generally upholds the elite traditions of private universities, through selective admissions, high-quality research, and training for elite professions. On the other hand, the flagships endeavor to democratize access, as they attempt to create diverse student cohorts, participate in community service, and devote significant energy to generating public goods.

The latter goals, while less prominent in public discourse and policy debates, are expressed in the flagships through a variety of historical roles and commitments, including:

- dedication to professional education and training for the public good
- relative democratization of access to education, knowledge, and training
- a "democratic" role in the reproduction of society through the inculcation of democratic values and through the creation and recreation of identities, shared beliefs; and norms
- commitment to equality and social justice
- commitment to critical inquiry and autonomous knowledge creation

As a consequence of pursuing these goals, the flagship university has also come to symbolize a site of strong state commitment to the public good through federal and local state funding, oversight, and reinforcement of institutional legitimacy.

Flagships at the Core: A Prescriptive Model

Over the past two decades, a number of authors have pointed to rapid changes in the nature of flagship universities in the United States, with an increased emphasis on applied research, graduate and professional training, and a status competition for elite students (Slaughter and Leslie 1997; Kirp 2003; Geiger 2004; Slaughter and Rhoades 2004). The titles and content of a set of reports and policy documents available on the Internet support this emerging vision as they suggest a different understanding of the notion of flagship university. Louisiana State University's *LSU campus* online news reports an agenda:

> The National Flagship Agenda is a seven-year plan focused on the historical significance of the year 2010, LSU's 150th anniversary. The agenda has been designed to build the University into a nationally competitive flagship university and serve the short- and long-term interests of Louisiana. Focusing on the action steps will increase research and scholarly productivity and will improve the quality and competitiveness of our graduate and undergraduate students.[4]

A similar commitment to competitiveness and funded research has begun to emerge at universities beyond the United States. The University of Edinburgh's 1999–2000 annual report calls for "A Flagship University for Scotland," stressing the importance of a "commitment to internationalism" and the need to attract international students from beyond the European Union in an "increasingly competitive environment."[5] A web search for flagship universities reveals other examples like these for the United States, Australia, and the United Kingdom.

These emerging mission statements reveal a different view of the flagship. From this perspective, a flagship university is a symbol of the changing contemporary relationship between the state and higher education and a vehicle for a new set of social and individual aspirations (Slaughter and Rhoades 2004). Contemporary university leaders, policymakers, and administrators cite similar characteristics of the emerging flagship ideal:

- knowledge production–centered (emphasis on research and graduate studies)
- strong ties to business and the knowledge economy
- competitive (for students and funds)
- focused on excellence and prestige

- productive and efficient
- locally grounded and internationally oriented
- autonomous through financial diversity

Not surprisingly, these emerging redefinitions of the flagship university are consistent with those that define a category of prominent universities variously labeled as entrepreneurial universities (Clark 1998), enterprise universities (Marginson and Considine 2000), or centers of academic capitalism (Slaughter and Leslie 1997; Slaughter and Rhoades 2004). What these redefinitions share in common is a portrayal of the most successful research universities in Europe and the United States in a global competition for greater resources, prestige, and legitimacy. Despite the rapid adaptation to the demands of globalization at elite universities, most retain one element central to the historical role of flagships: a discursive emphasis on service to the local community, state, and region.

Contemporary research on postsecondary organization and governance has also depicted flagship universities as political institutions (Pusser 2003; Ordorika 2003b). As such, they are sites of interest group competition over a range of issues, including student access, knowledge creation, funded research, and a myriad of social issues (Pusser forthcoming). As interest group competition has intensified, the flagships have increasingly aligned themselves with industry and the private sector, at increasing distance from their historical sources of legitimacy (Pusser, Slaughter, and Thomas forthcoming; Slaughter and Rhoades 2004).

The flagship is also a self-referential and self-replicating concept. As the leaders of the postsecondary arena, the flagships shape and give substance to the meaning of excellence in academe and in turn legitimize the entrepreneurial and political behaviors that solidify their positions as leaders. The concept of the American flagship university has become enticing to postsecondary institutions around the world on the strength of its success—where those global perceptions of flagship success, while genuine, are nonetheless shaped by the flagships themselves. In the words of Clark Kerr:

> The American research grant university has been an enormous intellectual success, particularly in the sciences: Since 1950, when the development of the federal research grant universities was in its infancy, 55 percent of all Nobel and Fields (mathematics) prizes have been awarded to scholars resident in the United States; in the 1980's, 50 percent of all citations in leading scientific journals around the world were to members of the same group; in 1990, 50 percent of all patents registered in the United States were of U.S. origin; and by

> 1990, the United States had 180,000 graduate students from foreign nations, clearly making it the world center of graduate study. Not since Italy in the early centuries of the rise of universities in western Europe has any single nation so dominated intellectual life. (Kerr 2001, 151)

The flagship model is a prescriptive model because of the power of the flagship concept in international higher education. The flagship form is so dominant in discourse, planning, and prestige rankings that the concept exerts an almost coercive force on institutions, systems, and policymakers. As Kerr noted, the hegemonic influence of the American flagship has been unrivaled for centuries. That dominance establishes global norms for postsecondary excellence and demands conformity from those institutions and systems that would emulate the success of the American flagship model. Ironically, despite a perpetual contest within the United States over the appropriate missions of the flagships, the idealized version of the flagship may reduce the traditional role of the university in the periphery as a site of social protest and contest. Instead, peripheral universities increasingly find themselves contesting demands to conform to the idealized norms of the American flagship. The prescriptive concept of the flagship also shapes the criteria for ranking postsecondary institutions and establishing international benchmarks for institutional performance.[6]

Flagships on the Periphery?

There is no doubt that American flagships are the source of the dominant postsecondary model in contemporary society and that they are the most successful institutions within that model. Yet, to understand whether it is appropriate to expect that model to establish itself on the periphery turns our attention to three key questions: (1) Is the flagship concept understood on the periphery in the same way as it is understood at the core? (2) Is it appropriate to adopt the American flagship model in peripheral countries? (3) If the flagship model can be adopted in the periphery, will it supplant the state-building institutions?

Where *flagship university* refers to the most notable, most important, finest, or even largest institutions in a country we see little conflict between the concept of a flagship and that of a state-building university. In either case the term used refers to the most distinctive colleges or universities at a state, regional, or national level.

Where the concept of the flagship diverges significantly from the state-building university is when each institution is considered in its own historical perspective and grounded in its specific context. The American flagship and the state-building universities on the periphery considered in historical context are quite distinctive, and distinct, from one another. This is largely due to the unique historical processes and events that have shaped individual institutional traditions, normative values, and organizational cultures and beliefs. The concept that distinguishes flagships and state-building universities as unique institutional archetypes and distinguishes one university from another within those archetypes is *historical centrality*. Historical centrality is shaped by social, political, economic, and cultural processes occurring within higher education institutions and between those institutions and other institutions of the state, social actors, and economic forces. It is also an outcome of the internal dynamics of the professions and the disciplines, as well as a consequence of teaching and knowledge-creation processes that take place within colleges and universities. Flagships and state-building universities have quite different degrees of historical centrality in their respective states. In part, this is due to the historical decentralization of higher education in the United States, where there are many unique and prominent state universities, but no national university. In many countries on the periphery there are national universities, with considerable historical centrality in the creation and sustenance of their respective states.

As noted earlier, the prescriptive influence of the flagship university generates coercive pressures on aspiring institutions throughout the world to conform to the norms of the American flagship and to adapt the structures and policies associated with the flagship. Those demands have historically been met with considerable contest and resistance. It is important in the case of institutions on the global periphery to focus on the dynamic concept of the university as a contested autonomous space, the process of opposition and resistance to demands to emulate the successful and dominant model from the core. The ways in which higher education institutions and constituents have resisted the prescriptive norms of the flagship model are central to understanding the distinction between flagships and state-building universities and the challenge that faces those who endeavor to create and sustain flagships on the periphery.

DISTINCTIVENESS, HISTORICAL CENTRALITY, AND CONTESTED AUTONOMOUS SPACE

A thorough understanding of most prominent public research universities on the periphery requires that we move away from implicit comparisons between universities on the periphery and the dominant institutions at the core. An effective comparison must be grounded in historical and contextual explanations for institutional distinctiveness and centrality on the periphery. Further, the university as a public sphere, an autonomous space for contest and resistance to conformity (Pusser forthcoming) has historically been a major component of the construction and shaping of colleges and universities on the periphery. In postcolonial peripheral countries, the university itself, as a concept and as an organization, is a historical product of contest entailing resistance and acquiescence to colonial powers and their hegemonic projects. This resistance to coercion by dominant models can be thought of as contested conformity. It can be located in any number of historical and contemporary struggles over higher education on the periphery (Ordorika 2003b).

Using UNAM as a lens for bringing clarity to these concepts, we turn attention to the historical contests, competing forces, and contradictions that have shaped UNAM's prominent position as a state-building university within Mexico. We then apply the insights from UNAM in an analysis of the role of distinctiveness, historical centrality, and the university as a contested autonomous space in distinguishing state-building universities from flagships.

La Universidad de la Nación as a Distinctive Institution

UNAM is the most legitimate and prestigious of all Mexican universities. It is also the most distinctive, distinguished by its unprecedented mix of academic programs and unique relationship to the state. The magnitude, centrality, and history of UNAM have firmly rooted the university within the Mexican society. UNAM is also involved in a wide array of activities beyond the realm of higher education, including government, economics, business, and health care. UNAM is truly Mexico's university.

As with other state-building universities, UNAM's distinctiveness, its historical centrality, and its legacy of resistance to conformity are key to its legitimacy and prestige. Legitimacy and prestige, in turn, are deeply related but distinct indicators of the status of UNAM. One cannot understand UNAM, or the nature of state-building universities, without understanding the sources of the legitimacy and prestige these institutions have long enjoyed.

The Attributes of UNAM

UNAM is a large and multifaceted institution. The university offers three levels of degrees: baccalaureate,[7] undergraduate (which includes professional schools), and graduate studies. These levels encompass 2 baccalaureate programs; 70 undergraduate and professional programs, as well as 9 technical and vocational programs; 45 doctoral, 110 master's, and 60 specialized study programs.

In the 2003–2004 academic year, nearly 270,000 students were enrolled at UNAM; 143,405 in undergraduate and professional programs, 104,554 in baccalaureate programs, and 18,987 in graduate programs. UNAM accounted for 3 percent of the nation's baccalaureate enrollments and 7 percent of its undergraduate enrollments. UNAM also held 13 percent of total national graduate enrollments, with 30 percent of the enrollments in specialized studies, 6 percent of the master's programs, and 26 percent of the doctoral programs.[8] According to data provided by CONACYT (Consejo Nacional de Ciencia y Tecnología [National Council for Technology]), Mexico's national science and research government agency, in 2003 UNAM awarded 30 percent of Mexican doctoral degrees.[9]

Research at UNAM is organized into two systems: the sciences (natural and physical) and the social sciences (including the humanities). Research takes place in 26 research institutes, 13 research centers, and many schools and departments. It is estimated that more than 50 percent of all research in Mexico takes place at UNAM. In 2003, the university produced 37 percent of all research articles in Mexico in the physical sciences that were published in international refereed journals,[10] and in 2004, faculty at UNAM comprised 29 percent of the nation's academic researchers. UNAM has also been entrusted with the National Seismologic System as well as the National Observatory and sails two research vessels along the Mexican coasts. The university is also a repository of Mexico's most important archives and book collections, held in the National Library administered by UNAM.

The university's reputation is further enhanced by the more than 60,000 extension programs and cultural events sponsored by UNAM each year. These presentations include musical concerts, theatrical performances, dance recitals, literary readings, movies, conferences, book presentations, guided tours, and seminars. UNAM has one of the nation's most prestigious classical music orchestras (Orquesta Filarmónica de la UNAM); a number of arts and sciences museums, several cinemas, theaters, and music halls; and even a professional soccer team that won the last two national league championships. Radio UNAM's two frequencies reach the entire country and TV UNAM, though not a channel on open access television, is a constant presence through private and public broadcasts.

The Ciudad Universitaria, the extensive campus built in the 1950s, is the center of UNAM's activities and a key site for public gatherings in Mexico City. Many of its buildings host murals by Mexico's most famous artists, including Rivera, O'Gorman, Siqueiros, and Chávez Morado. In addition to Ciudad Universitaria there are 14 baccalaureate and 5 graduate and undergraduate campuses in Mexico City, augmented by research and graduate campuses in other states and cities, including Cuernavaca, Ensenada, Mérida, Morelia, and Tlaxcala.

As is the case for other state-building universities, UNAM is more than a university—it is a distinctive institution of the state. The depth and breadth of its offerings demonstrate the extent of its intellectual, social, cultural, and political activities; and its essential contributions set it clearly apart from other institutions in the country. They also clearly distinguish UNAM from flagship universities on a number of dimensions. First, there are many flagships in the United States, but only one national university in Mexico. Second, while there are some flagships that have a complexity and breadth of academic and research offerings similar to what is available at UNAM, none approach the cultural, political, and social prominence of UNAM. It can be argued that all of the flagships of the United States taken together do not influence the national character to the degree that UNAM shapes the Mexican state. It is also the case that UNAM emerged as the sole higher education institution in Mexico and remained so for many years. As the system expanded and new universities were created, UNAM became the pinnacle of a relatively undifferentiated higher education arrangement. Unlike prominent universities in master-planned postsecondary systems, UNAM has evolved with many of the responsibilities of a differentiated system built into its own structure and processes. Finally, flagships in the United States differ in degree rather than in kind. The University of California, the University of Texas, the University of Michigan, Harvard University, and Yale University have a great deal in common. If one stands above the others at a particular moment, it is for the quality of its undergraduate education, the total size of its research productivity, and the excellence of its graduate schools; and those distinctions are subject to rapid change. UNAM, like many other state-building universities, has since its founding been like no other Mexican institution.

The historical centrality of the UNAM and much of its legitimacy can be explained by the fact that the institution has been closely linked to many of the most significant events in Mexican history. As is the case with other state-building institutions, UNAM has shaped the Mexican state and, in turn, its intense involvement with the country's key historical moments has shaped UNAM. This symbiotic process of shaping and being shaped, often through contest, is central to understanding the historical centrality of state-building institutions. While flagships in the United States have had significant influence upon the American political economy (Pusser 2003), the impact has been of an entirely different magnitude than the influence exerted by state-building universities.

Antecedents of the Universidad Nacional

UNAM in its contemporary form was established in 1945 by an act of the Mexican Congress. The antecedents of the university, however, can be traced to the Real y Pontificia Universidad de México, founded by a royal decree in 1551. In the aftermath of the war of independence and through the early years of the new republic, the Real y Pontificia Universidad suffered a long period of uncertainty and lack of stability leading to its closure in 1867. Despite the demise of this first incarnation of the national university, its memory stands as a powerful symbol of Mexican higher education, a tradition that predates the founding of Harvard College, with a lineage older than that of the contemporary Mexican state. The power of the symbol of the ancestral university, progenitor of the modern university and the modern state, has given UNAM an almost transcendental legitimacy in its conflicts with the various national regimes that have sought to use the state to shape the university.

Along with a powerful symbolic legacy, modern Mexican higher education inherited four strong principles of the colonial university that shape UNAM today. These were the principles of autonomy, internal election of university officials, student participation in university governance, and public funding for the university (Ordorika 2003b).

Autonomy and Academic Freedom

The university was reestablished in its modern form through the consolidation of existing postsecondary institutions in 1910, at the end of the 40-year dictatorship of Porfirio Díaz. The reconstituted university was called Universidad Nacional de México (Alvarado 1984; Marsiske 1985). That iteration of the institution reflected a complex mixture of philosophical traditions: conservative scholasticism, spiritual humanism, and positivism. The relationship between the national university and the populist governments emerging from the Mexican revolution was extremely confrontational. After considerable conflict, the tension between the university and the Mexican state was eased in 1929 by the formal granting of autonomy from the state to the university. The tension between the desire for self-governance by the *universitarios*[11] and the state's continuing interest in shaping national educational practices also gave rise to a powerful norm of academic freedom within the university.

Over time, the conflict between the university and the state emerged as a symbol of the struggle between urban middle classes that had been sidelined by the populist policies of the Mexican state and the leadership of the revolution. It was in every sense a political conflict involving definitions of society and the university (Ordorika 2003b). At such defining moments the historical centrality of the university as state-building institution comes into focus. The university becomes both site and symbol of broader national contests, shaping those contests as it is shaped by the conflict.

Developmentalism and Authoritarianism

In the ensuing years UNAM played a major role in the consolidation of the authoritarian political system and in the subsequent construction of a developmentalist state, one devoted to self-determination in economic and social improvement and increased independence in core-periphery relations (Marini 1994; Wallerstein 2004). The university was instrumental in the expansion of the urban middle class that accompanied national economic growth from the 1940s to the early 1960s (Guevara Niebla 1980). University credentialing and professional preparation were the vehicles for social mobility through which urban middle classes developed into a significant segment of Mexican society. The prestige of UNAM's degrees was widely advertised by professionals in urban and rural settings alike. To this day it is common to see physicians, engineers, and lawyers publicizing their UNAM degrees as a mark of expertise, merit, and high professional standards.

Universitarios were also instrumental in the creation of new public institutions of the state. Physicians from UNAM created the Ministry of Health as well as the most important National Institutes of Health. Engineers from the university organized and staffed the Ministry of Public Works, while lawyers trained at UNAM created the modern judicial system and wrote significant pieces of legislation that constituted the foundations of the Mexican state.

Beginning in the 1940s, UNAM also gave form and provided leadership for the Mexican political system. In 1946 Miguel Alemán was elected president of Mexico. He was the first president after the revolution who was not a member of the army, and he was a graduate of UNAM. Since that time *universitarios* have dominated government posts at every level. UNAM became the single most significant source of formal political leaders in the country (Smith 1979; Camp 1984, 1985). Roderic Ai Camp (2002) has argued that UNAM became the most important center for elite formation, as politicians, intellectuals, businesspeople, and a few members of the Catholic and military hierarchies were educated and recruited and then created networks at UNAM. From 1946 to 1994 every Mexican president was a graduate of UNAM.

Between 1940 and 1968, the Mexican state was governed by a powerful and politically stable authoritarian regime. A primary source of its legitimacy was its ability to incorporate professional expertise and intellectual networks from the national university. UNAM helped to shape, strengthen, and reproduce an authoritarian political system, and in turn UNAM was shaped by Mexican authoritarianism. These professional groups also became the most powerful actors within UNAM, as attorneys, physicians, and engineers controlled the governing board, the rectorship, and the university council (Ordorika 2003b).

The State-Building University and the Discourse of National Unity

The developmentalist state was grounded in a discourse of class collaboration and national unity. UNAM contributed in many ways to the creation and re-creation of this discourse and that society. Its very existence epitomized the notion of a unified, merit-based society as a vehicle of social mobility. This key attribute of UNAM is one that has been widely shared by state-building universities in other nations.

The role of UNAM as a state-builder, a distinguished institution of the developmentalist state, and a vehicle for social mobility earned it great legitimacy in the eyes of Mexican society. As a key function of the authoritarian state and a central source of legitimacy for that state, UNAM was held in great esteem by many sectors of Mexican society.

In this context, academic groups and intellectuals within UNAM expanded their research and related activities. Although there are important antecedents, organized research and knowledge production in Mexico are essentially products of the 1960s and 1970s. During these early years, research in the sciences and the humanities essentially took place at UNAM. Few other institutions, the National Institutes of Health among them, were active in research activities. While research in the sciences and humanities added to UNAM's prestige, research and knowledge creation were secondary to the professional degree orientation of UNAM in the opinion of the government, the public, and the university itself.

The University as a Contested Autonomous Space

Alongside its centrality in the academic, social, and economic life of Mexico, UNAM plays a critical role as a symbol, a site, and an instrument in relation to state political contests (Ordorika 2003a; Pusser 2003). In part, this function of UNAM emerged from the university's defiant stance toward the populist governments of the revolution. Since that time, while UNAM has by no means been a monolithic political entity, various constituencies within the university have been awarded a certain degree of leniency by the state despite their defiant stances and critical discourses at crucial political moments (Ordorika forthcoming). The university has also served as a central public sphere, which Pusser (forthcoming) has described as "a space that is at once physical, symbolic, cultural, political and semantic, not in relation to the State or the broader political economy but as a site of complex, autonomous contest in its own right." This concept of UNAM as a critical oasis in the midst of state contest further increased its legitimacy among vast segments of Mexican society. The role of the university as a public sphere is another defining characteristic of state-building universities. While it has been argued that a number of flagship universities have served as key public spheres at various historical moments (Pusser forthcoming), this characteristic is decidedly more prevalent at state-building universities. However, over the past four decades state-building universities and flagships have faced new and significant challenges to their autonomy.

THE END OF DEVELOPMENTALISM IN THE LATE 20TH CENTURY

The radical exercise of critique and the rebellious stance of university students in Mexico in the 1960s foreshadowed a coming crisis of developmentalism and a loss of legitimacy for the authoritarian political system. The miraculous economic growth that had characterized the developmentalist state was coming to an end, and the subsequent economic crises diminished the expectations of the professional urban middle classes. In 1968 the political expression of dissatisfaction took the form of a massive protest movement at UNAM, Instituto Politécnico Nacional, and other higher education institutions, where students challenged the foundations of the authoritarian political system (Gonzalez de Alba 1971; Guevara 1990; Martinez della Rocca 1986; Ordorika 2003b). The ferocious repression exercised by the government against students, faculty, and university buildings alike shattered the relationship between the *universitarios* and the Mexican state. In the wake of the economic crises of 1976 and 1982, the connections from the university to national economic development and the political system were further eroded. Government-enforced economic structural adjustment policies profoundly impacted public higher education[12] and UNAM was no exception. In spite of the increasing difficulties of the authoritarian political regime, UNAM's elites maintained their close ties with the government and the government party.

Over the past 25 years, efforts to impose structural adjustment policies and efficiency models have dominated the state-university relationship at UNAM and at state-building universities around the world (Ordorika 2004). During this period, traditional sources of legitimacy and prestige have been challenged, and, like many other public institutions, UNAM has become the object of neoliberal challenges. Under the guise of critiques of the efficiency and quality of the university, the traditional role of the institution has been called into question.

The State-Building University in Crisis

The past two decades have introduced a unique period of crisis for state-building universities, one that emerges from the end of developmentalism. The shift from developmentalist policies to neoliberal restructuring has entailed changes in form, process, and discourse that challenge the historical centrality, autonomous space, and distinctiveness of state-building universities. As these institutions increasingly emulate flagship universities, these shifts have also altered the relationship between the state and state-building institutions.

This crisis is clearly evident in the case of UNAM. Since the 1970s, in response to external demands, dominant groups within the university have redefined institutional priorities (Muñoz Garcia 2002; Díaz Barriga 1997b; Ordorika 2004). Research for economic development and elite professional education have been framed as the most appropriate objectives of UNAM. Though the university continues to serve vast numbers of students, undergraduate education has become secondary to research institutes and centers that have been redefined as the core of the university. Over the past decade even the hegemony of traditional research practices at UNAM has been challenged by demands for entrepreneurial postsecondary organization. As is the case at postsecondary institutions around the world, a rather nebulous discourse of efficiency and productivity has been adopted, with emphasis placed on commercial knowledge production, competitiveness, excellence, and economic development at the expense of undergraduate studies, democratization, and social justice (Marginson and Considine 2000; Slaughter and Rhoades 2004).

Along these lines, Mexican university administrators have established faculty evaluations and merit pay systems modeled on those used by successful flagships (Ordorika 2004; Bensimon and Ordorika forthcoming). Research has been privileged over teaching, and faculty members have been driven into intense competition for their salaries and research funds. Articles published in international journals have been more highly valued than those placed in refereed national or local academic publications with significant implications for national research, academic work, and the role of the faculty as a social body (Díaz Barriga 1997a; Canales Sánchez 2001; Acosta Silva 2004).

Under the banner of increasing quality, admissions regulations were changed and access to UNAM restricted. Calls for "financial diversification" were immediately translated into proposals for significant tuition increases. As the historical record demonstrates, state-building universities do not respond willingly to state coercion. The attempted transformations at UNAM generated intense conflicts in 1986, 1991, and again in 1999. After protracted public contest, tuition increases were reversed three times in response to student movements and prolonged strikes (Ordorika 2006).

The resistance at UNAM has come at a great cost. Attacks by government officials and the business community have increased throughout these contests. However, efforts to introduce the entrepreneurial model of postsecondary organization have contravened the historical understandings of UNAM as a state-building university with commitment to access and the redress of inequality. Knowledge creation and research, as a new source of prestige, is not immediately appealing to broad segments of the Mexican population. As the social responsibilities and aims of an institution like UNAM are redefined so that the institution becomes a site for state interaction with markets and global development, the historical centrality of the institution as the harbor of the aspirations of those traditionally excluded from higher education has been diminished. For a variety of reasons, the effort to move to a flagship model has alienated many of UNAM's constituencies, just as the move from developmentalism to neoliberal restructuring has alienated many constituencies on the periphery.

Flagships and the Future of Higher Education on the Periphery

The future of higher education institutions in the peripheral societies of a globalized world is unclear. Nascent adaptations to globalization and neoliberal restructuring have diminished the legitimacy of state-building universities. The purported benefits of the flagship model loom large in postsecondary planning on the periphery, yet we are reluctant to predict the evolution of state-building universities into flagships, and even more reluctant to predict success for such transformations. There are two fundamental reasons for caution. First, the flagships themselves are changing rapidly, moving in an intense drive for prestige toward ever-more-elite undergraduate training, professional credentialing, and commercially focused research (Geiger 2004; Slaughter and Rhoades 2004). In the process, public and private flagships have lost a considerable degree of the "public" character and legitimacy that could be traced, in the case of the publics to their land grant origins, and in the case of the private flagships to their role in the development of the political economy in the United States after World War II. As they have turned increasingly to private sources of funding, higher tuition, the commercialization of academic work, and demands for greater institutional autonomy, the flagships have also reduced their legitimacy as public spheres (Pusser forthcoming). Taken together, these shifts move the flagship model farther from the historically central and distinct projects of the state-building universities, broad access, the redress of inequality, and knowledge production for the benefit of society.

Our second caveat with regard to the transformation of state-building universities into flagships emerges from our understanding of historical centrality and distinctiveness as keys to understanding higher education on the periphery. We have argued here that the distinctiveness of a university like UNAM, its magnitude, moral authority, relevance, and impact, can only be understood as part of a dynamic historical process. The prestige and legitimacy of UNAM developed from historical interactions between the university, society, and the state in the political, economic, social, and cultural realms. It is the perception of its contribution to the public good at the national and the individual levels that has sustained the power of

UNAM as a state-building university. Although higher education institutions at the periphery have historically faced demands to conform to visions and models from the dominant countries, state-building universities have led the resistance. While their future is undoubtedly linked to the success of emerging political-economic forces pressuring states on the periphery, history suggests it is the distinctive character of state-building universities and their ability to serve as sites of contest that have enabled them to transcend pressures for adaptation across various epochs.

There is no doubt that UNAM remains the most important research institution in Mexico, as do other state-building universities in their respective contexts. The relevance of UNAM in this regard is widely recognized nationally and internationally.[13] However, the connection between postsecondary research, knowledge creation, and the public good for a peripheral country in the context of globalization is unclear. Prestige derived from international recognition of disciplinary excellence and significant external research funding is not enough to maintain the legitimacy of an institution like UNAM.

As sociohistorical products, legitimacy and prestige are not static concepts. UNAM and other state-building universities on the periphery are in a critical phase of their histories. The contemporary sources of prestige for universities at the periphery are not widely understood. Of more immediate concern, there is an intense contest over how to define the legitimate activities of these institutions. The dominant contemporary administrative approach, a comprehensive effort to emulate the flagship model, has had two distinct and negative effects. Demands for conformity to a flagship model have increased internal conflict, and they have weakened the internal cohesion of the university. In the case of UNAM these conditions have been exacerbated by the continuing adherence to authoritarian practices and structures of university governance, despite democratic changes occurring in the broader society and the Mexican political system. On balance, efforts to conform to the goals of the flagship model have widened the distance between UNAM and its traditional constituency, the Mexican people.

Nevertheless, UNAM and the other state-building universities face considerable pressure to emulate flagships. Without remarkable changes in the initial pattern of demands for adaptation, there is little likelihood for success in such a transformation. In pursuit of flagship status, UNAM and other state-building universities would be expected to increase their reliance on private funding and industry support. They would be encouraged to enhance their infrastructures to compete for partnerships with private commercial ventures, emphasize research with the potential for patent and licensing income, and establish partnerships with Mexican and multinational corporations for research and development. Revenues would have to be reallocated, shifting funds away from undergraduate and professional education in favor of investments in graduate studies and commercial research activities. Greater financial resources would need to be devoted to the hard sciences and technology development to the detriment of the social sciences and the humanities. Tuition would have to be increased. Student admissions practices and enrollment guidelines would need to be revised to increase selectivity and institutional prestige. As we have argued throughout this work, these policies run counter to the essential historical purposes and commitments of state-building universities.

In the final analysis, state-building universities differ from one another, and from flagships, in many of the same ways as the states from which they have emerged differ. The crises faced by state-building universities, and by flagships, reflect state crises in their respective national contexts. At the beginning of the 21st century the cradle of global flagships, the United States, faces exceptional political polarization and uncertainty over the future of public and private institutions of all sorts. As the flagships struggle to maintain their prestige and their historical commitments to public and private goods, they reflect the uncertainty at the center of globalization projects (Wallerstein 2004).

Postsecondary institutions that are distinctive, are historically central, and resist demands for conformity as they serve as sites for contest succeed by establishing themselves in mutually supportive relationships with the state. States that foster the centrality of public higher education, privilege the creation of critical discourse and knowledge production, nurture universities as public spheres, and are dedicated to the redress of social, economic, and political inequality can foster a symbiotic relationship with a state-building university. This sort of collaboration can be sustained for universities at the core and on the periphery. As the case of UNAM demonstrates, state-building universities on the periphery offer an important historical lesson for the flagships at the core. Despite repeated challenges from authoritarian regimes and a variety of internal and exogenous shocks and crises, UNAM has persisted by relying on its historical commitment to serve the people of Mexico and to build the Mexican state. When a state moves away from its commitment to support the missions of its essential institutions, it reveals its own crisis and moves away from its own history and sources of legitimacy. Our hope for the future is that the prominent institutions of higher education on the periphery and at the core will remain committed to those beliefs and activities that have long provided their legitimacy and sustained their centrality. We hope also that institutions of higher education and their respective states endeavor to serve as sites for critical inquiry and contest at this essential juncture and remain mindful that one cannot succeed without the other.

NOTES

1. *Máxima casa de estudios* can be translated as the "highest house of studies" or the "highest institution of knowledge."

2. This title can be translated as the "nation's university."

3. The nation and the people.

4. From the Louisiana State University, National Flagship Action Agenda, http://appl003.lsu.edu/acadaff/flagship.nsf/$Content/Action+Plans+&+Outcomes?OpenDocument.

5. See *The University of Edinburgh annual report 1999–2000*, www.cpa.ed.ac.uk/reports/annual/1999-2000/index.html.

6. The *Academic Ranking of World Universities* produced by the Institute of Higher Education, Shanghai Jiao Tong University (in 2005) as well as the *Times Higher Education Supplement World University Rankings* (in 2004).

7. In the Mexican case, baccalaureate (or preparatory) refers to a secondary degree that is required to move into the higher education system. This component of the secondary process is labeled Educación Media Superior (middle higher education) in the Mexican education system.

8. Enrollment figures are estimated based on data for UNAM provided by the Dirección General de Planeación (Sistema Dinámico de Estadísticas Universitarias, UNAM 2003, www.estadistica.unam.mx/2004/docencia/pob_escolar_2003-2004.html) and national enrollment data provided by Secretaría de Educación Pública (www.sep.gob.mx/work/appsite/princif2003/Princcif2003.pdf).

9. Calculated by the author based on graduate degrees awarded in 2003 at the national level; data provided by CONACYT (Indicadores de actividades científicas y tecnológicas, México 2004, Edición de bolsillo, www.conacyt.mx/dap/INDICADORES_2004.pdf). Data on doctoral degrees awarded by UNAM in 2003 data provided by Dirección General de Planeación (Sistema Dinámico de Estadísticas Universitarias, UNAM 2003, www.estadistica.unam.mx/2004/docencia/pob_escolar_2003-2004.html).

10. See sources in note 9.

11. This is the term used to refer to members of the university—it includes faculty as well as students.

12. Between 1982 and 1988 federal funding for all levels of education decreased 43.65 percent;. UNAM's budget was reduced by 49.47 percent between 1981 and 1987 (Martínez Della Rocca and Ordorika 1993).

13. UNAM was ranked among the top 100 universities by the *Times Higher Education Supplement*. According to this benchmark UNAM is the first institution in Latin America and also among the Spanish-speaking universities of the world. In 2004 UNAM was ranked among the top 200 universities in the world in the *Academic Ranking of World Universities* of 2004, by the Institute of Higher Education, Shanghai

Jiao Tong University. According the this ranking UNAM is first among Latin American universities and second among universities from Spanish-speaking countries.

REFERENCES

Acosta Silva, A. 2004. El soborno de los incentivos. In *La academia en jaque*, ed. I. Ordorika. Mexico City: Miguel Angel Porrua.

Alvarado, M. L. 1984. La Escuela Nacional de Altos Estudios. Sus Orígenes. In *Memoria del Primer Encuentro de Historia sobre la Universidad*. Mexico City: CESU/UNAM.

Bensimon, E., and I. Ordorika. Forthcoming. Mexico's *estímulos*: Faculty compensation based on piece-work. In *The political economy of globalization: The university, state and market in the Americas*, ed. Robert A. Rhoads and Carlos Alberto Torres, 250–74. Stanford, CA: Stanford University Press.

Berdahl, R. M. 1998. The future of flagship universities. Remarks at the convocation, Texas A & M University. (October 5). http://cio.chance.berkeley.edu/chancellor/sp/flagship.htm.

Camp, R. A. 1984. *The making of a government: Political leaders in modern Mexico*. Tucson: University of Arizona Press.

———. 1985. *Intellectuals and the state in twentieth-century Mexico*. Austin: University of Texas Press.

———. 2002. *Mexico's mandarins: Crafting a power elite for the twenty-first century*. Berkeley: University of California Press.

Canales Sánchez, A. 2001. *La Experiencia Institucional con los Programas de Estímulo: La UNAM en el período 1990–1996*. Mexico City: DIE, CINVESTAV.

Clark, B. R. 1998. *Creating entrepreneurial universities: Organizational pathways of transformation*. Oxford and New York: Published for the IAU Press by Pergamon Press.

Díaz Barriga, A. 1997a. La comunidad académica de la UNAM ante los programas de estímulos al rendimiento. In *Universitarios, institucionalización académica y evaluación*, ed. A. Díaz Barriga and T. Pacheco, 62–81. Coyoacán: CESU/UNAM.

———. (1997b). Los programas de evaluación (estímulos) en la comunidad de investigadores. Un estudio en la UNAM. In *Universitarios, institucionalización académica y evaluación*, ed. A. Díaz Barriga and T. Pacheco, 37–52. Coyoacán: CESU/UNAM.

Douglass, J. A. 2000. *The California idea and American higher education: 1850 to the 1960 master plan*. Stanford, CA: Stanford University Press.

Flexner, A. 1994. *Universities: American, English, German*. New Brunswick, NJ: Transaction.

Geiger, R. L. 2004. *Knowledge and money: Research universities and the paradox of the marketplace*. Stanford, CA: Stanford University Press.

González de Alba, L. 1971. *Los días y los años*. 4th ed. Mexico City: Ediciones Era.

Guevara Niebla, G. (1980). La educación superior en el ciclo desarrollista de México. *Cuadernos Políticos* 25 (July–September).

———. (1990). *La rosa de los cambios*. Mexico City: Cal y Arena.

Kerr, C. 2001. *The uses of the university*. 5th ed. Cambridge, MA: Harvard University Press.

Kirp, D. L. 2003. *Shakespeare, Einstein, and the bottom line: The marketing of higher*

education. Cambridge, MA: Harvard University Press.
Levin, J. S. 2001. *Globalizing the communtity college*. New York: Palgrave Press.
Marginson, S. 1997. *Markets in education*. Melbourne: Allen & Unwin.
Marginson, S., and M. Considine. 2000. *The enterprise university: Power, governance, and reinvention in Australia*. Cambridge: Cambridge University Press.
Marini, R. M. 1994. La crisis del desarrollismo. *Archivo de Ruy Mauro Marini*. www.marini-escritos.unam.mx/026_crisis_desarrollismo_es.htm.
Marsiske, R. 1985. La Universidad Nacional de My la Autonom. In *La Universidad en el tiempo*, ed. UNAM/CESU. Mexico City: UNAM/CESU.
Martínez Della Rocca, S. 1986. *Estado y universidad en México, 1920–1968: Historia de los movimientos estudiantiles en la UNAM*. Mexico City: J. Boldó i Climent.
Martínez Della Rocca, S., and I. Ordorika. 1993. *UNAM, espejo del mejor México posible: La universidad en el contexto educativo nacional*. Mexico City: Ediciones Era.
Muñoz García, H. 2002. La política en la universidad. In *Universidad: Política y cambio institucional*, ed. H. Muñoz García, 39–80. Mexico City: Seminario de Educación Superior, CESU-UNAM, Grupo Editorial Miguel Angel Porrua.
Ordorika, I. 2001. Aproximaciones teóricas para un análisis del conflicto y el poder en la educación superior. *Perfiles Educatios* 23 (91): 77–96.
———. 2003a. The limits of university autonomy: Power and politics at the Universidad Nacional Autónoma de México. *Higher Education: The International Journal of Higher Education and Educational Planning* 46 (3): 361–88.
———. 2003b. *Power and politics in university governance: Organization and change at the Universidad Nacional Autonoma de Mexico*. New York: RoutledgeFalmer.
———. 2004. El mercado en la academia. In *La academia en jaque: Perspectivas políticas sobre la evaluación de la educación superior en México*, ed. I. Ordorika, 35–74. Mexico City: CRIM-UNAM/Miguel Angel Porrua.
———. 2006. *La disputa por el campus: Poder, política y autonomía en la UNAM 1944–1980*. Mexico City: CESU-UNAM/Plaza y Valdés Editores.
———. Forthcoming. Universidades constructoras de estado: Un modelo distintivo. *Perfiles Educativos*.
Pusser, B. 2002. Higher education, the emerging market, and the public good. In *The knowledge economy and postsecondary education*, ed. P. A. Graham and N. G. Stacey, 105–25. Washington, DC: National Academy Press.
———. 2003. Beyond Baldridge: Extending the political model of higher education governance. *Educational Policy* 17 (1): 121–40.
———. Forthcoming. Reconsidering higher education and the public good: The role of public spheres. In *Governance and the public good*, ed. W. G. Tierney. Albany: State University of New York Press.
Pusser, B., B. Gansneder, N. Gallaway, and N. Pope. 2005. Entrpreneurial activities in nonprofit institutions: A portrait of continuing education. *New Directions for Higher Education* 129 (Spring): 27–42.
Pusser, B., S. Slaughter, and S. L. Thomas. Forthcoming. Playing the board game: An empirical analysis of university trustee and corporate board interlocks. *Journal of Higher Education*.
Rhoads, R. A., and N. Durdella. 2005. Review of *Power and politics in university governance: organization and change at the Universidad Nacional Autónoma de*

México, by I. Ordoriko. *Journal of Higher Education* 76 (2): 234–37.

Rudolph, F. 1965. *The American college and university: A history*. New York: Vintage Books.

Slaughter, S., and L. L. Leslie. 1997. *Academic capitalism: Politics, policies, and the entrepreneurial university*. Baltimore: Johns Hopkins University Press.

Slaughter, S., and G. Rhoades. (2004). *Academic capitalism and the new economy: Markets, state, and higher education*. Baltimore: Johns Hopkins University Press.

Smith, P. H. 1979. *Labyrinths of power: Political recruitment in twentieth-century Mexico*. Princeton, NJ: Princeton University Press.

Wallerstein, Immanuel. 2004. After developmentalism and globalization: What? Keynote

address at the conference Development Challenges for the 21st Century, Cornell University, October 1.

10

The Role of Research Universities in Mexico

A Change of Paradigm?

Salvador Malo

In Mexico's higher education system, the rapid pace of expansion has produced new and often conflicting views regarding leading institutions. Today, the different opinions as to what constitutes leadership are not only linked to the new universities and higher education institutions competing for students, academics, funding, and prestige. These perspectives also arise from the new educational paradigms, as well as the existence of new actors, arenas, and rules: assessment and certifying organizations, media surveys and marketing, selection processes and rankings, and new political power players. In this context, there are no generally accepted criteria to assess the importance and leadership of Mexican universities.

Mexico experienced significant demographic, social, economic, and political changes during the second half of the 20th century. Thus, while a high demand for education already existed in the early 1950s, due to the small number of schools then available in relation to those needed, demand was pushed even further by population growth, trade liberalization, women's participation, urbanization, industrialization, and other phenomena that began to take place. This trend gave way to a remarkably dynamic education system, which had to meet the various needs and cope with differences in quality (ANUIES 2000a).

The growth of Mexico's population from 27 million in 1950 to over 105 million in 2005 indicates that the education system had to multiply itself many times over. This is certainly noticeable at the higher education level, where total enrollments rose from 30,000 students in 1950 to over 1.2 million in 1990 (OECD 1997) and to over 2.4 million in 2005 (SEP

2005a). These figures are also an indication that the growth and diversification of the sector has brought and continues to bring new players to the field. In the early years of development (1950–1980) the growth was absorbed mainly by the public universities, while in the past 25 years it has taken place mostly within the private sector.

These factors have not greatly modified society's general appreciation of the role and importance of higher education, which is still perceived as a public good and something every young person should complete. However, the significantly larger student population now attending the expanded number of higher education institutions (close to 2,000) has shifted public views on the quality of higher education and the comparative quality of the institutions providing the education.

While the rate of higher education enrollment in the country is still low (22 percent) in comparison to that of the Organization for Economic Cooperation and Development (OECD) countries, the ever-increasing numbers of first-degree graduates leaving universities each year have expanded the supply side to a level in which their relative labor market value has dropped. There are indications that many university graduates do not find jobs, while others cannot pursue their chosen professional careers due to the increasing competition. Some graduates must take jobs that require lower credentials, displacing those with less schooling and training (ANUIES 2003). Thus, notwithstanding the comparatively reduced proportion of enrollments in higher education, the most common explanation given for the low intake of university graduates by the labor market is that they are ill prepared for it—that the quality of teaching has decreased and universities' standards have dropped.

The federal and local (state) public universities were the ones that suffered the most from this perception, particularly during the 1980s and 1990s. Years ago these public universities attracted the best students, generally from upper-income population brackets. However, the expansion, brought about by a fast-growing population and a continuously increasing demand for higher education, transformed them into large, sometimes huge, institutions receiving less-qualified students from all segments of society and frequently having an oversized structure, multiple constituencies, and diverse functions.

Furthermore, government financial support and policies toward public institutions took a turn in the mid-1980s. Money became less readily available, while accountability demands and expressions of concern about teaching quality became more commonplace. At these public institutions, however, where research activities and doctoral programs began, the larger fraction of scientific and scholarly production in the country currently takes place and the majority of doctoral degrees are granted.

The above-mentioned factors indicate that while public research–oriented universities represent an important asset, they are also overstressed and experience difficulties that reduce their leadership and hinder their role in society. In addition, the visibility and weight public universities still have can be attributed more to their history or size than to the quality of their research or graduates, and their leadership loss is probably due to factors unrelated to graduate teaching or research performance.

THE HIGHER EDUCATION SYSTEM

University education in Mexico at the undergraduate level is different from what is offered by American colleges and universities. Deriving its origins from 19th-century continental Europe (Spain and France), undergraduate education is generally organized in a five-year period of study leading to a professional degree in which students are expected to follow specialized course syllabi centered on the subject matter of their selected field. The syllabus structure offers few possibilities for students to take courses that would provide them with a better general education, and regulations make it difficult to change to another field of study. Upon completion of their coursework, students obtain a *licenciatura,* a professional degree that enables them to practice their chosen profession or pursue graduate studies.

Even though most students (80 percent) enroll in *licenciatura* programs, one-third of them at private universities, there are other forms of tertiary education: vocational schools, technical universities, and teacher training institutions. Many of these institutions are also called universities, although with an added qualifier such as technical, technological, pedagogical, or polytechnic. On the other hand, some higher education institutions called polytechnics or technological institutes are in fact similar to universities, offering *licenciatura* and graduate programs and even pursuing research.

In contrast, graduate education follows that of the United States and is structured around three alternative paths: specialized studies (e.g., medicine) master's programs, or doctoral programs. Doctoral programs usually require significant involvement of candidates in research activities.

Research-Oriented Universities

Given the confusing scenario regarding names of institutions, classifications of higher and tertiary education do not help much to identify research-oriented universities.[1] The federal government differentiates tertiary education institutions based on the nature and duration of the undergraduate programs they offer (vocational training, two-year technical, teacher training, or *licenciatura*); by the level and ratio of the federal government's contribution to the institution's total funding in comparison to that provided by local (state) governments; and by the degree of the government's involvement in the institution's management (SEP 2005b).

The best-known classification of higher education institutions, that of the Asociación Nacional de Universidades e Instituciones de Educación Superior (ANUIES), uses both research and the level and diversity of degrees offered as institutional differentiators (ANUIES 2001). However, the non-quantitative definition of what is required in research and the degrees, plus the continuously varying situation of universities,[2] make this classification of little use.

Having graduate study programs does not necessarily indicate a university is research oriented. In 1998, ANUIES stated that 402 out of the 1,533 higher education institutions offered at least one specialized studies, master's, or doctoral program (ANUIES 2000b). Four years later, this number had increased to 526 institutions, but if only those having doctoral programs were counted, the number of institutions would be reduced to 120 (CONACYT 2004).

On the other hand, research activities alone do not confer on universities a special status, nor does defining themselves as research-oriented universities clearly indicate that institutions actually undertake research at a meaningful level. Most public universities have had research in their founding charters or in their mission statements for many years. Yet, in 2001 Ricardo Arechavala concluded that few Mexican higher education institutions possessed the organization, facilities, and attitudes required to qualify as the research universities discussed in that report (Arechavala 2001).

Some Mexican scholars argue that differentiation between research-oriented and teaching universities is not the result of deliberate institutional specialization or tertiary education stratification policies but rather the outcome of quality assurance instruments provided by the Sistema Nacional de Investigadores (SNI, National System of Researchers), the Padrón Nacional de Posgrado (National Registry of Graduate Programs), or the Comités Interinstitucionales de Evaluación de la Educación Superior (CIEES, Peer Review Evaluation of Academic Programs). According to this perspective, by generating quantitative information on scientific productivity, accredited professional and doctoral programs, and other data these instruments enabled the establishment of competitive funding mechanisms. These accomplishments, it is said, have brought about institutional differentiation.

Rankings

Ranking practices in Mexico are controversial. This does not mean that quality is not considered relevant. Students, academics, and, to a certain extent, society at large all seek to distinguish high-quality institutions. But since the most publicized institutional rankings, so far, are those made by the media (newspapers, *Reader's Digest*, etc.) or by government agencies, there is a broad perception that rankings are either a marketing exercise, an elitist practice, or at best a policy instrument. Furthermore, the contrasting perceptions of prestige that different sectors (business, government, and academia) have and that vary according to areas of study (social sciences, hard and life sciences, and engineering and technology) and levels of education (*licenciatura*, specialized studies, master's, and doctoral) make available rankings difficult to follow and accept.

In recent years new players have come to the forefront in the ranking arena. Those from the media rely on surveys, while others like the independent organization, Centro Nacional de Evaluación de la Educación Superior (CENEVAL, National Assessment Center for Higher Education), rely on standardized entrance and exit examinations. Although the surveys and tests do not consider graduate programs, scholarly activity, or research productivity, public perception of the quality of Mexican universities continues to be based largely on the results of the media rankings rather than of studies based on hard data and evidence.

Academic Evaluation and Accreditation

The number of externally evaluated academic programs at each institution is slowly becoming an indicator of institutional quality. At the *licenciatura* level of studies, the assessment and accreditation agencies and organizations such as the CIEES, the Consejo para la Acreditación de la Educación Superior (COPAES, Accreditation Council), and the Federación de Instituciones Mexicanas Particulares de Educación Superior (FIMPES, Association of Private Universities) periodically publish lists of accredited programs. These lists constitute a sort of ranking of universities, as can be illustrated by the fact that 10 universities with accredited programs decided to form a consortium. However, assessment and accreditation are not compulsory, and as yet the total number of programs evaluated is a small fraction of the total number of programs in the country.

For graduate education, the Consejo Nacional de Ciencia y Tecnología (CONACYT, National Council for Science and Technology) and the Subsecretaría de Educación Superior (SES, Undersecretariat for Higher Education) periodically list institutions having well-evaluated doctoral and master's programs (SEP 2005c). SES also publishes the names of the institutions that receive competitive funds for institutional, academic staff, and graduate studies development.

LEADING (FLAGSHIP) RESEARCH-ORIENTED UNIVERSITIES

In addition to program quality, the number of degrees awarded each year provides an indication of the relative institutional strength. In 2002, Mexico's total number of graduates at the doctoral level was 1,217. This number was attained by over 50 higher education institutions, three of which account for half of all the degrees awarded and seven of which represent three-quarters of the total number.

Most doctoral degrees awarded are in programs strongly linked to scientific and social research, technological development, or discipline advancement. Thus, the institutions that grant a significant number of doctoral degrees can be considered to be research-oriented universities. Based on these indicators, there are some 40 institutions awarding at least 10 PhD degrees every year. The number of private universities in this group is rather small considering that these universities absorb one-third of all *licenciatura* students in the country. Since their foundation in the early 1940s, two well-known private universities—ITESM (Instituto Technológico de Estudios Superiores de Monterrey) and the Iberoamericana University—have offered graduate study programs and in later years produced some 25 PhDs (ITESM 2005; Universidad Iberoamericana 2005). Some other private institutions have joined them, but the majority either do not offer graduate programs or limit them to master's degree programs in a few selected areas.

In 1984, the federal government created SNI, a program to which interested scientists could apply. Selection is decided by peer-review committees that assess applicants' merits by the quantity and quality of their research and scholarly productivity. Successful applicants are accepted for a fixed time span (three or four years), at the end of which their permanent membership in the program is decided by a peer review of their scientific productivity in the period.

Since SNI membership brings both prestige and significant pecuniary benefits to its members, few research-active academics can afford to be left out of it. Although open to all researchers in the country, more than three-quarters of the 10,000-strong members belong to higher education institutions.

The data from SNI constitute the oldest and more often used university ranking in Mexico regarding research-oriented universities. In 1986, SNI began publishing data indicating the institutions to which its members belonged (Malo 1986). Since then, the number of academics each university has in SNI has become a generally accepted indicator of its strength and quality of research.

Using the above indicator, there are at present some 150 higher education institutions that can be classified as research-oriented universities in the country. Table 10.1 lists the top 10 universities based on the number of SNI members in their staff, only one of them (ITESM) private. The small number of private institutions having SNI members reflects both their limited research activities and the fact that SNI's financial rules favor public universities.

A strong correlation exists between the institutions that have the highest number of accredited graduate programs, award more PhDs, or have more SNI-recognized academic staff members. Thus, either singly or together these indicators are a sign of leadership in research.

World-Class Research-Oriented Universities

In addition to SNI membership, quality graduate programs, and doctoral degrees, internationally measured scientific productivity has also been used as a means of differentiating research-oriented universities from the rest. By considering the total number of scientific papers produced by Mexican institutions as reported by the Institute for Scientific Information (ISI) over three time periods (1990–1994, 1994–1999, and 1999–2003) CONACYT (2004) reported that 6 of the top 10 were research-oriented universities, 5 at the same level in the three periods considered.

The Academia Mexicana de Ciencias (Mexican Academy of Sciences 2004), repeated CONACYT's approach and identified the top 10 institutions by the number of scientific papers produced in an equal number of different fields of research from 1980 until 1999. Some 35 research-oriented universities are mentioned: the Universidad Nacional Autónoma de México (UNAM, National University) and the Universidad Metropolitana (UAM) appear 10 times each—UNAM always at the top of the list while UAM is 8 times in the first four places; the Centro de Investigación y Estudios Avanzados (CINVESTAV) and the Instituto Politécnico Nacional (IPN) appear 7 times each—CINVESTAV 6 times in the first four places while IPN is 4 times in the first five; Benemérita Universidad Autónoma de Puebla appears 5 times, one of them in the first four; Universidad Autónoma de Nuevo León 4 times; Universidad de Guadalajara, Universidad Autónoma del Estado de Morelos, Universidad Autónoma de Baja California, El Colegio de México, and Universidad de las Américas 2 times each. Besides this last university, only 3 other private universities are mentioned: ITESM, the Instituto Tecnológico Autónomo de México, and the Centro de Investigación y Docencia Económica.

Table 10.1 Universities with a Minimum of 100 SNI* Members, 2004

Institution	SNI Members
Universidad Nacional Autónoma de México	2,718
Universidad Autónoma Metropolitana	597
Centro de Investigación y Estudios Avanzados	512
Instituto Politécnico Nacional	320
Universidad de Guadalajara	269
Benemérita Universidad Autónoma de Puebla	250
Colegio de Postgraduados	178
Universidad Autónoma de Nuevo León	177
Instituto Tecnológico de Estudios Superiores de Monterrey	168
El Colegio de México	144
Universidad Michoacana de San Nicolás Hidalgo	144
Universidad Autónoma del Estado de Morelos	135
Centro de Investigación Científica y Educación Superior de Ensenada	130
Universidad Autónoma de San Luis Potosí	119
Universidad de Guanajuato	111
Universidad Autónoma del Estado de Hidalgo	104
Centro de Investigación y Estudios Superiores en Antropología Social	101

Source: Data provided by the Sistema Nacional de Investigadores.

* Sistema Nacional de Investigadores (National System of Researchers)

The limited presence of the private universities in most research-related indicators can be attributed to their relative novelty; but the panorama is fast evolving and there are indications that in some cases this situation might change soon.[3]

Taken with other data all the above institutions have a relevant position within Mexico's research-oriented universities. Nevertheless, the figures and data do not necessarily reflect their overall leadership within the country's higher education system, since many other factors contribute in giving them social prestige, academic leadership, or public image.

Finally, the "world-class value" of Mexican research-oriented universities can be assessed from international comparisons. The ISI indicates that the 5,783 papers Mexico produced in 2003 represented 0.72 percent of world publications. Since UNAM was responsible for roughly half of those publications, this means it produced 0.36 percent of the world's scientific papers that year.

A less orthodox but equally convincing evidence of UNAM's world-class position in research can be derived from a comparison of the number of times a contribution to the scientific weekly journal *Nature* was deemed worthy, by the editors, of making it to the journal's cover page. UNAM was among the 39 institutions whose research papers made it to the cover of *Nature* at least five times in the 1985–1995 period.[4]

PUBLIC POLICY CONCERNS AND EXPERIENCES

All the above data show that Mexico has about 100 research-oriented universities, some of which can be said to have a leadership role in this field. The evidence also proves the country has, from a research-output standpoint, at least one world-class university. However, from a public policy perspective, the central question is whether obtaining flagship universities is the best route middle-income and developing countries should follow.

Stated in another way, the question is not whether Mexican scientists, research groups, or research institutions can be as good as their counterparts in advanced countries but whether the resources and efforts could be better used in other ways to bring about more significant and broader development for the nation. A proper answer to this question cannot be derived merely from a country's or institution's number of scientists, academic programs, degrees awarded, or papers published. While having good science and high-quality degrees is important, it is equally important to ensure that they return more than they draw from their societies.

In order to seek the best answer to this policy question, quality research has to be seen as a requisite rather than as a goal, as a means to reach non-research goals rather than as an end in itself. These concerns also apply to the decisions and policies to be made within specific institutions, their overall purpose, organization, and growth. Assuming these initiatives share an interest in research, analyzing the characteristics that differentiate them—rather than their common features—can be more relevant and useful.

University Development

Mexico provides an interesting case study for international comparison. The de facto higher education policy Mexico followed to the end of the 20th century was one that relied on just a few universities, rather than on creating conditions to foster the establishment and development of many. In the 1950s there was only a handful of universities; most of them were publicly funded and located in different states (King 1971).

UNAM—the national university located mostly in the Mexico City area—played a flagship role for many years, and by the end of the 1960s most states in the country had established a state university following its model. Its leadership was so strong that even those universities and higher education institutions not created based on its model were influenced by it.[5] The higher education expansion that took place in Mexico was first felt at UNAM in the 1960s but was soon experienced by the rest of the state universities.

Unbridled growth gave way to large universities providing education to more students than they were prepared for. The concerns about the impact this expansion had on quality were disregarded, intent as most universities and state officials were on taking advantage of the momentum to make their higher education institutions more important. The belief was that public university education as practiced by UNAM and other public state universities was a model to be kept unchanged and extended to embrace many more students.

Even after Mexico's repeated financial crises,[6] and notwithstanding several efforts to develop other higher education paradigms, the traditional model remained strong. By the turn of the century each of the 32 states had a state university. While the universities differed from one another, all repeated the pattern laid out by UNAM; they enjoyed a special status in their states in comparison with other higher education institutions in terms of public image or political weight. In a manner of speaking, these institutions became flagship universities within their higher education regions of influence, while UNAM was considered by many to be the standard-bearer of them all. In that sense, Mexico's higher education developed following a pattern that fostered and relied on flagship universities.

The First Signs of a Paradigm Shift

The fast pace of expansion gave way to concerns regarding the quality of public higher education: many universities had opened their doors to students they would not have previously accepted, sometimes even at the expense of their traditional constituencies; some of the additional enrollments were approved thinking that the resources to support them would come later; and the increasing number of first-degree university graduates began to create unemployment in certain fields and cities.

In addition, the financial constraints began to limit the response public universities could give to an ever-increasing demand that came as a consequence both of demographics and the belief that *licenciatura* studies should be given to all.

This state of affairs began to affect government policies. Following recommendations derived from national studies or heeding international advice, the federal government began to focus on diversification of higher education, higher education accountability, graduates' employability, and market and international forces.

These initiatives have not been wholly successful. It is true that new tertiary institutions have been created, that private higher education has expanded at a fast pace, and that evaluation and accreditation mechanisms have begun. But the new institutions have not yet attracted a significant number of students; the private sector has also created a number of small self-named universities of dubious quality; and the pace of acceptance of evaluations and accreditations has been slow.

Public universities have not generally been responsive to these policies, which are seen as an excuse for not supporting public education. While surveys and other signals indicate that some private universities are considered to have a better quality, some observers from the public universities point to the fact that private universities concentrate their teaching programs in market-driven fields, and have almost no research activities and few doctoral programs and graduates. Earning a professional degree, especially in selected key fields such as law, medicine, and engineering is still considered prestigious by the majority of social sectors in the country. These perceptions result in high competition for admission into the best-known higher education institutions. CENEVAL's university entrance examinations are now used by half of the applicants to higher education in Mexico. However, the preferential treatment the large universities give to students coming from their own high schools, as well as the different entrance examinations used in the selection process, demonstrates that students are not selected on an equal basis.

As stated before, there is also a growing perception—fueled by the media, political interests, ideological positions, and aggressive marketing campaigns—that some private universities are better than the public ones. This is gradually becoming a two-tier competition: one for entrance into the large public universities, the other for entrance into the most prestigious private institutions. The situation does not apply to doctoral studies or research-oriented master's programs, in which places available exceed the demand and the most prestigious institutions continue to be the public research-oriented universities.

The Research Function

Perhaps due to Mexican higher education's strong professional character during the first part of the 20th century, the research function has remained associated more with graduate teaching than with undergraduate professional training. The faculty at professional schools—many of whom are part-time professors—not having been trained for the academic world, had their main interests outside the university walls and viewed the newcomers (PhDs trained elsewhere) with a distant polite interest. The academic staff in charge of the first doctoral programs soon grouped themselves in organizational units with research as their primary objective.

These two types of professors coexist at UNAM, where now some 5,000 academic staff work in 45 institutes and research centers. These categories of faculty also exist at CINVESTAV, which has integrated itself as a research and graduate training institution. At both institutions, undergraduate and professional teaching can be described as at least one step distant from research professors. This arrangement has been, and continues to be, followed by other institutions.

The most noticeable exception is UAM. It was established 30 years ago as an alternative university model. To emphasize the connection between teaching and research, it was created as a decentralized university with full-time professors, a departmental structure, and a coursework schedule per quarters (terms).

Since as recently as 1996 only 8 percent of the total number of academic staff in the country had a PhD; this meant that having a doctoral degree provided hierarchical advantage. As of 2005, the proportion of faculty with a PhD has grown to 19 percent, as that qualification is now a requisite for an academic position at most public state universities (SEP 2005d).

GOVERNMENT POLICIES

All public universities in Mexico need federal or state government funding to operate. Tuition fees are negligible, and attempts to increase them have been fraught with problems and have led to conflicts between students and institutions. In academia, the most common view is that governments (federal and state) pay lip service to research-oriented universities but do not provide them with the resources they need to perform and develop properly. Most of this criticism is directed toward the federal government. The main arguments are related to the low level of resources the country devotes to R&D and the small number of scientists it has in comparison with other countries. Relations between academia and government are, therefore, cold and difficult.

There are two federal government bodies directly related to higher education and scientific research: SES and CONACYT.

Undersecretariat for Higher Education (SES)

It is true that, in the national budget appropriation considerations this office presents to Congress every year, there has not been an explicit special treatment of research-oriented universities. It is also true that, while the funding of public universities has not increased, SES has supported the creation and development of many new two-year technological universities and other institutions, thus reducing the amount of public resources that could be allocated to the public research-oriented universities.[7]

Notwithstanding this policy of institutional diversification, the other programs and policy instruments this government office has been promoting can all be said to favor public universities, since most of them have academic staff, graduate studies, and research as objectives.

For the past 15 years SES has promoted and funded the establishment and development of many different nongovernmental quality assurance and accreditation agencies, with CIEES, COPAES, and CENEVAL being among the better-known ones. Many of them have become fully independent, as is now the case regarding CENEVAL. At the same time, SES has supported diverse programs providing universities with financial support, for both institutional development and attaining the quality requirements the above agencies establish.

Finally, competitive funding mechanisms were created for institutional and graduate studies development. Significant sums were allocated, and institutional progress was systematically monitored. In spite of all these actions, SES is perceived in academia as a bureaucratic and distant office.

National Council for Science and Technology (CONACYT)

CONACYT is also a key player providing research funds in the form of grants, most of the graduate studies (master's and PhD) scholarships, and financial aid for students attending Mexican and overseas universities.

In addition, CONACYT operates SNI, which recognizes the research productivity of researchers and grants salary bonuses that can double or triple the university base salaries of faculty at public institutions,[8] and the Padrón Nacional de Posgrado (National Registry of Graduate Programs), which carries out an assessment exercise that recognizes the best (in terms of quality) master's and doctoral programs in the country, including those it identifies as "world-class programs" (understood to be equivalent to those offered by the best universities abroad).

CONACYT is also responsible for overseeing a group of 25 research centers with graduate teaching responsibilities and for establishing the general policy framework and the coordination of the strategic programs for Mexico's R&D efforts.

Most of CONACYT's actions and programs are related to graduate education and science development. Its main focus in the past several years (2000–2004) has been directed toward (1) having a new science and technology law that will facilitate more coordinated activities of the various government departments and a greater involvement of the business and industrial sectors in R&D and also providing a forum for academia, government, and business to work toward the generation of an innovative attitude and system; (2) creating R&D funds with state governments and with different government departments favoring research in areas of national and regional interest. Notwithstanding these initiatives, in recent years (as with SES) the gap between the public universities' science groups and CONACYT seems to be widening.

While the government can point to the increasing numbers of PhDs and scientific papers published as an indication that the national policies are making progress, public universities can claim the relevant numbers are proof that these universities could do more if they only had more resources.

Several issues are involved in this debate, among which university autonomy is a key factor. In addition to giving universities full independence with regard to teaching and academic matters, including decisions to open *licenciatura* and graduate programs, autonomy also allows the university to administer government subsidies with complete independence and to decide on its organizational structure and development programs.

Autonomy is a two-faced shield: it prevents emerging government policies from disrupting the universities' academic and administrative organization but it also makes it difficult for innovative, long-term government policies to influence the course of action and the university outcomes. For example, Mexico has a saturated demand for professionals in certain areas, but universities keep graduating and enrolling large numbers of students in those fields. There are few incentives to modify student flow at some schools.

University autonomy manifests itself not only in an unwelcome attitude toward government initiatives, strategies, and policies perceived as an "interference" in the university's internal affairs that will erode its independence. Autonomy has also generated an inward-looking attitude in academic communities with regard to any "external" influence that does not come from academia and also to regulations that foster this corporative attitude.[9]

The visibility and autonomy top administrators of large public universities have in comparison to other prominent local, regional, or national figures foster universities' involvement in political debates and strategies rather than in using their advantages to generate public policies conducive to the nation's development. For example, universities have not addressed, let alone contributed to solving in any meaningful way, Mexico's reduced technical capacity in all fields; nor have the larger institutions used their own mechanisms, science units, and personnel as long-term planning tools for the selective advancement of knowledge, the greater flow of scientific knowledge toward other sectors in society, or the development of applied research and local or national innovation systems.[10]

CONCLUSION

While the concept of flagship university in Mexico has become blurred, it is true that some universities are better known, have a higher reputation, or are more attractive to students than others. But it does not necessarily follow from any of these descriptions that these institutions are now exerting leadership over other universities or working to advance higher education to new levels or new forms in a meaningful way. Thus while the credibility of former paradigms has been eroded, there is no evidence that new concepts have taken the place of the old ones.

The fast pace of Mexican higher education expansion in the past 50 years, together with the still limited coverage of the population, means the system is still in the making. Mexican society is also experiencing huge transformations, which means that higher education will continue changing, that new educational approaches will have to be tried, and that significant comparisons and analyses of what has worked and what has not (and why) will have to be made in order to decide on the future of higher education.

Striking a proper balance between what Mexican society needs and how universities perceive its needs is difficult—as difficult as matching the perceptions of academia with those of society at large regarding what higher education as a whole is in fact delivering. The distance between these views in part explains why there are successful universities that do not yet exert any significant leadership within Mexican higher education.

World-class research-oriented universities are indeed a sign of development, but it remains unclear whether when positioned in less-developed societies their contribution to national development is smaller, equal, or greater than that in advanced societies. Another question concerns the cost of having institutions that play in the big leagues and providing them with appropriate financial backing and a supportive policy environment and whether the resources could not be more effectively used for institutional diversification, building a strong scientist/technician interface, reducing adult illiteracy, fostering vocational qualifications, increasing undergraduates' "employability," or developing a solid information technology society.

With regard to alternatives closer to current roles of higher education, middle-income (and other) countries have many other possible courses of action open to them. Mexico could benefit by paying more attention to the core skills and knowledge that will be needed in the future and to the training and retraining of the labor force; by ensuring the existence of a solid national innovation system; by developing strategies to increase collaborative and interdisciplinary work and new modes of knowledge production; and by modifying teaching and learning methods with information and communications technologies. Many of these goals are urgently needed together with support for the development of research-oriented universities.

This is not to say that international comparisons and assessments cannot be made. On the contrary, international comparisons can make significant contributions to higher education policies worldwide. However, the use of universities' performance indicators as the basis for an international comparison on the role these institutions play in their respective societies must begin by providing a precise definition of the role we expect of them, as well as on the way these and other indicators will help determine whether this role is being fulfilled. Thus, a proper examination of the needs and potential in the developmental sense becomes mandatory.

NOTES

1. While this book's theme is studying "flagship universities," it should be kept in mind that this concept has lost the meaning it once had and now is generally not understood or used in the country.

2. Both federal and state public universities have the authority (which they exercise) to open and close *licenciatura*, master's, and doctoral programs without permission from other bodies or in consultation with other institutions.

3. For example, in 2005 the Instituto Tecnológico de Estudios Superiores de Monterrey had over 1,100 PhDs and will soon have 200 SNI members on its academic staff (ITESM 2005).

4. The source was a private conversation with Jorge Flores, Centro de Ciencias Físicas, UNAM.

5. Several public and private universities created completely independently had been in existence since before the middle of the last century.

6. In 1976, 1982, and 1994 the Mexican peso was subject to strong devaluations and had difficulty meeting its international obligations to the world banking community.

7. The federal government—not necessarily in consultation with SES—has also endorsed or allowed policies to be implemented that favor the proliferation of private universities.

8. Professors' total monthly income at most public universities can be several times larger than those formally stated.

9. For example, rectors and deans of public universities have to be elected from within their own academic staff.

10. UNAM, for example, operates a grant system comparable in magnitude to the research grants program of CONACYT.

REFERENCES

Academia Mexicana de Ciencias. 2004. *At las de la Ciencia Mexicana*. www.amc.edu.mx/atlas.htm.

ANUIES. *See* Asociación Nacional de Universidades e Instituciones de Educación Superior.

Arechavala, R. 2001. Las universidades de investigación: La gran ausencia en México. *Revista de la Educación Superior* 118:173–81.

Asociación Nacional de Universidades e Instituciones de Educación Superior (ANUIES). 2000a. *La Educación Superior en el Siglo XXI*. Mexico City: ANUIES.

———. 2000b. Anuario Estadístico 2000. *Licenciatura y posgrados en universidades e institutos tecnológicos*. Mexico City: ANUIES.

———. 2001. *Tipología de Instituciones de Educación Superior*. Mexico City: ANUIES.

———. 2003. *Mercado Laboral de Profesionistas en México. Diagnóstico (1990–2000)*. Primera Parte. Colección Biblioteca de la Educación Superior. Mexico City: ANUIES.

CONACYT. *See* Consejo Nacional de Ciencia y Tecnología.

Consejo Nacional de Ciencia y Tecnología (CONACYT). 2004. *Informe General del Estado de la Ciencia y la Tecnología 2004*. www.conacyt.mx/dap/indicadores2004 /index.html.

ITESM. *See* Instituto Tecnológico y de Estudios Superiores de Monterrey.

Instituto Tecnológico y de Estudios Superiores de Monterrey (ITESM). 2005. *La investigación y el Posgrado 2003–2004*. Mexico City: Instituto Tecnológico de Estudios Superiores de Monterrey.

King, Richard G. 1971. *The provincial universities of Mexico*. New York: Praeger.

Malo, S. 1986. El Sistema Nacional de Investigadores. *Ciencia y Desarrollo* 67 (12): 55–73.

OECD. *See* Organization for Economic Cooperation and Development.

Organization for Economic Cooperation and Development (OECD). 1997. Reviews of national policies for education: Mexico, higher education. Paris: OECD.

SEP. *See* Secretaría de Educación Pública.

Secretaría de Educación Pública (SEP). 2005a. *Infome de Labores, September 2005*. Mexico City: SEP.

———. 2005b. *Aspectos financieros del sistema universitario de Educación*. http://sesic.sep.gob.mx/sesic/financieros/afes/AFES2005.pdf.

———. 2005c. *Padrón Nacional de Posgrado SEP-CONACYT*. http://sesic.sep.gob.mx/pe/pfpn /pfpn.htm.

———. 2005d. *Programa de Mejoramiento del Profesorado*. www.sep.gob.mx/wb2/sep _PROMEP_Programa de Mejoramiento del Profesorad.

Universidad Iberoamericana. 2005. *Primer Informe del Rector 2004–2005*. Mexico City: Universidad Iberoamericana.

11

Are There Research Universities in Chile?

Andrés Bernasconi

The gigantic public universities one finds in other parts of Latin America do not exist in Chile. By the sheer force of their tradition, output, size, and political clout, for better or worse these universities occupy a central position in their national higher education systems. The Universidad de Chile could perhaps have become such an institution, albeit smaller, had it not been fragmented under the military dictatorship of Gen. Augusto Pinochet (1973–1990). Established in 1842 and the nation's oldest university, the Universidad de Chile remained the premier university in the country throughout the 20th century, educating the professional and political elites and supporting the arts. Since the 1950s, the university added some incipient research to its main professional training role. In the 1960s, it started to build graduate programs and a small professional cadre of full-time academics with advanced degrees. In the same decade, the university created a network of regional branches that were to perform the function of feeder colleges to the main campuses in Santiago (Levy and Bernasconi 1998). The 1967–1968 national university reform introduced the typical Latin American system of "co-governance" by faculty, students, and administrators; the replacement of professorial chairs by a departmental organization; and a great expansion of enrollments, from 27,000 in 1967 to almost 66,000 in 1973 (Brunner 1986, 31–40).

But the 1973 military coup hit the Universidad de Chile hard. Faculty, students, and administrative personnel were purged; eight academic units were eliminated and their personnel dismissed; and enrollments shrank to 48,800 in 1980 (Brunner 1986, 49). Moreover, the military regime's 1981 higher education reform severed from the university all of its regional branches and almost half of its schools in the capital city of Santiago, turning them into small, independent public universities. By the time democracy returned in 1990, the Universidad de Chile had campuses only in Santiago, the student body was reduced to 18,000 students, and the share of public funding in its budget had dropped to 37 percent (Consejo de Rectores 1990).

The other Chilean universities predating the expansion of the system in the 1980s were not primarily created as leaders of the higher education system or as models of new approaches to teaching or research. The Pontificia Universidad Católica de Chile emerged in 1888 as a conservative response to what the Catholic Church perceived as the onslaught of liberal, secularizing ideas in the government and in the Universidad de Chile. (The separation of church and state was not formalized until 1925.) The other private universities established during the first half of the 20th century emerged instead to meet the desire of regional elites to have local universities for professional education and the dissemination of culture. Universidad Técnica del Estado, the second public university, was founded in 1947 to offer technical and vocational programs, pedagogical education for the technical schools, and engineering degrees.

This history possibly explains why the notion of "flagship" university has not caught on in Chile. Some evidence (Bernasconi 2003) indicates that when looking at a local university for inspiration, contemporary Chilean university leaders would consider instead the research-oriented Pontificia Universidad Católica de Chile, which throughout the 1980s and 1990s led a most spectacular process of academic development and administrative reform (Clark 2004, 110–21; Bernasconi 2005). But, in any case, in a small country with 15 million inhabitants and an open economy, models for everything are most often sought abroad, not locally. Moreover, because of its affiliation—which it takes very seriously—the Catholic university is an unlikely candidate for flagship status within the system.

Instead, the favorite term used nowadays by university administrators, scholars, and government officials to denote excellence in the pursuit of a genuine university mission is *research university*. Even this term is of recent origin—in the 1990s, a handful of Chilean universities, including Universidad de Chile, Pontificia Universidad Católica de Chile, Universidad de Santiago (the current name of the Technical University, founded in 1947), and a few others—began to embody some of the attributes of the expression. The term emerged after the increasing entropy of the Chilean higher education system (which in the 10 years after 1981 went from 8 universities to 63 extremely diverse institutions of that name) made it necessary, especially among university people, to differentiate classes of universities.[1]

Once the first classifications and rankings of universities made their appearance in Chile in 2000, the concept of research university had become academic leaders' standard form of grouping Chile's most prestigious universities. Accordingly, the rankings began to call the topmost group research universities. This group has always been composed either of the same five universities, which are the ones with the greatest numbers of research grants and publications in the mainstream academic literature, or of the top three among these, when the rankings are based on a more restrictive set of criteria for membership in the research university group. The adoption of the idea of the research university as a category to describe some of Chile's leading institutions of higher education is now a rather unproblematic practice and continues to be deployed to characterize a segment of the university sector (see Brunner et al. 2005, 147–48).

Aside from local usage, however, do these Chilean institutions meet the international standards for research universities? If they are not yet research universities, are they on a path of development that may eventually transform them into that type of institution? To answer these questions we need, first, to identify the essential, universal elements of the notion of a research university and then use that definition to measure Chile's best-performing institutions in terms of research. In this chapter I, therefore, begin by presenting an analytical construct of a research university, an ideal type of sorts (Weber 1949, 89–112), abstracted from US and international experience. I next explain why, in spite of the great progress of research in Chile in the past decade or so, there are still no research universities in this country. Finally, I elaborate on the trends that have to date propelled the research agenda in Chile and are likely to remain driving forces in the thrust of Chilean research-oriented institutions to become research universities.

Data for this chapter include, first, publicly available national and institutional statistics on research funding, personnel, and output; and second, qualitative data from earlier work (Bernasconi 2003), collected through site visits to four research-oriented Chilean universities between October 2001 and January 2002. The qualitative material deals mostly with the profiles of professors in those universities and with the changing nature of their jobs as the institutions strengthen their scientific capabilities.

THE IDEA OF THE RESEARCH UNIVERSITY

The idea of the research university is now best exemplified by institutions at the apex of the US higher education system, but the institution is, of course, not native to the United States. From the German philosophers to whom we owe the modern idea of the university and its first model, the University of Berlin, there is a long and winding road to the reluctant adoption of the German model in the United States in the second half of the 19th century (Geiger 1986); the solidification in the decades of the 1920s and 1930s of research as the central mission of US universities; and the worldwide prominence achieved after World War II of universities like Harvard, Chicago, California, Michigan, Yale, Wisconsin, and the Massachusetts Institute of Technology (MIT).

As a consequence of these developments, the American idea of the research university took hold, becoming the gold standard according to which universities throughout the world compare themselves and are assessed.

The ISI Web of Knowledge search engine for academic articles in peer-reviewed, mainstream journals allows for the following exercise: if one enters "research university(ies)"[2] in the *topic* search field, the search engine returns 431 articles published between 1970 and 2005, in which the expression "research university" or "research universities" appears in either the title, the abstract, or the keywords. The same kind of search, using the expression "elite university(ies)," produces 17 results. "World-class university(ies)" yields 4 pieces, while the query "flagship university(ies)" retrieves only one. As we can see from the data, across the world of indexed scholarship, "research university" is the most current designation for institutions at the top echelon of higher education. Moreover, a review of the abstracts of the items in the list for "research university(ies)" reveals that in approximately 85 percent of them research university is but a category for defining the type of higher education institution that served as a fieldwork site, a control group, or the setting in which the problem of interest had been studied (be it race relations, salary of professors, safety of laboratories, use of instructional technology, public health issues, and many more), or an independent variable in a regression model. Only about 15 percent of the articles included the functions, characteristics, problems, or missions of research universities, as such, as the topics of interest. In other words, the notion of a research university is more often taken as a given than turned into a research question.[3] Only a relatively minor part of the research effort deals explicitly with the definition of a research university.

This usage of the term *research university* is not restricted to US scholarship. Ten percent of the articles on research universities retrieved by the search engine refer to universities in countries outside the United States (including Australia, Canada, Chile, China, France, India, Israel, Italy,

Japan, Korea, the Netherlands, Russia, Singapore, Switzerland, and the United Kingdom). In 2002, 12 prestigious universities in Europe formed the League of European Research Universities, an "association of twelve research-intensive universities sharing the values of high-quality teaching within an environment of internationally competitive research."[4] Another association of research universities exists in Australia.[5]

The classification of US institutions of higher education by the Carnegie Foundation for the Advancement of Teaching cannot be overlooked in terms of its influence on the worldwide dissemination of a model for a research university. With its precise quantitative standards for citing universities with the strongest research orientation, the Carnegie Foundation has provided scholars, policy analysts, clients, and stakeholders in general, in the United States and abroad, a clear, simple, and widely used tool to identify the institutions that merit the name of research university.

Defining Features

What constitutes a conceptual construct for "research university," against which real universities may be fruitfully compared for purposes of description and analysis? Geiger (1985, 371) groups the defining features into three categories—*faculty, money,* and *students*—to which I would add as a fourth element an overall *research ethos*.

Faculty. A research university is composed of full-time faculty members who have been trained as researchers, are experts in a field of knowledge, devote most of their time at work to research, and contribute with their publications to scholarship in their field. Intellectually, they see themselves as members of an international disciplinary community (Jencks and Riesman 1968). Professionally, they belong in a guild with norms for such factors as career structure, academic freedom, and job description that remain outside the legitimate power of the employer to alter in their essential elements (Geiger 1985, 380; Goodchild 1991, 3). Faculty are organized in academic units staffed with sufficient numbers of colleagues with the same profile within each field of specialization so as to make academic dialogue possible and rewarding.

Money. The institutions require the economic resources to support research, in the form of salaries sufficient to secure a full-time dedication of faculty members to their university jobs, state-of-the-art laboratories, supplies, bibliographic resources, and other material infrastructure necessary for research. These resources are chiefly obtained through funds allocated on the basis of the merit of the proposed research project or program (Thelin 2004, 356–57).

Students. This category is essential because otherwise we would be in the presence of a research institute, not a university. But not just any kind of student will do. First, students are needed at both the undergraduate and graduate levels. A sizable group of graduate students are working at the doctoral level.[6] Finally, students at research universities are highly selected, since ample resources and a reputation for quality, both associated with research achievements, attract the best applicants (Braxton 1993).

Research ethos. Freedom of inquiry and freedom of teaching are a must, of course, but the culture of a research university reaches beyond academic freedom. The difference between a research university and a university carrying out research is that, in a research university, scientific achievement is the overarching goal of the institution and its requirements, processes, and values suffuse the whole of the functions of the university. These elements are institutionalized within the organization—that is, they constitute parts of the everyday, taken-for-granted features of the university.

These days, research universities in the United States and elsewhere in the developed world find themselves increasingly challenged by the growing need to make their research economically relevant, become more entrepreneurial, and get more closely linked to their markets. At this point, since they seem to pertain not to the ideal concept of the research university but to its current form of embodiment, these phenomena are not considered part of the ideal type.

How would the most research-intensive Chilean universities measure up against this mental construct of the research university? We turn next to this question.

RESEARCH-ORIENTED UNIVERSITIES IN CHILE

Scientific research emerged at Chile's universities relatively late, not only in comparison with the developed world but also with neighboring countries such as Brazil and Argentina. By the late 1960s, Chilean universities were almost exclusively undergraduate teaching institutions. Although higher education engaged 80 percent of the nation's incipient research and development personnel, in 1965 there was only one doctoral program in Chile, and in 1967 only 5 percent of the faculty at the Universidad de

Chile had doctoral degrees. Data for 1966 also showed that 68 percent of the professors at the Universidad de Chile worked there part-time (Brunner 1986, 18–30). Only since the 1980s have some of Chile's universities begun to match their rhetoric about a research mission with actual scientific accomplishments, and the process of institutionalizing research is still in progress.

Table 11.1 Profile of the Five Research-Oriented Universities in Chile, 2004

Indicators	(1)	(2)	(3)	(4)	(5)	Average
Students						
Numbers[a]	26,470	19,829	18,411	17,555	9,295	18,312
High scores[b] (%)	94	94	51	75	41	71
Graduate[c] (%)	11.7	10.0	5.1	3.2	3.9	6.8
PhDs conferred[j]	50	37	34	8	5	27
Faculty (2003)						
Numbers[d]	3,392	2,349	1,430	2,425	784	2,076
Full time[e] (%)	35.9	43.4	57.1	25.0	67.2	45.7
PhDs[f] (%)	20.7	48.9[k]	25.5	13.9	22.6	26.3
Full-time PhDs[g] (%)	34.3	71.6[k]	40.8	38.8	31.7	43.4
Research						
Projects[h]	569	393	222	157	95	287
Publications[i]	2,322	1,432	928	546	376	1,121

Source: Consejo Superior de Educación (2004); Departamento de Medición (2005), for the class of 2004; Consejo de Rectores 2003; *El Mercurio* (2004).

Note: Column headings are as follows: (1) Universidad de Chile; (2) Pontificia Universidad Católica de Chile; (3) Universidad de Concepción; (4) Universidad de Santiago; (5) Universidad Austral.

[a]Head count of undergraduate and graduate students.

[b]Percentage of freshmen among the 27,500 students with the best scores in the national standardized admissions test.

[c]Proportion of graduate students in total enrolments.

[d]Total head count.

[e]The proportion of faculty who are full-time.

[f]The proportion of faculty with a PhD degree.

[g]The proportion of full-time faculty who are PhD holders.

[h]"Projects" are all externally funded, and competitively assigned, research grants.

[i]The sum of all the Thomson Scientific ISI-indexed articles published in the previous three years.

[j]Number of PhD degrees conferred in 2003.

[k]Includes faculty with a medical specialization degree—if those are excluded, the proportion of Pontificia Universidad Católica de Chile faculty with doctorates reported by Qué Pasa (2004) is 29.7 percent, and full-time faculty with PhDs is 47 percent.

Since 1982, the bulk of funding for academic research in Chilean universities has been channeled through FONDECYT, the main competitive research fund of the National Council for Scientific and Technological Research (CONICYT). As a peer-reviewed competitive mechanism for allocating research funds in all fields of inquiry, the FONDECYT program looks like a good place to start identifying the universities most active in research. The distribution of FONDECYT research funds in the 1982–2000 period shows that five universities acquired almost 80 percent of all funding: the Universidad de Chile (37.4 percent); the Pontificia Universidad Católica de Chile (21.5 percent); the Universidad de Concepción, founded in 1919 (8 percent); the Universidad de Santiago (6.4 percent); and the Universidad Austral, founded in 1954 (6 percent). The next university on the list appears with half the amount obtained by the Universidad Austral (CONICYT 2000, 45). These five universities also turn out to be the ones with the highest research output, measured by the number of ISI-indexed publications between 2002 and 2004, as seen together with other indicators in table 11.1.

Table 11.1 provides a quantitative profile for the five universities with the most research resources and output. Had the universities ranking sixth, seventh, and eighth in research output (measured by the number of indexed articles published) been included, the list would have encompassed all eight of the oldest universities—precisely those founded prior to the expansion of the system in the 1980s.

The indicators in table 11.1 correlate with some elements of the ideal model of a research university. On average, only 45 percent of faculty at these universities have full-time appointments—ranging from 25 percent at the Universidad de Santiago to 67 percent at the Universidad de Concepción. Regarding faculty credentials, on average less than half of full-time professors have PhD degrees. This probably explains why the faculty at the Universidad de Chile (3,392) produced just 2,322 ISI-indexed articles in three years, at a rate of two-thirds of an article per professor in three years. This productivity rate is similar to those at the Pontificia Universidad Católica de Chile and the Universidad de Concepción. At the Universidad de Santiago and the Universidad Austral the figures are even lower. These numbers can be contrasted with the reported 4,450 ISI-indexed articles in 2003 for the 4,953 professors at the Universidade de São Paulo.[7] Another comparison can be made with the average of 4,316 Science Citation Index (SCI) and Social Science Citation Index (SSCI) articles published annually by the top 20 Chinese universities.[8] Another Brazilian institution, closer in size to the Chilean universities presented here, is the Universidade Estadual de Campinas. It has some 1,800 professors, 90 percent of them full-time and 94 percent with doctoral degrees. Their output is 2,264 ISI-indexed articles per year, in 2001 (UNICAMP n.d).

Given the figures in table 11.1, it is hard to make a case for these Chilean universities meeting the research university criteria set forth earlier in this chapter of being "composed of full-time faculty members who have been trained as researchers, are experts in a field of knowledge, and contribute with their publications to scholarship in that field." A similar judgment needs to be made with regard to doctoral students. The number of students in graduate programs reaches 10 percent or more only at the Universidad de Chile and the Pontificia Universidad Católica de Chile, and typically only one out of every three or four graduate students is in a doctoral program. This configuration is reflected in the numbers of doctorates conferred in 2003 (see table 11.1).

The quality of incoming students at three of the five institutions in table 11.1 seems to conform with one feature of the ideal type of a research university, and the Universidad de Chile and the Pontificia Universidad Católica de Chile are the most selective institutions nationally in this regard. But of course, in the absence of the other attributes of research universities, this dimension alone is not enough to support a research status for these institutions.

Site visits conducted at the Universidad de Chile, the Pontificia Universidad Católica de Chile, the Universidad de Santiago, and the Universidad Austral between October 2001 and January 2002 (Bernasconi 2003) provide some insights into the standing of scientific work at each institution. At all these universities, highly research-oriented units (schools,[9] departments, centers) coexist with others—especially in professions, the social sciences, and the arts—centered on teaching undergraduate students. The qualified staff resources for research, economic resources, doctoral students, and the scientific ethos that exists in these universities are not evenly spread across each institution. There are some units, typically in the natural sciences, where the proportion of full-time faculty with doctorates reaches 100 percent, doctoral programs are well established, and the research output equals between one and two ISI-indexed journal articles per capita each year (Krauskopf 1999), alongside others, usually in the professions, the social sciences, and the arts, with little or no research capacity. These differences across academic units greatly influence the overall research output of a university. Moreover, the more academic units with cadres of full-time faculty with doctoral degrees, research grants, and a zest for publication in international outlets one finds in a university, the stronger the overall research output of the institution.

Another underlying element of the uneven research profile and performance within each university is the governance structure. The Universidad de Chile is an extreme example, but it serves to illustrate trends that, albeit less forcefully, are nonetheless also present at the other universities. Decentralization is so strong that this university is usually conceived by its members as being a federation of schools—some of which are excellent, some of only average quality, but all sharing a common brand name. The Universidad de Chile shares this form of internal diversification with the Latin American giants the Universidad de Buenos Aires and the Universidad Nacional Autónoma de México.[10] Harvard University is often brought up as an example of this federation model, but unlike Harvard, the Universidad de Chile lacks common minimum standards, not all the schools have a nationally recognized critical mass of scholars, and the central administration does not have the financial clout to steer the university toward strategic goals.

Unlike the Universidad de Chile, which emerged from a tradition of almost independent schools, decentralization at the Pontificia Universidad Católica de Chile resulted from a deliberate effort to move away from centralization. Starting in the mid-1980s, a new model was introduced that gave deans autonomy to manage their budgets and their human resources, create new programs, and raise funds. This transfer of power has enabled some schools to make significant progress toward integrating the practice of academic work typical of a research university, while others continue to maintain a traditional teaching profile. The Universidad de Santiago has also embarked on a process of administrative and financial decentralization to give its schools more room and better incentives to generate resources through consulting, continuing education, and graduate programs.

A second governance feature, present at all universities introduced here, with the exception of the Pontificia Universidad Católica de Chile, is the election of school deans and department heads by the faculty. Elected officials are generally not able or willing to introduce necessary but unpopular measures regarding their colleagues' work. Department chairs and deans are usually beholden to their constituencies, and if these are not researchers, then research suffers. This is, in part, why the rules governing the composition of professors' workloads emphasize teaching over research: many tenured professors are not capable of undertaking research. The feasibility of a more incisive enforcement of research productivity is met with skepticism by administrators, who doubt the measure would be effective because of the conflict-avoidance mentality that prevails among elected department chairs and deans.

A TRANSITION FROM TEACHING STAFF TO RESEARCH FACULTY

Recruitment of new faculty tends to work in the opposite, research-oriented direction. Increasingly, academic units are seeking to hire new faculty with doctorates. This heightened standard has been introduced due to the greater availability of young people with PhDs, the need for accreditation of doctoral programs, the consideration of academic prestige, inter-institutional comparisons, performance indicators–based funding, and reputation rankings.

The difference in expectations about the credentials and work of senior and younger academic staff creates a sort of "generation gap," which also contributes to the varied outlook on research across units in the same institution. For example, in the natural sciences, the doctorate has for a generation already been a requirement for membership in academia. In other disciplines, and in the professions, it is increasingly considered as the earliest step in a junior faculty member's career. Large numbers of professors with non-terminal degrees, however, who were hired before universities took on a research orientation in the 1980s, will most likely remain in the social sciences, the humanities, the arts, and the professional schools (law, architecture, social work, education, etc.) until retirement.

At the Universidad de Santiago, for instance, there still remain among the senior faculty many who were originally trained as school teachers in science. They continue to be excellent teachers, a dean points out, but have never during their careers engaged in research, nor will they do so in the future. Indeed, research is a new focus at the Universidad de Santiago. This approach started in 1971, trailing the Pontificia Universidad Católica de Chile, the Universidad de Chile, and the Universidad de Concepción by several years, mostly in the form of graduate training for the faculty. While the Universidad de Santiago ranked seventh in terms of research productivity nationally in 1990, today it has risen to fourth place. The rapid development of a research mission has divided the faculty into two generational groups: older faculty are mostly devoted to teaching, while researchers are largely found among younger faculty. The Physics Department, for instance, began hiring young PhDs in 1990 and now has some 20 young faculty, giving the department a strong research profile. This university had 606 full-time faculty in 2003 (see table 11.1), 50 or 60 of whom are highly productive in research and another 60 to 80, only moderately productive, according to one top university administrator I interviewed.

Another factor of relevance is the expedited manner in which faculty acquire permanency of employment, especially at public institutions like the Universidad de Chile and the Universidad de Santiago. The US idea of tenure is not a concept found in Chile. Yet, while public universities cannot fire their staff without a legal cause, other universities, autonomous to regulate this matter as they see fit, have established in their statutes and bylaws a similar right for their faculty and created a status equivalent to tenure. It is, however, necessary to distinguish two concepts of tenure: (1) "civil service"–type tenure is the right to permanency of employment, barring suppression of the position (retrenchment) or dismissal for moral turpitude or criminal behavior; (2) "academic"-type tenure includes, in addition to the aforementioned limits to permanency of employment, unsatisfactory academic performance.

All four Chilean research-oriented universities for which data have been obtained (the Universidad de Chile, the Pontificia Universidad Católica de Chile, the Universidad de Santiago, and the Universidad Austral) offer tenure to their professors. The Pontificia Universidad Católica de Chile offers academic tenure only for professors at the two highest ranks, but at the other three institutions, a professor can get tenure in any faculty rank. The Universidad de Chile is in a somewhat intermediate position between academic- and civil service–types of tenure. Although its General Code of Academic Evaluation contemplates poor performance as grounds for dismissal, it is unclear if this provision is actually enforced. In any case, this university grants tenure to professors with indefinite appointments regardless of category or rank, although it often makes short, initial, probationary appointments. The Universidad Austral grants civil service–type tenure after a two-year probationary period during which the new professor, in any rank, has a fixed-term contract. The Universidad de Santiago provides civil service–type tenure with initial appointments. Additionally, there is no terminal ("up or out") probationary period for faculty on the lower rungs, except at the Pontificia Universidad Católica. In other words, someone can become a tenured assistant professor for life.

At the Universidad de Chile and the Universidad de Santiago, the problem of an overly quick path to tenure is compounded by the absence of a mandatory retirement policy. Their regulations do not cite reaching retirement age (65 years for men, 60 years for women) as a cause for terminating tenure nor is there any incentive for faculty to retire voluntarily since the result would be an enormous drop in income. A few faculties, such as the physical and mathematical sciences (engineering) at the Universidad de

Chile, do force people to quit at age 65 by means of sheer peer pressure, although the law protects those who do not wish to retire.

At the Pontificia Universidad Católica retirement is mandatory at age 65. Faculty are offered a compensation equal to what their severance pay would be in case of unilateral termination of their contracts. Extensions up to age 70 must be approved by the faculty council and by the superior council, beyond that. In general, senior faculty choose to retire at 65, and many of them later find employment at new private universities. At the Pontificia Universidad Católica all faculty appointments carry a 10 percent tax on the salary that goes into a university-wide severance fund, the purpose of which is to enable academic and administrative units to provide severance pay for people they wish to dismiss. This fund has been a key enabler of this university's strict enforcement of productivity standards and of its mandatory retirement policy (Koljatic 1999, 356).

Salary policy also favors a diversity of faculty profiles. Base-level salaries are generally commensurate with average private-sector professional wages for staff with equivalent qualifications and are, thus, generally sufficient to support a modest middle-class lifestyle without the need for a second job, although universities offer numerous forms of variable salary connected to extra teaching, consulting, or research. Even for those who are disinclined or unable to benefit from these extra funds, there is always the possibility of part-time teaching at private universities.

Several universities with rigid and—for young PhDs conscious of their new value—unattractive salary scales connected to academic rank have devised appointment systems parallel to the regular tenured and tenure-track paths. This policy makes it possible to pay new faculty with doctorates salaries above the level prescribed for a junior faculty member in the rank-based salary scale.

However, it is important to point out that at all universities visited, except for the Universidad de Santiago, some measurement of opportunity cost (what the professor would make outside the university) is considered to establish salary policies. This institutionalized acknowledgment of the influence of the professional market on faculty salaries authorizes a professor of economics or law to earn more than a professor of equal rank in, say, history or philosophy. As such, this approach constitutes a radical departure from the ideology of equal salary for equal rank prevalent in Latin American public universities. The concept, however, continues to exist except that now the claim is defended by faculty only for salary equalization within a school. Salary differentials across schools within the same university are mostly presumed to be a (hard) fact of life.

The abundance of incentive schemes provides an intriguing contrast to the paucity of evaluation mentioned above. When it comes to stimulating performance among professors, Chilean research-oriented universities seem more prone to the carrot than the stick. They all have internal competitive research funds intended to prepare researchers for or to complement FONDECYT, the national research grants program. Another common policy related to research is to pay monetary bonuses or otherwise reward publication in the mainstream scientific literature (usually defined as journals indexed by ISI).

Salary supplements tied to good overall performance are offered at the Universidad de Santiago and the Pontificia Universidad Católica de Chile. To be eligible, faculty also have to pledge "exclusivity," which bans teaching at other universities generally but is essentially aimed at curbing part-time teaching at private institutions. In the late 1980s, exclusivity was created by the Pontificia Universidad Católica, which by setting the example made it legitimate to curb part-time teaching among full-time faculty. Subsequently, other universities with the financial clout to offer more salary in exchange for exclusive dedication followed suit.[11] At the Universidad de Santiago, one of the requirements to obtain "excellence in teaching" or "excellence in research" salary bonuses is to sign an affidavit relinquishing outside teaching. The Universidad de Chile demands no exclusive commitment of its faculty, due to freedom of work and lack of financial incentives to back up a prohibition. The university had briefly tried out a policy of exclusivity, with a salary bonus, but the approach failed because the faculty the university wanted the most were too expensive to retain at the university full-time. Ideology (mixed with self-interest) also plays a role: one perspective states that professors at tax-funded public universities have to be freely available to disseminate knowledge in society beyond the walls of their university. Another argument claims that control of products works better than control of time, and that, therefore, a tight performance evaluation should suffice to ensure productivity.

Salary policy has become a crude but effective tool for accountability—the point being that professors are not exempt from showing results in exchange for their salary. Several officials I interviewed indicated that the emergence of private universities, where the relationship between work and salary is generally regarded as close and unambiguous, has helped reinforce the notion that salary is remuneration for work and those who perform more effectively deserve higher salaries.

In general, an upgrade of the qualifications of faculty throughout a university is still several years away at these four institutions. At some professional schools, moreover, it is unclear whether the universities will totally replace their professional practitioners with academicians, given that the training in professional skills and familiarity with the professional markets encompass much of these schools' mission and are also what students demand. Rather than relying solely on full-time researchers, most leaders of professional schools I interviewed would be happier with a mix of academics with PhDs and a research portfolio as well as practitioners active in their professional markets who teach part-time.

This chapter has explored the reasons why one cannot, in light of the ideal type of research university proposed, regard even Chilean research-oriented institutions as research universities. Decentralized governance allows schools with different degrees of commitment to science to coexist under the same roof. Another factor is the weak university-wide expectations and requirements concerning faculty research productivity or lack of generalized enforcement of such expectations and requirements where they exist. Rapid access to a tenure system offers little chance to monitor a tenured professor's accomplishments over time or to act upon such evaluation. Salary and workload policies accommodate the interests of both research and nonresearch faculty. Holding permanent positions on campuses across the nation, a generation of professors reached tenure without a doctorate or a research track record, do not engage in research, and are unlikely to retire voluntarily to open up space for research-trained and -oriented younger colleagues. And, finally, because of the training demands of professional education, dedication to knowledge creation is unevenly rooted across schools in the most-research-oriented universities in Chile. What some Chilean universities do have, however, are schools, departments, or centers that function as islands of scientific research within universities that are striving, with more or less emphasis and urgency, to infuse the whole institution with the research-centered organization and culture of their research units.

From the present context, what is the outlook for research-oriented universities in Chile? Will a Chilean university become a research university in the near future? In pondering these questions we only have the past to go by, and the overall trend of the past 20 years looks generally auspicious.

THE RISE OF RESEARCH IN CHILE

The military government in power in Chile between 1973 and 1990 was bad news for universities. The institutions' autonomy was stifled by the military rectors, who assumed all governance functions. Repression was unleashed against faculty, students, and administrative personnel. Entire fields—sociology, political science, anthropology, and political economy—were practically wiped out from the university. Institutional autonomy, freedom of speech, academic freedom, and pluralism disappeared; the structural and governance reforms of the late 1960s were abolished, and the university was put under permanent surveillance (Brunner 1986, 41–46).

Public spending in higher education decreased between 15 and 35 percent (depending on the estimate) between 1974 and 1980. Universities were required to abandon gratuity, charge tuition, and seek other outside sources of funding. Self-financing at Chilean universities grew from 13.5 to 26.9 percent, on average, between 1965 and 1980 (Brunner 1986, 46–47).

Drastic economic reforms resulted in years of socially painful adjustment to a new political economy in which the engine of growth was no longer the state but rather the export-driven private sector until Chile's economy took off in the mid-1980s, beginning what 20 years later is widely regarded as one of the most spectacular recent periods of steep and sustained economic growth of a developing country anywhere outside of Asia. The size of the Chilean economy tripled, purchasing power-adjusted per capita income reached close to US$10,000 (5.25 million Chilean pesos), poverty was cut by half, and extreme poverty was reduced to single digits. The return to democracy in 1990 brought freedom and political stability, while leaving the legacy of economic reforms largely untouched.

Higher education took the same path as the economy: the system was privatized and deregulated, and competition imposed upon its institutions as the only possible strategy for survival. Twenty years after Chilean higher education was reformed, "privateness" has come to be its dominant feature, with the private sector representing 93 percent of institutions and 70 percent of enrollments. Funding has also been privatized, with nonpublic sources accounting for some three-quarters of the total national expenditures in higher education. These figures set Chile among the world's leading countries in the extent of private-sector participation in tertiary education.

This trend hardly seems a fitting scenario for science to blossom. Yet, between 1979 and 1990, the year of Chile's return to democracy, public funding for research and development increased by 30 percent in real terms, the numbers of ISI-indexed publications doubled, and faculty with graduate degrees tripled.[12] This is partly a result of research being largely spared from the budgetary cuts for higher education decreed in the 1980s by the military government of General Pinochet. The absence in Chile of major research centers outside the university system also helped the development of science in universities.

Since 1990, the democratic governments have continued to expand funding for research, doubling public expenditures in R&D between 1990 and 2002, while overall funding (public, private, and international) also increased in the same proportion over that span. In the two-and-a-half decades from 1979 and 2002, overall expenditures in R&D grew almost fivefold[13] (see table 11.2).

Table 11.2 University Publications, R&D Expenditures, and Faculty Productivity in Chile, 1979–2002

Indicators	1979	1985	1990	1995	2000	2002
Publications[a]	427	657	878	1,166	1,583	1,751
R&D expenditures[b]						
Ch$[c] (millions)	26,548	40,414	58,754	91,256	107,665	115,050
US$ (millions)	31.0	38.7	71.9	164.1	183.0	162.5
Faculty with graduate degrees	1,021	2,408	3,353	4,395	5,634	6,234
Publications per person[d]	0.42	0.27	0.26	0.27	0.28	0.28

Source: CONICYT, *Indicadores*, Santiago de Chile, www.conicyt.cl/bases /indicadores/index.html.
[a]University publications in ISI-indexed journals.
[b]Government, international, and private expenditures on university R&D.
[c]Chilean pesos in 2003.
[d]Faculty with graduate degrees.

Faculty productivity, however, remains rather low, at one-fourth of an article per year for faculty with PhDs. The uneven research productivity across schools and institutions discussed earlier includes the fact that publishing in English and in indexed outlets remains alien to the scientific communications tradition of vast areas of knowledge in Chile. Thus this measurement of productivity omits much of what is produced in the social sciences, the humanities, and the arts.

In Chile, as research develops with government support, so do graduate programs. Enrollments of only 2,000 students in graduate programs offered in 1983 increased to close to 12,000 in 2001. While in the early 1980s doctoral programs offered by Chilean universities were concentrated at a few universities and almost exclusively in the natural sciences and the humanities, the 1990s saw the expansion of these programs. While 80 doctoral programs were offered in Chile in 1999, 126 were available in 2004. In the same period, student numbers rose from 1,144 to 2,237, while doctoral graduates, numbering 75 in 1999, reached 238 in 2004.

The latter figure represents 15 doctoral graduates per million inhabitants, a figure higher than the proportion in Argentina and Mexico, but lower than that in Brazil (Reich 2005).

Graduate degrees of faculty are increasing as well: in 1965, at the most advanced university in this respect, the Universidad de Chile, 12 percent of the faculty had graduate degrees (master's degrees or doctorates). In 1985, 22 percent of faculty at Chilean universities had graduate degrees, according to census data (Brunner 1986, 112). A similar figure (18 percent) was reported from a survey in the study of the academic profession in 14 countries, including Chile,[14] carried out by the Carnegie Foundation for the Advancement of Teaching; the data for Chile were collected in 1991 and 1993 (Boyer et al. 1994; Schiefelbein 1996, 286). The latest census figures for degrees earned among faculty at all universities, public and private, show that the proportion of faculty with graduate degrees (master's degrees and doctorates, since no separate figure exists for doctorates alone) had climbed to 38 percent by 2004.[15]

Another glimpse into these trends, this time at the institutional level, can be obtained by examining publication output in recent years across the five research-oriented universities of Chile. The Universidad de Chile went from 516 ISI-indexed articles in 1998 to 855 in 2003, while mainstream publishing at the Pontificia Universidad Católica de Chile, in the same period, increased from 303 to 529. The Universidad de Concepción, with less than a dozen articles in 1999, registered 346 in 2003. The Universidad de Santiago almost doubled its output in four years, starting in 2000.

Even though no research universities exist in Chile,[16] the ones considered in this chapter and many others have embraced, rhetorically if not entirely in practice, a research orientation as their main pathway to national preeminence and, eventually, world-class distinction. Reasons for this shift toward a scientific mission include well-known global factors, such as the emergence of the knowledge economy or the response in Chile, as in the rest of the world, to the influence of the US research university model.

There are also indigenous developments, which include a sustained government policy of strong incentives for research productivity, the emergence of rankings and classifications of Chilean universities (based on the US model), the rise of the full-time research scholar as the archetype of a faculty member, and, more recently, the widespread dissemination of the idea that training at the doctoral level and research are essential for improving Chile's competitiveness in the world economy. I briefly describe these local stimuli for research.

As I explained earlier, CONICYT is the main public funding agency for research. Between 1990 and 2002, CONICYT's budget increased fourfold, reaching the equivalent of US$71 million, which represents 18 percent of overall government higher education expenditures. Direct funding for research and doctoral programs has not been the sole means for fostering the universities' research missions. Additionally, the government allocates 5 percent of the total subsidy to universities based on performance indicators. The indicators mostly reward high graduate enrollments, faculty with graduate degrees, externally funded research projects, and ISI-indexed articles.

Another area of higher education public policy with heavy impact on research is the accreditation of graduate programs, carried out by a public accrediting agency. The policy also requires faculty with doctorates, indexed publications, and FONDECYT projects. Graduate programs need accreditation for their students to become eligible for government scholarships. As with the 5 percent performance indicators, the relatively narrow scope of accreditation has expanded its reach so as to permeate the whole system with its standards of good practice.

In sum, public policy created markets for research, publications, and graduate degrees in a system where there was not much of a demand for such achievements. The policy instruments used reinforced each other by consistently rewarding the same things: doctoral degrees, full-time contracts, research, and publications. It was not long until universities started replicating these instruments in their own internal policies, so as to align their results with those rewarded by the government and thus enter into a virtual cycle of incentives.

If these government messages alone are not influential enough, there is also an official guide concerning universities and programs for higher education applicants, called INDICES, and the unofficial rankings prepared for massive consumption by the news media. These listings also count and publish the numbers of faculty with graduate degrees, faculty who are full-time, numbers of indexed publications, and FONDECYT research projects.

ISI indexes have been criticized for underreporting scholarly production originating outside the United States and, especially, research generated in developing countries and published in languages other than English (Altbach 2003, 6). The university research directors I interviewed showed an awareness of these criticisms—as well as of the tradition in Chile of publishing in local scholarly outlets in the social sciences, the humanities, and the professional fields—and were willing to take them into account. Yet, in great measure as a result of the financial consequences, these research directors were determined to press ahead for ISI-indexed publications. Thus, publication in the mainstream international literature is increasingly becoming the most recognized way to publish, and not only at institutions where funding depends on their performance levels. As with full-time faculty, externally funded competitive research, and graduate degrees, ISI-indexed publications have become institutionalized as markers of academic rigor and success throughout the university system. What started as a set of standards imposed by the funding policies of the government has become a systemwide institutional norm.

In a similar process of institutionalization, the idea of an academic as a successful practitioner in a profession who teaches part-time has been effectively replaced by a new gold standard that sees an academic as a researcher with a doctorate, a full-time commitment to his or her university, and a demonstrated ability to obtain research grants and publish in the international mainstream literature. Moreover, these research faculty have acquired an increasingly strong voice and influence over their institutions' and the government's policies for resource allocation. What started as a supply-side effort, so to speak, to create research capacity in universities, now seems to be turning into a demand-driven cycle of increased resources and instruments to support research.

Over the past 10 years a labor market has evolved, where the monetary value of the services of professors from different backgrounds and fields can be readily ascertained and used to shape compensation policy. With the development of market values, greater mobility of human resources has ensued. The need to recognize an academic's other opportunities appears increasingly more pressing. Universities where salary policy ignores this notion are constantly struggling to recruit and maintain qualified faculty in high-income fields.

Requirements for entering an academic career have inched upward as the quality of applicants rise. There is increased interest in graduate studies among young people. Accordingly, the past decade has seen a sizable expansion of the number of people with doctorates in all disciplines and in the professions, from biology to mathematics and from law to journalism. As credentials improve, full-time academic work, long the only form of academic work in the natural sciences in Chile, is permeating such traditional strongholds of part-time teaching by successful practitioners as schools of law and engineering.

Finally, there is little doubt in the Chilean scientific community, or in the government, that increasing the qualified human resources, strengthening the country's scientific base, and working more closely with the business sector are essential for transforming the nation's economy in tune with the demands of the knowledge society. Accordingly, scientific research is "marketed" by its constituencies to the larger community as a booster for competitiveness. This is the thinking behind, for instance, the latest World Bank science and technology project in Chile, for US$100 million. These funds would increase CONICYT's budget by 25 percent annually, for six years, to be invested in research programs, doctoral training, and post-doctoral internships in industries. The strategy is to reach the goal of 400 doctoral degrees granted annually by 2010 (and 800 by 2015), increase the proportion of full-time faculty with doctoral degrees to 50 percent of the staff in research-oriented universities, foster the incorporation of PhDs in the industry, and expand the share of private-sector funding in research and development.

This "mode 2" perspective, of knowledge for economic advantage (Gibbons et al. 1994; Etzkowitz and Leydesdorff 2000), may represent an impoverishment of the mission of the university, considering that it leaves behind goals so dear to the Latin American idea of the university as fostering new power structures, performing the role of society's critical consciousness, deepening democracy, extending high culture to the masses, and the like. But it offers the university two considerable benefits: first, it provides an extremely effective case for the need of vigorous science even in peripheral countries unlikely to ever become scientific powerhouses; second, it serves to fill with a transcendent sense of purpose the life of an institution that—after the meltdown in the 1970s and 1980s in Chile and elsewhere in Latin America of the social transformation agenda represented by the elevated goals recounted above—has had to justify itself on the grounds of its most immediate and rather inglorious products (professionals trained, concerts staged, national treasures saved from neglect or oblivion, etc.) rather than on a grand discourse of social progress or redemption. Knowledge as a provider of competitiveness puts the university back in the company of the national actors in whose hands the fate of the nation is molded.

CONCLUSION

I have argued that there are no research universities in Chile, regardless of the great impulse directed toward scientific research since the mid-1980s. Unlike some Asian nations, the government in Chile chose not to single out one or two institutions on which to concentrate research resources, allowing instead open competition for research grants and across-the-board funding for doctoral students. The strategy has been, and will continue to be for the foreseeable future, one of generalized support for research across institutions, with relatively more resources flowing to the handful of the most competitive universities. Over time, this strategy has helped a few universities get closer to the research university ideal, but as Chile's economy continues to grow the question of the possibility of the emergence of a research university becomes more pressing. What still needs to be done to get there?

One limitation is funding. Chile invests 0.6 percent of its gross domestic product (GDP) in research and development, at a rate of US$29 per capita, lower than Brazil's and Argentina's comparable figures. The World Bank estimates that this level of investment would have to double to match Chile's economic outlook. Moreover, private investment in this area is only 22 percent of the total, whereas it reaches 40 percent in Brazil and 69 percent in the United States (World Bank 2004, 10).

Chile's research-oriented universities need to complete their transition from the legacy of the full-time teaching staff or the faculty members who are successful professional practitioners and teach part-time to the full-time, research-trained scholars. (Of course, there will still be space for practitioners in the clinical or practical curriculum of the professions.) To achieve this goal, doctoral training in Chile will need to expand substantially, as planned by the government, and universities will have to be assisted financially to offer their faculty of retirement age attractive compensation packages.

Universities could also help by strengthening their regulations for faculty productivity, or enforcing them if they already have them on the books, by granting tenure only to those who have shown the capacity to do research and by continuing to monitor a tenured professor's accomplishments over time.

On the positive side of the ledger, Chile's universities can rely on their capacity to adapt to new environments—honed after 30 years of change in the political economy of national higher education, their low level of politicization, and their near monopoly over research in the country (since there are only a few major research institutes outside the universities in Chile).

The majority of Chilean universities, however, are far removed from these concerns. For universities, public and private, research is either the province of a small group of faculty members, a sporadic activity, or a completely alien one. The majority of private universities fit into the latter category. They are teaching institutions with no qualified, dedicated faculty hired to carry out research. But there is an intermediate group of some 20 universities, including two or three private ones, where a few nuclei of active researchers can be found. The rationale for sustaining this effort is not connected to any plan of becoming a research university, which would be unreasonable except for the longest term. It has to do, in part, with the prestige associated with scientific accomplishment (reflected, as explained earlier, in rankings, among other forms of recognition). It also derives from the enormous modeling power of the research university ideal, which although impossible for most universities to follow closely at least calls for some form of symbolic representation. Finally, there are some leaders at universities self-described as teaching institutions who nonetheless believe research is needed for students to be educated in an atmosphere of critical inquiry and at least some faculty can show their students what it is like to work at the knowledge frontier. Based on this rationale, research is not sought mainly for the sake of generating results but chiefly as an enrichment to education—an inspiration that somehow reminds us of Humboldt's idea of a research university.

NOTES

1. Indeed, I couldn't find one incidence of the phrase "research university" in a report on scientific development goals and results in Chile, covering the period from 1965 to 1985, published in 1987 under the auspices of the Chilean Academy of Sciences (Corporación de Promoción Universitaria 1987). Yet, just six years later, another study of the status of research in Chile appeared (Krauskopf 1993) in which the author, after referring to the case of research universities in the United States, and looking back to the situation in Chile, said: "it becomes increasingly difficult to share in the progress of the most advanced nations, without strengthening in our country a significant number of universities genuinely committed to research" (32, my translation), while the book's chapter 5 (133–52) bore the telling title "Research Universities: A Challenge." A slightly earlier occurrence of the name "research university" in Chile appears in a 1992 book by Mario Letelier, cited by Krauskopf (1993, 135).

2. Actually, I used the truncated form, universit*.

3. Of course, several caveats are in order. First, ISI-indexed articles do not exhaust published research. Aside from books, there are also articles not covered in ISI, typically those in outlets published in languages other than English, and outside of the United States, the British Commonwealth, and continental Europe.

4. The Web site of the **League of European Research Universities (LERU)**, www.leru.org.

5. The Web site of Innovative Research Universities, Australia, www.irua.edu.au.

6. This makes it possible, among other things, to increase scientific output, as illustrated by the cases of top Chinese universities, where more than half of the first authors of academic publications are graduate students (see Chapter 3).

7. These numbers are presented in Chapter 8.

8. These numbers are presented in Chapter 3.

9. A semantic note is necessary here: the larger academic units in Chilean and

Latin American universities are called *facultades*, which roughly correspond to US schools. I use the English word *school* to refer to *facultades*, to avoid confusion with the word *faculty*, in spite of the fact that in Spanish university nomenclature, schools (*escuelas*) are the teaching units within *facultades*.

10. The Universidad de Buenos Aires is discussed in Chapter 12; the Universidad Nacional Autónoma de México is discussed in Chapter 9.

11. An outright ban on outside work would be against the legal protection of the freedom of work and is likely to meet fierce resistance by faculty who teach part-time at private universities.

12. Data from CONICYT's Indicators of Science and Technology (Chile), www.conicyt.cl/indicadores/gasto/nacional/xls/T1-5.xls.

13. Data from CONICYT's Indicators of Science and Technology (Chile), www.conicyt.cl/indicadores/gasto/nacional/xls/T1-6.xls.

14. Australia, Brazil, Chile, Germany, Hong Kong, Israel, Japan, Korea, Mexico, the Netherlands, Russia, Sweden, the United Kingdom, and the United States.

15. Data from Consejo Superior de Educación's (Chile) *INDICES* database (2004) www.cse.cl/asp/WEB_CSE_Indiceshistorico.asp.

16. *The Academic Ranking of World Universities* published in 2004 by Shanghai Jiao Tong University placed the Universidad de Chile in the 401th to 450th-range position as the sole Chilean university. No Chilean universities appeared in the *Times Higher Education Supplement* World University Rankings, the same year.

REFERENCES

Altbach, P. G., ed. 2003. *The decline of the guru. The academic profession in developing and middle-income countries*. New York: Palgrave Macmillan.

Bernasconi, A. 2003. Organizational diversity in Chilean higher education: Faculty regimes in private and public universities. PhD diss., Boston University.

———. 2005. University entrepreneurship in a developing country: The case of the P. Universidad Católica de Chile: 1985–2000. *Higher Education* 50 (2): 247–74.

Boyer, E. L., P. G. Altbach, and M. J. Whitelaw. 1994. *The academic profession: An international perspective*. Princeton, NJ: Carnegie Foundation for the Advancement of Teaching.

Braxton, J. M. 1993. Selectivity and rigor in research universities. *Journal of Higher Education* 64 (6): 657–75.

Brunner, J. J. 1986. *Informe sobre la educación superior en Chile*. Santiago, Chile: FLACSO.

Brunner, J. J., G. Elaqua, A. Tillet, J. Bonnefoy, S. González, et al. 2005. *Guiar el Mercado. Informe sobre la educación superior en Chile*. Working paper, Universidad Adolfo Ibáñez, Escuela de Gobierno (March).

Clark, B. R. 2004. *Sustaining change in universities: Continuities in case studies and concepts*. Maidenhead, UK: Society of Research into Higher Education and Open University Press.

CONICYT (Consejo Nacional de Investigación Científica y Tecnológica). 2000. *Programa FONDECYT: Impacto y desarrollo 1981–2000*. Santiago, Chile: CONICYT.

Consejo de Rectores de las Universidades Chilenas (CRUCh). 1990. *Anuario Estadístico*. Santiago, Chile: CRUCh.

———. 2003. *Anuario Estadístico*. Santiago, Chile: CRUCh.

Consejo Superior de Educación. 2004. *Indices*, www.cse.cl/asp /WEB_CSE_Indiceshistorico.asp.

Corporación de Promoción Universitaria. 1987. *El desarrollo científico y tecnológico en Chile. Un análisis cualitativo 1965–1985*. Santiago, Chile: Corporación de Promoción Universitaria.

Departamento de Medición, Registro y Evaluación, Universidad de Chile. 2005. *Distribución del Aporte Fiscal Indirecto 2005*. Santiago, Chile: Universidad de Chile.

El Mercurio. 2004. *Revista El Sábado* no. 322, November 20.

Etzkowitz, H., and L. Leydesdorff. 2000. The dynamics of innovation: From national systems and "Mode 2" to a triple helix of university-industry-government relations. *Research Policy* 29 (2): 109–23.

Geiger, R. 1985. After the emergence: Voluntary support and the building of American research universities. *History of Education Quarterly* 25 (3): 369–81.

———. 1986. *To advance knowledge: The growth of American research universities, 1900–1940*. New York: Oxford University Press.

Gibbons, Michael, et al. 1994. *The new production of knowledge*. London: Sage.

Goodchild, L. F. 1991. What is the condition of American research universities? *American Educational Research Journal* 28 (1): 3–17.

Jencks, C., and D. Riesman. 1968. *The academic revolution*. Garden City, NY: Doubleday.

Koljatic, M. 1999. Utilidades, orientación al mercado y descentralización: "Nuevas" ideas para la administración universitaria en Latinoamérica. *Estudios Públicos* (Santiago de Chile: Centro de Estudios Públicos) 73 (Summer): 335–58.

Krauskopf, M. 1993. *La investigación universitaria en Chile: Reflexiones críticas*. Santiago, Chile: Corporación de Promoción Universitaria.

———. 1999. Los doctorados en Chile. Perfil y capacidad científica de los programas den ciencias acreditados en Chile. *Estudios Públicos* (Santiago de Chile: Centro de Estudios Públicos) 76 (Spring): 359–408.

Levy, D. C. 1986. *Higher education and the state in Latin America: Private challenges to public dominance*. Chicago: University of Chicago Press.

Levy, D. C., and A. Bernasconi 1998. University of Chile. In *The International dictionary of university histories*, ed. C. Summerfield and M. E. Devine, 464–67. Chicago: Fitzroy Dearborn.

Reich, R. 2005. Postgrado en Chile. *Informativo MECESUP*. No. 294. Santiago, Chile: Ministerio de Educación, Programa MECESUP.

Schiefelbein, E. 1996. The Chilean academic profession: Six policy issues. In *The international academic profession: Portraits of fourteen countries*, ed. P. G. Altbach, 281–306. Princeton, NJ: Carnegie Foundation for the Advancement of Teaching.

Serrano, S. 1994. *Universidad y Nación: Chile en el siglo XIX*. Santiago, Chile: Editorial Universitaria.

Shanghai Jiao Tong University, Institute of Higher Education. 2005. The academic ranking of world universities, http://ed.sjtu.edu.cn/en /index.htm.

Thelin, J. R. 2004. *A history of American higher education*. Baltimore: Johns Hopkins University Press.

Times Higher Education Supplement. 2004. World university rankings, www.thes.co.uk/worldrankings/.

UNICAMP. n.d. *Informaciones*. Campinas, Brazil: Universidade Estadual de Campinas.

Weber, M. 1949. *The methodology of the social sciences*. New York: Free Press.

World Bank. 2004. *Chile: New economy study*. Report no. 256666-CL, vol. 1. Washington DC: World Bank, Finance, Private Sector and Infrastructure, Latin America and Caribbean Region.

12

The Challenge of Building Research Universities in Middle-Income Countries

The Case of the University of Buenos Aires

Ana M. García de Fanelli

In Argentina, a differentiated higher education system serves as a way to meet the complex, and sometimes conflicting, demands for universal access to education and top-quality research and elite-training opportunities. Argentina now has almost 2 million students studying at 100 public and private universities and at more than 1,700 other small postsecondary institutions. The higher education system is as yet undefined. Aside from the goal of providing greater access to higher education for the growing population of secondary school graduates, the higher education system expanded without any plan. Its parts are neither functionally differentiated nor suitably articulated. Moreover, the considerable increase in enrollments was not matched by a rise in the quality and the quantity of highly skilled scientists and technologists. This situation has restricted the country's ability to reach the standards of the more technologically advanced ones, leaving Argentina distanced from the international knowledge frontier. An opportunity exists for at least one, or a few, top-quality, research-oriented universities among Argentina's higher education institutions. Such a university is vital for producing high-level scientists, technologists, and professionals to enable the country to meet the challenges of a knowledge-based society in the 21st century. Moreover, the literature on national systems of innovation mentions the relevance of these institutions as an especially important node in a network of many interrelated actors involved in innovation and technology within each country.

One of the universities with greater potential to play the role of leading academic institution in Argentina is the University of Buenos Aires (UBA). Although it is not a research-oriented institution, UBA is highly segmented and some of its academic units more closely fit this definition. Moreover, it is a major player in elite and professional training.

Other traditional public universities exist in the principal cities of the provinces. At the regional level, these institutions tend to play a similar role to UBA's at the national level. That is, they enjoy high academic prestige but show functional weaknesses that are equivalent to those observed at UBA. Thus, many observations made about UBA could also apply to these universities.

This chapter concentrates on the case of UBA, based on the hypothesis that it is a national "flagship" university albeit not a canonical "research university." UBA plays the de facto flagship role in the Argentine university system because of its importance as a fully mature institution. Consequently, its institutional policy decisions and organizational functioning are permanently under the scrutiny of public opinion. UBA's complexity, together with its key role in the Argentine university system, has historically been a daunting challenge to the governments that were determined to introduce changes into the system: while governments assumed that a successful reform of UBA was crucial in terms of the "demonstration" effect that could influence the rest of the public and private universities, they were powerless to introduce the required changes given the organizational complexity of the institution, its monumental size, and the political sensitivity surrounding this problem.

INSTITUTIONAL MISSIONS AND SOCIETAL CONDITIONS

Established in 1821, UBA is the largest higher education institution in Argentina, with an enrollment of about 300,000 undergraduate students. Located in the country's capital and wealthiest city, it consists of 13 faculties (*facultades*), located throughout the city, and two top-quality secondary schools with about 5,000 students. The provincial government founded UBA just five years after Argentina had gained full independence from Spanish rule. At the time, it was created to satisfy the demands of wealthy merchants and public officials who sought the prestige of a university education for their sons that would award them degrees in medicine or law. From the beginning, UBA's principal mission has been the education of professionals and political leaders.

Under the influence of the Napoleonic university model, the undergraduate level at UBA includes both the *licenciado* degree (on average, five years) and professional degrees (generally with a longer duration—six to seven years) in fields such as medicine, engineering, public accountancy, architecture, psychology, and law. In many respects, these undergraduate degrees are equivalent to a professional Anglo-Saxon master's degree. A university chair is the main teaching unit within each faculty, and the chair holder enjoys a great deal of teaching and administrative autonomy.

Research activity is concentrated in institutes, laboratories, and centers within each faculty. The most important sites at UBA are located in the Faculties of Exact and Natural Sciences, Pharmacy and Biochemistry, and Philosophy and Literature. Moreover, the majority of the doctoral students are also found in these three academic units. Nonetheless, considering the concentration of the undergraduate student population in some professional degrees (especially medicine, law, and public accountancy), UBA still maintains the professional character that has marked the institution from its beginning. At the same time and according to national research indicators, UBA has been, and still is, the most relevant higher education research institution in Argentina.

Halperín Donghi—in his book, *The History of the University of Buenos Aires* (1962)—shows how UBA's development has been shaped by recurring political and economic crises and the struggle between two visions of the university, the scientific and the professional. The tension between these two different institutional missions has paved UBA's entire trajectory and played a role in turning university governance into a federation of faculties. In particular, the traditional professional schools—such as those of medicine, law, or public accountancy—have maintained strong identities and their autonomy.

In this decentralized structure, professional and scientific units barely interact, and none of them are strong enough to promote their cultural identities over the others. However, the crucial question remains why UBA has not developed an institutional strategy to strengthen its research-oriented and elite-training activity, as some Brazilian or Chilean universities have done. A range of exogenous and endogenous factors may have affected UBA's institutional development—such as a volatile political, economic, and public policy context; UBA's own role in the politics of society and government, as an informal school and platform for future political leaders and an arena in which national political parties resolve their conflicts; and the structure of governance that restricts UBA's institutional ability to develop an adequate response to state and market pressures.

In the early 20th century, after a period in which restrictive democratic governments took office through corrupt electoral practices, electoral reforms helped lead the first Argentine middle-class political party to victory in 1916. During this administration, a significant student movement, the 1918 Cordoba Reform, took place at the oldest public university, the National University of Cordoba. Student leaders criticized the elitist, traditional, and conservative university and the intellectually mediocre level of the faculty. The student movement quickly spread to UBA and to other public universities in Argentina, as well as across the rest of Latin American higher education institutions. The main outcome at Argentine public universities was the introduction of important changes in governance and faculty appointments.

First, the 1918 Cordoba Reform institutionalized student participation on university councils, joining professors, students, and alumni in a three-party system known as co-governance. This system means that students and alumni have an important voice as political actors in the building of the national university system. In particular, student movements have exerted great pressure on university authorities to guarantee access to the growing number of middle-class high school graduates. This had some positive impact on equity, but in the context of restricted financial resources it also affected quality levels.

Second, the changes also promoted the selection of the faculty through open, competitive, and periodic renewal reviews to counteract nepotism and patronage. In this area, the Cordoba Reform supported building a top-quality teaching staff by guaranteeing academic freedom and the use of meritocratic procedures for faculty selection. UBA's current statute, approved in 1966, also included another condition to assure the recruitment of top-quality faculty: most professors were to work full-time, and part-time faculty were only an exception to the rule. Nonetheless, as will be discussed below, the social practices do not follow these formal institutional measures.

Finally, the 1918 Cordoba Reform supported institutional autonomy with respect to the state.

Since the late 1920s the rising participation of the middle class as a political actor has also resulted in greater social demand to broaden institutional opportunities for social mobility. UBA—the only university in a city with 17.5 percent of the total population, according to the 1935 National Census—began its dramatic development in response to this demand. Halperín Donghi (1962, 99) clearly illustrates this expansion process that in certain ways has continued into the present: "The University grows, like the Nation in which it was born, in a blind and powerful expansion process sustained with almost biological vigor" (author's translation).

Throughout the 20th century (1906–2000)—a period characterized by economic and political instability—national university enrollments grew at an average annual rate of 7 percent, absorbing the increased demand generated by the expanding number of secondary school graduates (García de Fanelli 2005).

UBA underwent many economic crises and political upheavals. In particular, from 1930 to 1983 Argentina was subject alternately to civilian and military rule, with military governments in place 22 of those 53 years. Following some years of economic growth in the 1960s and early 1970s, Argentina experienced a period of stagnation, deindustrialization, high inflation, dramatic foreign indebtedness, and increasing inequality in income distribution between 1975 and 1984.

This unstable environment directly affected UBA's evolution in three ways. First, the military dictatorships obstructed academic freedom, fired many professors or forced them to resign, and incorporated reactionary intellectual views. Second, the economic crises undermined the financial resources needed to sustain both the increasing student demand and investment in research and development. Finally, UBA's weak capability to steer itself and the lack of a clear-cut institutional mission merely mirrored the absence of a national development policy for the entire country. In particular, the first seeds of scientific activity at UBA were sown under a development project: during Arturo Frondizi's democratic administration (1958–1962), UBA increased the number of full-time professors (from only one full-time professor to 160), expanded the system of scholarships for their students, raised the funding for research, and founded the EUDEBA (UBA's publishing house). In 1958, the government also created the National Council for Scientific and Technical Research (CONICET), and Bernardo Houssay, the 1947 Nobel Prize winner in medicine, was appointed its first director (Halperín Donghi 1962). Emulating the French CNRs (national centers of research) model, CONICET allowed the professionalization of research in the form of the "research career" and through competitive procedures to allocate research grants. During the Frondizi administration, these activities enhanced research activity in public universities, since most CONICET researchers were also professors at these higher education institutions.

Under the military government of Juan Carlos Onganía (1966–1970), CONICET research activity began to move away from the university. In 1966, Onganía authorized the police to storm UBA, especially the Faculty of Exact and Natural Sciences, forcing out students and professors in what became known as the "Night of the Long Sticks." From 1976, the military government strengthened the role of CONICET in its scientific policy through the creation of many public research institutes under its jurisdiction outside the university domain. Military governments feared the public university's political activism. This measure weakened the research activities at public universities. Many CONICET research institutes are associated with public universities, and most of their researchers hold teaching positions at both UBA as well as other public and private universities.

The 1918 Cordoba Reform and the memories of the 1960s as UBA's "golden years" have created the most relevant institutional models of how the university should be run. The Cordoba Reform set up the democratization of university governance via the participation of students, alumni, and professors in a collegial body and introduced the open competitive procedure to hire the faculty. During the 1960s, UBA fostered research activities through the hiring of full-time faculty and the election of highly prestigious academic leaders as executive authorities. In particular, UBA's president between 1957 and 1962, Risieri Frondizi, was a respected Harvard graduate and many of the executive deans were academics with renowned international reputations, like Rolando García, dean of the Faculty of Exact and Natural Sciences.

Democracy was restored in 1983, together with the process of consolidating democratic institutions. For the higher education system this meant a respect for the academic freedom to teach and conduct research. Nonetheless, the political and economic environments have remained quite unstable. After the 1989 hyperinflation and a period of high growth from 1993 to 1998, the economic situation deteriorated in 2001, resulting in an economic crisis and depression. Labor market conditions worsened substantially, income distribution became far more skewed, and the Argentine global socioeconomic situation deteriorated. The macroeconomic volatility throughout the 1980s, 1990s, and early 21st century dramatically affected the level of higher education expenditure.

In sum, the unstable political and economic context and the internal governance structure—often co-opted by national political parties—influenced UBA's capability to build a research-oriented university. Over the past two decades, UBA has continued to absorb most of the secondary school demand in the region. As a result of this development, in 2003 there were 14 public and 33 private university institutions[1] in the area comprised of the capital city of Buenos Aires and its periphery—the so-called AMBA or metropolitan area of Buenos Aires. In the AMBA, UBA alone attracted 51 percent of undergraduate enrollments, 45 percent of the first-year student intakes, and 39 percent of the undergraduate alumni in this region (see table 12.1).

Table 12.1 Enrollments, First-Year Student Intakes, and Alumni, by Sector and Region, in Argentina, 2003

	AMBA[b]			Entire Country	
	UBA[c]	Other Public (13 HEI[d])	Private (33 HEI[d])	Public (45 HEI[d])	Private (55 HEI[d])
Undergraduate enrollments[a]	289,526	146,005	133,795	1,278,284	215,272
First-year student intakes	66,533	41,194	38,599	305,820	63,617
Undergraduate alumni	13,780	8,537[e]	12,655[e]	56,441[e]	18,357[e]

Source: Ministry of Education, Science and Technology (MECyT 2004), UBA 2004.
[a]Undergraduate enrollments include first-year student intakes, second-year students, and others.
[b]Metropolitan area of Buenos Aires.
[c]2004, UBA census.
[d]HEI (higher education institutions) includes universities and university institutes.
[e]2002

UNIVERSITY-SECTOR DIFFERENCES

In Argentina, no national rankings of universities exist. For this reason, the premise that UBA is one of the most important universities or the national "flagship" public university is based only on the scant information available. Some dimensions of difference in the Argentine university sector exemplify UBA's importance in relation to student quality, research activity, and the training of professionals.

Educational Selectivity

Access to the public university sector becomes open upon completion of secondary school. Some public or private universities, and some schools within them, administer entrance examinations or require students to take specific courses—in particular, the medical schools (Trombetta 1999). With some exceptions, such as the admissions policy of the Faculty of Medicine at the traditional National University of La Plata, all other cases reveal the absence of a clear selection process seeking qualified applicants or of an openings strategy that defines the maximum number of students to be admitted to a degree program. Only selective admissions criteria with restricted numbers plus a large number of applicants can guarantee recruiting highly qualified students. Under this assumption, although the UBA admissions policy is not openly and formally selective, it could become such a one. Table 12.1 shows UBA to be the only university in the metropolitan area of Buenos Aires that has this queue of qualified applicants. It is determined by UBA's prestige, the variety of the programs, and its tuition-free policy (García de Fanelli 1997). The index of UBA's reputation is also reflected in the fact that the majority of UBA's secondary school graduates attend UBA faculties. This is a relevant indicator because the Colegio de Buenos Aires is one of the oldest and most prestigious secondary schools in the country. Moreover, it is highly selective through a vigorous entrance examination and the restricted student numbers. Only about one-quarter of the applicants are admitted.

The open admissions process at UBA does include the subtle selection process during the first year, the so-called CBC (general cycle of basic knowledge). Although the CBC is formally considered the first year of the degree program, all first-year students must pass it to be able to continue their program of study in each faculty. An average of only 46.5 percent of CBC students were admitted annually to the faculties from 1985 to 2004, and half of the students who complete the first year (CBC) eventually graduate within a five-year period (UBA 2005a, 2005b).

In sum, as Altbach (1999) said, the graduation rates at UBA are based on the Darwinian principle of survival of the fittest. Unfortunately, owing to the lack of good remedial courses and scholarships to cover student costs, the institution does not guarantee the survival of the most talented but economically disadvantaged students.

The Research Function

The majority of Argentine universities are more profession oriented than research oriented. Nonetheless, the level of research activity is highly developed in some hard science fields, such as biomedicine, biology, and chemistry—especially at a few traditional public universities. Among them, UBA stands out,[2] having (1) the largest number of faculty members who teach and conduct research at national universities—17.2 percent of the total public university "faculty-researchers"; (2) the most students working on advanced degrees (13,780 graduate students in specialization, master's, and doctoral programs in 2004)—27 percent of the total public university sector; (3) the largest proportion of graduate courses with the highest ranking (A or B) according to the National Committee of University Assessment and Accrediting (CONEAU) accreditation procedure—22.7 percent of the total;[3] (4) the largest amount of national research grants in the public university sector, between 1997 and 1999—32.7 percent of the total;[4] and (5) 29 percent of the total number of Argentine scientific publications and 8 percent of the total indexed publications in South American universities (MECyT 2004; García de Fanelli 2005; UBA 2005a).

Data regarding research products also show that this activity at UBA is concentrated in some academic units and in certain fields—such as biology, biotechnology, chemistry, and physics. For example, in the field of chemistry, UBA researchers published 268 out of 1,412 articles in indexed journals produced by the entire Argentine chemistry community during 1999–2000. Only one faculty at the UBA, the Exact and Natural Sciences one, published 65 percent of these 268 articles (Albornoz et al. 2005).

Some other research-intensive schools, especially those devoted to the basic sciences, exist at other traditional and large national universities located in the main cities of the provinces, such as the National Universities of Córdoba, La Plata, Tucumán, Litoral, and Rosario, and in other smaller ones, such as Cuyo and Sur. Then the most important research groups and doctoral programs at the higher education level are concentrated at fewer than 10 of the 45 public universities (García de Fanelli 2005).

Of the 55 private universities, there are also a few elite institutions, mainly founded in the 1990s. Unlike most public universities, these institutions have higher expenditures per student, as well as full-time professors, full-time students, high-quality facilities, and good libraries. Nonetheless, they depend almost entirely on private funding (donors, the Church, firms) and student tuition and fees. This explains why, with the exception of one technological institute and a few medical schools, undergraduate and graduate programs and research activities in these elite-type institutions are concentrated in the lower-cost fields of the social sciences and humanities.

Although the scarce empirical evidence shows the significant place UBA has in the Argentine academic market, this institution occupies an intermediate position with respect to other public universities in middle-income countries. According to the academic ranking of world-class universities carried out in 2004 by the Institute of Higher Education at Shangai Jiao Tong University, which especially focuses on research indicators, UBA ranked among the top 300 institutions of the top 500 universities in the world (Institute of Higher Education 2004). While UBA's inadequate financial situation is not the only factor that led to its position in this international ranking, a satisfactory institutional budget for providing top-quality teaching and research activities does seem to be a necessary element for developing a research-oriented university. As stated in a report on top US research universities, "All other things being equal, the amount of money available to invest in attracting and retaining human capital will set a limit on a university research campus' success" (Lombardi, Capaldi, Reeves, and Gater 2004, 11). In the UBA case, the total operating budget in 2003 was scarcely US$537 million (in parity purchasing power [PPP]). Taking into account total enrollments (both full-time and part-time students), the expenditure per student at UBA in 2003 (public and private resources) comprised just about US$1,606 (MECyT 2004). With universities becoming increasingly more central to Argentine competitiveness in the knowledge-based economy, data on UBA's expenditures suggest that a tremendous effort must be made to overcome the history of institutional underfunding.

The Professions

Among the professional units we particularly highlight the faculties of law, economics (mainly devoted to the training of public accountants), medicine, architecture, psychology, and engineering. Even though some research centers, institutes, and laboratories exist in all of these units, the majority of the faculty members do not conduct research.

Although no formal institutional ranking of professional programs exists, there is an incipient institutional market of reputations. The origins of this market can be traced to the early 1990s and attributed to the foundation of a few elite-type private universities that offer professional programs; the increasing competition arising from the expansion of advanced degree programs that charge tuition and fees at both public and private universities; and CONEAU's ranking of graduate studies (as A, B, or C). At the undergraduate level only tacit knowledge circulates among students and families about the ranking of institutions and programs.

According to the media, UBA alumni are highly regarded in the labor market. Some scattered opinions from the business sector, disseminated by the press, show that they value the ability of UBA alumni to confront adverse conditions. This is considered another by-product of the so-called Darwinian method of selection (Altbach 1999). Moreover, as some human resources consultants confirmed, the common awareness is that employers and clients prefer the services of UBA professionals in such fields as public accountancy, law, engineering, medicine, dentistry, and architecture. Clearly, more empirical evidence is needed to draw any solid conclusions on this issue. Nonetheless, it should be taken into account that UBA produces yearly more than one-third of the total graduates in the metropolitan area of Buenos Aires (see table 12.1).

One example of UBA's prestige in the Argentine professional market is the result of the Buenos Aires city government's contest to select applicants for medical residencies. The contest was based on a multiple-choice test and graduates' total grade averages. Of the applicants who graduated from UBA, 14.3 percent acquired residencies, a statistically significant difference concerning total private universities in Buenos Aires (5.3 percent) and the public universities in the rest of the country (3.5 percent). Of the total applicants who were granted residencies, 82 percent graduated from UBA (Neuman, Questa, and Kaufmann 2004).

Most professors at these professional faculties teach on a part-time basis, making their living principally via their professional work. One important incentive for teaching at this university (given that the average wage level for part-time faculty is quite low) is the prestige they obtain for being professors at UBA. Also, the faculty at some professional faculties can earn extra income thanks to external activities like consultancies, teaching graduate courses, or technical assistantships. Finally, many alumni have returned as teachers as a way to voluntarily pay the university back for the tuition-free education they received.

INSTITUTIONAL CONDITIONS

As was indicated in the previous section, UBA's relative position in the Argentine academic and professional markets is good. Nonetheless, if no changes are made in the medium term, UBA will continue to deplete its stock of physical and human capital.

Public universities in Argentina enjoy considerable academic and institutional autonomy. They have control over the admissions process, curriculum, management of human resources, allocation of public and private funds, and the election of the collegial and executive authorities.

Following the 1918 Cordoba Reform movement, UBA's formal governance was left in the hands of the executive and collegial authorities elected in equal proportions by professors, undergraduate students, and alumni. This kind of structure has important democratic and academic advantages but also has some organizational disadvantages. First, executive authorities, elected by the representatives of these three groups, have neither the incentives nor the power to make decisions that may displease some of these university actors. For example, an institution's decision to promote excellence in an individual faculty or department could generate opposition from the teaching staff (if it implies the reallocation of scarce resources to some centers of excellence) or from the students (if selective admissions policies are implemented to improve the quality of a program). Second, relying on collegial decision-making processes slows down management decisions, and the short-term and "urgent" matters are likely to displace more relevant medium- and long-term issues. Third, individual faculty autonomy tends to be high, to the point that the structure of governance takes the shape of a federation of faculties. Hence, the university council and the rector cannot establish an institutional project. As the dean of the Faculty of Social Sciences said, referring to UBA, it resembles Greek mythology, something like a hydra-headed monster (UBA 2003a).

The structure of governance is also quite atomized because professors, undergraduate students, and alumni are not the only actors with a say in the entire process through which institutional policies are formulated, adopted, and implemented. In the special case of profession-oriented faculties, for example, professional councils greatly influence the setting of the academic structure, the duration of the programs, and the curricula. In research-oriented faculties, another relevant actor is the disciplinary community. The invisible disciplinary community, or the academic network of problem-oriented researchers, defines relevant research according to the international research frontier and the teaching and research methods and quality assurance standards based on internationally accepted principles.

In all faculties, the administrative staff labor unions and the student movement also exercise important political power. At a public university like UBA, the power of the administrative staff labor unions is usually stronger than that of the faculty labor union. Professors show less commitment to their posts because they generally work part-time. In addition, given what they receive from the university, their remuneration is unlikely to affect their personal income structure.

Informal constraints on the structure of governance also affect UBA's ability to implement change. One feature that further complicates the decentralized decision-making process is the relationship between many of these actors and the leading national political parties. Moreover, for some university authorities and student leaders, the position held at the university is considered a stepping stone in their political careers. Another obstacle to change is the rigid academic organization that the chair system imposes. In particular, this affects chances to innovate the curriculum.

While change in the basic undergraduate curriculum and structure is extremely difficult, some transformations have occurred through "an expanded developmental periphery" (Clark 1998). As have other public universities, UBA has been facing strong pressures from the market and the state to make changes in two directions: to increase the supply of graduate courses and to diversify the core funding base. Market transactions have given rise to professional and academic master's and PhD programs, which have not been properly articulated with the undergraduate level (García de Fanelli 2001). Moreover, unlike the undergraduate level, graduate education at UBA is principally financed through tuition and fees. This has allowed an outstanding rise in entrepreneurial activity at this level. Between 2000 and 2004, graduate student enrollments at UBA increased by 53 percent (Echeverry 2004).

Something similar has occurred between the university and the productive sector. The relationships between the different UBA faculties and the productive sector take place through consulting activities, technical services, human resources training, and, to a lesser extent, application-oriented research (García de Fanelli 1993). All these activities help increase new streams of funding to faculties and the university. At the majority of the national universities, they are managed through new offices and via foundations outside the university structure. Serious internal opposition to these developments does not exist since they function parallel to the core undergraduate structure of governance. The resources generated by UBA increased from 19.6 percent to 29 percent of the total budget between 1996 and 2003 (MECyT 1999, 2004). As illustrated by the entrepreneurial cases that Burton Clark (1998, 2004) researched, the scarcity of resources has driven many of these changes.

The Academic Profession

In the tradition of the 1918 Cordoba Reform, the UBA statute guarantees academic freedom and stipulates that "regular" and "ordinary" faculty (professors or junior teaching staff) are to be appointed on the basis of periodic open competitions held every seven years. The statute also establishes that full-time and half-time positions should be standard contractual appointments. Part-time and half-time faculty generally only perform teaching. By and large, full-time faculty conduct research, in addition to their teaching activities.

Although the legal framework determines the institutional conditions for the development of permanent and limited-term labor contracts, social practices do not follow these formal institutional agreements. At UBA, 60 percent of professors have a regular position (a stable tenure-like status). The situation is worse for the assistants. Only 45 percent of this group have stable tenure-like posts. Moreover, some of these so-called regular or ordinary faculty are really working under de facto tenure contracts without periodic performance evaluations. These positions have not been renewed through a formal, open competitive procedure following the seven-year period legally fixed by the statutes. This state of affairs results from failures in the open competitions that can be attributed to the fragile financial scenario in the face of increasing demand and an open-admissions policy, the lack of incentives to sit on a jury, the lengthy bureaucratic procedures, the rigidity of the chair system, and the presence of corporative and political vested interests. Given this complex set of factors, a large proportion of UBA faculty are currently employed as "interims," under de facto tenure contracts, without having been appointed through open competition and without the periodic reviews of their performance. These conditions affect university teaching, research quality, and upward mobility in the academic ranks. Furthermore, the democratization of institutional governance has been impacted because only regular faculty have the right to choose and be chosen to participate in executive and collegial governments (García de Fanelli 2004).

To cope with the rising demand for access resulting from an open-admissions policy as well as public financial constraints, the UBA has adopted the policy of hiring more part-time and volunteer staff—especially, but not only, for the lowest academic positions (junior teaching staff). In 2000, full-time and half-time remunerated faculty represented 13 and 15 percent, respectively, of the total (UBA 2005b). Thus, most academics at UBA (72 percent) are part-time teachers, with research and service taking up a minor part of their work.

Nonetheless, within each academic unit, the academic profession differs. Although the proportion of full-time faculty at UBA is remarkably low—quite similar to the average in the public university sector—labor conditions are clearly different. For example, in the Faculty of Exact and Natural Sciences, 64 percent of the senior faculty members work full-time and 84 percent hold PhD degrees, while only 23 percent of the UBA faculty have achieved this academic level (UBA 2000). Moreover, wages make up the largest item on the university budget, explaining why these more research-oriented faculties have about four times UBA's average public expenditure per student. While public expenditure per student at UBA was US$1,066 in 2003, expenditure at the Faculty of Exact and Natural Science totalled US$4,200 (MECyT 2004; UBA 2005a).

In sum, in units with superior research outputs the labor conditions of the faculty more closely fit the normal standard defined by the model of a research-oriented university.

The Graduate Level

Compared to higher education structures in Europe and in other Latin American countries such as Brazil, the undergraduate level in Argentina is quite developed. On the other hand, graduate education is radically underdeveloped. The ratio between undergraduate and graduate students in 1998 was only 0.03 in Argentina in comparison to 0.11 in Brazil and 0.28 in the United States (UNESCO 1998; MECyT 1999). At UBA, this ratio resembles the average of the Argentine higher education system: 0.034 in 2000 (UBA 2005a). In particular, the number of doctoral dissertations granted by UBA per year amounted to only 213 in 2003 (UBA 2004). Some institutional and financial conditions explain the underdevelopment of UBA's graduate level.

First, although the average annual number of first-year student intakes at the undergraduate level was about 54,000 during the 1985–2004 period, the average annual number of undergraduate alumni totalled only 13,000 (UBA 2004; MECyT 1999, 2004).

Second, although not at the undergraduate level, at the graduate level UBA charges tuition and fees. The absence of an important national scholarship program for master's or PhD students—like the one developed by CAPES (Coordenaçao de Aperfeiçoamento do Ensino Superior [Office for the Improvement of Higher Learning]) in Brazil—explains the smaller numbers of master's and PhD graduates at UBA.

Third, neither the PhD nor the master's degree became a requirement for entry into and promotion within an academic career until the 1995 higher education act. As a consequence, the vast majority of university teachers, especially in the social sciences and technological fields, entered the profession without graduate education or research experience. The situation is clearly different in the basic sciences faculties that have a long tradition in doctoral training.

Fourth, in Argentina the undergraduate level of instruction and degree completion places more emphasis on specialization and professional qualifications in all fields. Physicians, lawyers, and public accountants are particularly overrepresented among higher education graduates, and the labor market conditions in these professions do not require a doctoral degree. Within these groups, specialized graduate courses have only become important since the 1980s.

Finally, the graduate training level is a relatively neglected area in terms of political visibility. As university authorities are elected by professors, undergraduate students, and alumni, the undergraduate level is the only one that counts in the political process. Moreover, the power of university authorities to negotiate annually the funding with Parliament and the Ministry of Education depends on the number of undergraduate students enrolled in the faculties, not on the number of graduate students.

GOVERNMENT POLICY ENVIRONMENT

Within the turbulent social, political, and economic environment described in the first section of this chapter, governments have been more concerned about putting out fires than focused on strategic planning of the system as a whole. Thus, working on increasing highly skilled human capital and investing in R&D have not ranked among the government's priorities until recently.

The external factors that explain past failures and the current challenges regarding forming a research-oriented university sector are: (1) inadequate financial resources; (2) the allocation of public funds determined by inertia and lobby mechanisms; and (3) different perspectives regarding the strategic role of public universities in the new national system.

Inadequate Financial Resources

The data regarding higher education finance show that deficient public and private funds for university teaching and research in Argentina are hampering the university from catching up with frontier research in fields of knowledge in which the country could have a competitive edge. Moreover, the funding is not only insufficient but also volatile, affecting long-term planning (García de Fanelli 2005).

Additionally, the percentage of 2003 gross domestic product (GDP) dedicated to R&D (0.41 percent) fell far below the levels of industrialized countries and significantly below the levels of other Latin American countries, like Brazil or Chile (see table 12.2).

From an institutional perspective, the scarcity of public and private resources has several impacts on the structure and functioning of public universities, especially because they depend almost fully on national public funding. First, the faculty incentive structure[5] created within this financial scenario does not promote effective teaching, commitment to research, self-investment in PhD degrees, and the design of incentive-compatible contracts at the institutional level to reward high academic achievement (García de Fanelli 2004). Second, the funding available for research activity alone cannot strengthen centers of excellence. Third, the number of scholarships to attract talented students to research-oriented fields has been almost negligible. Finally, few private funds compensate for the scarcity of public funding. Argentina has little tradition of philanthropy as a means of encouraging alumni and the private sector to support public universities or of significant private investment in R&D, as occurs in other industrialized countries (Balán 1993).

Table 12.2 R&D Indicators in Selected American Countries, 2003

Countries	R&D as a % of GDP[a]	Number of Researchers in R&D[b]	Expenditure in R&D per Researcher[b] (US$)	Number of ISI Publications (2002)
Argentina	0.41	27,367	19,100	5,581
Brazil	1.04	64,577	96,600	15,854
Canada	1.87	107,300	127,400	40,513
Chile	0.57	6,447	55,800	2,655
Mexico	0.39	25,751	95,300	5,995
United States	2.62	1,261,227	193,500	331,538

Source:SECyT (2004).

[a]Data correspond to the year 2000 for Brazil, and 2001 for Chile and Mexico.

[b]Data (in US dollars PPP) correspond to the year 1999 for the United States; 2000 for Brazil and Canada; and 2001 for Chile and Mexico.

Allocation of Public Funds

UBA's political visibility, as a consequence of its tradition, prestige, and, especially its size, has made it a relevant political actor in the higher education system. Nonetheless, this does not mean that UBA has been privileged regarding the allocation of public funds. On the contrary, the growth of UBA's national support during the 1990s fell below the average increase in the higher education sector. Between 1991 and 1998, total government funds allocated to national universities rose 78 percent in real terms but the increment to UBA was only 42 percent (MECyT 1999).

Before the 1990s, the allocation of public funds among the national universities was based almost exclusively on historical proportions (determined mainly by the number of undergraduate students and without any consideration of average unit costs in different academic or professional fields), as well as lobbying activity in Congress. This funding mechanism promotes the growth of less costly fields in the social sciences and humanities at the expense of the more expensive ones in the hard sciences. If a university seeks to grow by augmenting its political will, it offers programs in law or public accounting. This approach allows expansion at a low cost per student. Since the 1990s, new mechanisms have been introduced. Public universities receive block grants, small portions of which are determined through a funding formula, and an increased amount of public funding has been earmarked on a competitive basis or, more recently, via noncompetitive mechanisms to improve quality. Nonetheless, most public funds are still allocated in response to the number of students and lobbying activities by the university authorities or provincial governments where these institutions are located. Some national universities in the provinces or in Greater Buenos Aires have developed political alliances with their local members of Congress.

Within the same political rationality, when the national government has allocated resources through the funding formula or contracts, the tacit rule to avoid conflicts and gain political support ensures that all public universities receive some kind of funding.

In sum, funding mechanisms applied since the 1990s depended either on the principle of horizontal equal treatment of all public universities (the functions of national universities are seen as homogeneous) or on the arbitrariness of public funding allocated via political lobbying. Since UBA's authorities have either been politically loyal to the Radical Party (the political opposition for 14 years) or (like the present rector) politically independent, UBA's lobbying activities have not been very successful. Other small national universities had been more successful in lobbying Congress for extra funding. Of course, given the size of UBA, an increase in funding would require huge resources compared to the increased budgets for other smaller universities.

Since the 1990s the higher education sector has not witnessed any intentional policy for top-down state control to promote excellence through the allocation of resources, although some bottom-up lobbying mechanisms on behalf of the hard sciences have been effective.

At the national research agencies and at UBA, hard science researchers have been able to exert a major influence in promoting competitive national research grants and national research fellowship programs. This ability stems from the weight of their full-time academic and research activities and the country's tradition of high-level qualifications in such fields as biomedicine, biology, chemistry, and physics. At UBA, for example, the Faculty of Exact and Natural Sciences, with only 6,023 undergraduate students, is allotted the same public funds as the Law Faculty, with more than 31,316 undergraduate students (UBA 2005a). The hard sciences also won the support of a competitive mechanism to improve the quality of undergraduate teaching at public universities—the Fund for the Improvement of Quality in Universities (FOMEC)—that operated from 1995 to 1999. FOMEC was a mechanism that supported the reform process and the improvement of the national universities to enable them to provide enhanced education. The distribution of resources was determined through competitive procedures to back proposals with well-established goals. The basic science faculty was FOMEC's main beneficiary, receiving most of the scholarships for graduate training, funds to acquire new equipment to improve teaching activities, and resources to enhance the university libraries and laboratories. With the smallest proportion of undergraduate students, the basic sciences obtained support for 27 percent of the total projects and 38 percent of the more than US$200,000 allocated through this mechanism. As a result of these funding mechanisms, the total FOMEC funds per student in the basic sciences amounted to more than US$2,000, while the same ratio for the social sciences was barely US$30 (García de Fanelli 2005). In sum, FOMEC was a useful mechanism to foster excellence in the research-oriented academic units via better quality conditions, but it could not promote change in the professional units (García de Fanelli 2005).

Perspectives on Research at Public Universities

In Argentina, a portion of research activity is carried out at public institutes outside the universities, many of which fall under the jurisdiction of CONICET, or through the CONICET "research career" and via other public agencies. In response to these aspects of the Argentine science and research system, at least three different views—presented by public authorities, academic experts, and university authorities—developed regarding the public policy of strengthening research-oriented universities (CONEDUS 2002): (1) all universities should be research-oriented with equal levels of quality; (2) a stratified system should be developed in which the majority of the public universities meet the increasing demand of students and concentrate on teaching activities, while a few others specialize in top-quality research activities; and (3) research at the advanced level should preferably be carried out outside universities, especially in public research institutes. The public policy perspective (2) is the only one that could eventually bolster one or more research-oriented universities in Argentina.

In the particular case of UBA, its relationship with governments since the restoration of democracy in 1983 reveals clear tensions and mutual mistrusts. Clearly, its huge size alone is considered a pending problem. As has happened with the leading universities in other countries, UBA is not yet willing to allow the national government to coordinate the system. For example, UBA did not accredit the medical and engineering undergraduate degrees through CONEAU's mandatory process, as most of the other public universities had done. Although different governments may recognize the crucial importance of transforming UBA into a top-quality university, most have surrendered this idea because of the difficulty of modifying such a large public institution. Moreover, no government officials want to put their public positions or political power at risk by seeking to overhaul UBA, with the subsequent danger of confronting a major social conflict with students and faculty labor unions.

The government that took office in May 2003 has neither a special stance on the strategic role of "top-quality universities" nor a clear intention to boost UBA's research-oriented character. However, there is a strong commitment to increase the amount of public funds devoted to R&D and the number of scholarships available for PhD students in certain priority fields. At the same time, the government recognizes that beyond the difficulties in supporting excellence in research in all areas, the public university should improve its social, cultural, and economic relevance. Additionally, a new program has been implemented to increase the number of full-time positions at national universities and to improve the quality of those professional programs accredited by CONEAU (like medicine and engineering). The current public policy is also targeting the repatriation of Argentine scientists. The National Secretariat of Science and Technology offers two programs (Raíces and Becas de Reinserción de CONICET) for this purpose. All of this is taking place in a more favorable economic scenario. The economy stabilized in mid-2002. GDP has expanded by more than 8 percent yearly since 2003, and inflation has fallen to single-digit levels.

Although none of the policies of the new government focuses on UBA as a political target, many of them might help to strengthen its research-oriented character. For example, the increase in the number of full-time posts will benefit universities with a higher proportion of faculty-researchers, and UBA has the highest percentage of faculty in this situation. However, all of these initiatives will not be enough to produce the key changes UBA needs to improve its position among the leading universities in the world.

CONCLUSION

In summary, perspectives deserve highlighting. UBA is a national flagship university, albeit not a canonical research university. That is, although UBA is the most prestigious, mature, and preeminent public university in the country, the institution as a whole has not achieved the standard indicators of a research-oriented university. Its trajectory has been strongly affected by conflicting missions: whether to be the most important university to educate professionals with deficient research training, or to be the principal institution devoted to the advancement of teaching and research activity in some key fields—such as the basic sciences, agronomic sciences, and the humanities.

To increase international competitiveness, promote economic growth, and achieve a better quality of life, Argentina needs one or a few top-quality universities to train scientists, technologists, and professionals at the highest level. In this context, it can be argued that UBA should play a central role in any strategy to strengthen the research capacity of the Argentine university system. Two reasons justify UBA's transformation into a research-oriented university. First, as a result of its visibility and social prestige, UBA is in a privileged situation to induce demonstration effects. The strengthening of top-quality research and elite-training activities at UBA could generate a strong and positive impact on the rest of the system. Second, UBA's indicators reveal that it is one of the Argentine public universities with greater potential to become a research-oriented institution.

The challenge of closing the gap between the ideal model and reality poses two key questions: what kind of research-oriented university Argentina needs and can afford given the constraints on social and economic development; and whether UBA would be able to become a research-oriented and elite-training institution. These two questions are critical to guiding the direction of future research efforts.

Regarding the first issue, the current paradigm of a research-oriented university is designed based on the American model. However, there is no way UBA or, for that matter, any other Argentine university, can clone the top-American research universities. The gap is too wide between the availability of financial, human, and physical resources in the Argentine and American institutions. Additionally, the Argentine system cannot achieve the international scope of the institutional fabric of American higher education. Moreover, even if the Argentine system were able to imitate some successful features of the American structure and functioning, some of the flaws highlighted by the critics of the American system—such as not giving undergraduate education the attention that it deserves, rewarding research productivity far more than teaching, and producing irrelevant research—could have a much more perverse effect, given the structural weakness of the Argentine system. Thus, what type of research university developing countries should strive for depends on the precise interaction between the university and other key actors of the national system of innovation, especially the government and local industry. Likewise, it is critical to take into account Argentina's specific growth challenges. A research university could make several important contributions in this regard: the increase of exports to ensure growth and external sustainability, the formation of a stronger entrepreneurial class, and the strengthening of the still weak institution building and organizational abilities. Argentina faces two obstacles to increase exports: (1) the country still shows comparative advantages that are strongly biased toward agricultural products in a world characterized by agricultural subsidies and protectionism; (2) real wages and per capita GDP are too high to compete with newly industrialized countries such as China or India. In this context, research universities that are fully articulated with the innovation system could help the economy to develop new competitive advantages. Technology-based academic research initiatives should aim to exploit the existing niches of excellence—for example, biomedicine and biotechnology. In this way, research universities could contribute to the creation of high-productivity jobs and to the success of institutional initiatives to promote startups and expanding businesses, thereby strengthening the formation of entrepreneurs. Finally, this process could give rise to and sustain a process of learning-by-doing in the institutional and organization fields and contribute to training highly skilled professionals, institutional entrepreneurs, and leaders for diverse social activities.

Placing UBA on the right track to become a research university, nonetheless, would certainly demand complex transformations, and many of the issues involved are not well known. One key issue that demands further research concerns the internal and external restrictions on institutional innovation. In Argentina, the governance structure appears to constitute the most important internal constraint on institutional change. Research findings have shown formal constraints on institutional governance—such as failures in the collegial decision-making processes, weak executive leadership, the absence of incentive-compatible contracts to reward institutional innovation—as well as informal ones, like the connections between many of the key actors in university organizations and the leading political parties. An analysis of the elements that impinge on institutional governance suggests that any policy initiative aimed at changing the core undergraduate governance structure will face strong obstacles. Introducing changes into the periphery (e.g., graduate programs and the relationships with the productive sector), on the contrary, would likely be much more feasible. In fact, the increasing importance of an expanded developmental periphery is producing a hybrid university—that is, an organization with two different functioning logics, one more conservative, the other more entrepreneurial. Taking this situation into consideration, one politically feasible pathway to improve the research-oriented character of UBA could be to foster the graduate level via the allocation of public funds through contract programs that the university or some of its academic units negotiate. These contract programs would allow the government to support a strategic plan to increase research activity and graduation rates at the graduate level. At the same time, increasing public funds should be devoted to raising the percentage of full-time professors at the undergraduate level as a way to improve the quality of both academic and professional programs.

Some Argentine higher education experts often say that were it possible to expand the amount of public funding devoted to public universities, the main problems would remain unresolved. Yet the question remains of how institutional reforms could be implemented without increasing funding. It is clear that, although this rise is not a sufficient condition for improvement, it does appear to be necessary for increasing research activity, changing the incentive structure to improve teaching quality through better academic labor conditions, and encouraging equal opportunity through scholarships or loans. In all three cases (research grants, funds to improve labor conditions, and student financial support), an increase in institutional funds is a necessary condition for making public policy financially and politically feasible. But it should be stressed that economic incentives become an issue only when there is a feasible plan to be carried out and a pattern of behavior to be followed. So, UBA should define its institutional objectives in today's context of economic, political, and social transformations and should improve its management capability to implement the necessary changes successfully. Given the prevailing formal and informal constraints at the core undergraduate structure of governance, this is the most difficult obstacle to overcome in the process of institutional change.

Beyond the aspects of the policies specifically oriented to changing the university, nonetheless, it is crucial to take into account the impact of the general political environment. Until 1983, the overall policy environment not only impeded the strengthening of UBA's research activity but was also an obstacle to institutional modernization and cultural advancement. This is why the status of some issues, like academic freedom and institutional autonomy, has been substantially improved as a consequence of the consolidation of the democratic regime since 1983. The counterpart of this was the growing importance of other pressing issues, like financial resources, quality control, and market coordination. This chapter highlighted the factors that are most relevant to understanding the current challenges that UBA faces. More specifically, the main exploratory hypothesis is that there are three factors that restrict the path to excellence in UBA: inadequate financial resources for teaching and research activities at top-quality levels; the negative influence of inertia and lobbying on the allocation of public funds to national universities; and different government views concerning the role of public universities in the national system of innovation.

Argentina is now leaving behind the period of economic stagnation that began in 1998 and culminated in the 2001/02 deep economic crisis. The economy has been growing steadily for three years. These developments on the economic front have been accompanied by policy. In particular, the new economic policy emphasizes that strengthening the country's international competitiveness is key to achieving sustainable growth, thereby avoiding the stop-and-go pattern that has characterized the evolution of the economy in the past decades. This new economic and public policy scenario is much more favorable to introducing reforms aimed at improving the functioning of the university system, building a stronger research capacity, and strengthening its ability to meet an increasing demand for human capital. It remains to be seen whether these changes in the Argentine economic and policy context are strong enough and whether the design and implementation of policies will meet the challenge of overcoming the budget constraints, the institutional restrictions, and the organizational weaknesses that have restrained the transformation of the university system in the past.

NOTES

1. University institutions include both universities and university institutes. University institutes are specialized in single fields of knowledge, such as engineering, medicine, or psychology.

2. The following former students of UBA received a Nobel Prize in sciences: Bernardo Houssay (physiology 1947); Luis Federico Leloir (chemistry 1970); Cesar Milstein (physiology 1984).

3. Since 1995, CONEAU must accredit graduate courses at public and private universities. Those that voluntarily accept will be graded as excellent (A), very good (B), and good (C).

4. This figure corresponds to the competitive grants allocated to individual researchers or groups by the national research agency, Agencia Nacional de Promoción

Científica y Tecnológica.

5. The incentive structure is reflected in the level of remuneration, the types of labor contracts (full-time, part-time, *ad honorem*, or hourly basis), the possibilities of upward mobility, and the adequacy of the facilities (García de Fanelli 2004).

REFERENCES

Albornoz, M., et al. 2005. Producción científica argentina en química [Argentine scientific production in chemistry]. *Ciencia Hoy* 85:17–26.

Altbach, P. G. 1999. The University of Buenos Aires model for the future of higher education: A neglected perspective. *International Higher Education*, no. 14:8–9.

Balán, J. 1993. Políticas de financiamiento y gobierno de las universidades nacionales bajo un régimen democrático: Argentina 1983–1992 [Funding policies and governance of the national universities under a democratic regime: Argentina 1983–1992]. In *Políticas comparadas de educación superior en América Latina*, ed. H. Courard. Santiago, Chile: FLACSO.

Clark, B. 1998. *Creating entrepreneurial universities.* Oxford: Elsevier Science.

———. 2004. *Sustaining change in universities.* Berkshire, UK: SRHE and Open University Press.

CONEDUS. 2002. *Informe Final de la Comisión Nacional de Educación Superior.* [National Commission of Higher Education, final report]. Buenos Aires: Ministerio de Educación, Ciencia y Tecnología.

Echeverry, J. 2004. *Palabras pronunciadas por el Rector de la UBA en oportunidad de presentar el informe de gestión 2002-2004* [Address of the UBA rector on presenting the Management Report 2002–2004]. From www.uba.ar/download/institucional/rector/discursos/discrec141204.pdf (University of Buenos Aires website).

García de Fanelli, A. M. 1993. Articulación de la Universidad de Buenos Aires con el sector productivo [The interrelationships of the University of Buenos Aires with the productive sector]. *Documentos CEDES. Serie Educación Superior.* Buenos Aires: CEDES.

———. 1997. Las nuevas universidades del conurbano bonaerense: misión, demanda externa y construcción del mercado académico [The new universities in Greater Buenos Aires: Mission, external demand, and building of the academia market]. *Documentos CEDES. Serie Educación Superior.* Buenos Aires: CEDES.

———. 2001. Los estudios de posgrado en la Argentina: una visión desde las maestrías de ciencias sociales [Graduate studies in Argentina: A view from the social sciences master's programs]. In *Los posgrados en las ciencias sociales: la experiencia de Argentina y México tras los impulsos reformadores de los años ochenta y noventa*, ed. A. M. García de Fanelli, et al., 129–96. Mexico: ANUIES.

———. 2004. *Academic employment structures in higher education: The Argentine case.* Paris: International Labour Organisation.

———. 2005. *Universidad, Organización e Incentivos* [University, organization, and incentives]. Buenos Aires: Fundación OSDE–Miño & Dávila.

Halperín Donghi, T. 1962. *Historia de la Universidad de Buenos Aires* [History of the University of Buenos Aires]. Buenos Aires: EUDEBA.

Institute of Higher Education, Shanghai Jiao Tong University. 2004. *Academic ranking of world universities—2004.* http://ed.sjtu.edu.cn/rank/2004/top500list.htm.

Lombardi, J. V., E. D. Capaldi, K. R. Reeves, and D. S. Gater. 2004. The top American research universities. http://thecenter.ufl.edu/research2004.pdf.

Ministerio de Educación, Ciencia y Tecnología (MECyT). 1999. *Anuario de Estadísticas Universitarias* [Annual University Statistics]. Buenos Aires: MECyT.

———. 2004. *Anuario de Estadísticas Universitarias*. [Annual University Statistics]. Buenos Aires: MECyT.

Neuman, M., U. Questa, and R. Kaufmann. 2004. Concurso de residencias médicas en la ciudad de Buenos Aires: Importancia de género y universidad [Medical residencies contest in Buenos Aires City: Importance of gender and university]. *Educación Médica* 2:90–96.

SECyT (Secretariat for Technology, Science, and Productive Innovation). 2004. *Indicadores de Ciencia y Tecnología* [Indicators of science and technology]. Buenos Aires: Ministerio de Educación, Ciencia y Tecnología.

Trombetta, A. 1999. El ingreso en las universidades nacionales argentinas [Access to national Argentine universities]. In *Sistemas de Admisión a la Universidad. Seminario Internacional*, 121–49. Buenos Aires: Ministerio de Cultura y Educación.

United Nations Educational, Scientific and Cultural Organization (UNESCO). 1998. *Statistical yearbook*. Paris: UNESCO.

University of Buenos Aires (UBA). 2000. *Censo de Docentes 2000 [Faculty Census]*. www.uba.ar/institucional/censos/Docente2000/default.htm (University of Buenos Aires Web site).

———, 2003a. Entrevista al Licenciado Federico Schuster [Interview with Federico Schuster]. www.uba.ar/comunicacion/difusion/entrevistas/d-05.php (University of Buenos Aires Web site).

———. 2004. *Informe de Gestión 2002-2004. Consejo Superior y Rectorado de la UBA* [Management report. 2002–2004. University Council and UBA Rectorade]. www.uba.ar/download/instituciona l/destacados/informedegestion.pdf (University of Buenos Aires Web site).

———. 2005a. *Censo de Estudiantes 2004. Datos Preliminares* [2004 Student Census. Preliminary Data]. www.uba.ar/academicos/destacados/cestudiantes/index.php (University of Buenos Aires Web site).

———. 2005b. *Serie de Estadísticas* [Statistical series]. www.uba.ar University of Buenos Aires Web site).

Vest, Ch. M. 2005. World-class universities: American lessons. *International Higher Education*, no. 38:6–7.

13

Higher Education Policy and the Research University

In Asia and Latin America

Jorge Balán

This chapter provides a comparative examination of government policy, building upon the preceding descriptions and analyses of research universities in Asian and Latin American countries. The focus is on the development of policy frameworks and tools aimed at strengthening research and advanced training in the university while facing the challenge of institutional diversity in complex higher education systems. The comparison between Latin America and Asia might prove useful due to contrasting histories—the influence of continental European models since independence in Latin America and of a recent colonial past, wars, occupation, and the strong American and British presence in Asia. Countries in a region also look closely at their neighbors, borrowing experiences and often competing with one another. These two sets of countries, however, are very heterogeneous.

Given the increased competition in the global knowledge economy, the need for further institutional differentiation[1] has been stressed by governments and intergovernmental agencies all over the world. The European Commission considers insufficient differentiation as a bottleneck for achieving "world-class" excellence and increasing access to a broader range of students (Vught et al. 2005). Initiatives to concentrate public investment in research and doctoral training have been proposed in countries previously reluctant to consider differences in the university system, such as Germany (Kehm 2006). Many Asian governments, but not in India, have wholeheartedly embraced the goal of building world-class, research-oriented universities. Governments in Latin America have been less committed to this strategy to achieve international competitiveness through selective funding and institutional concentration on research and advanced training, with the partial exception of Chile.

Until recently, universities in developing countries gained public confidence and support by addressing the perceived needs of government—such as the education and licensing of lawyers and civil servants, teachers, doctors, and other skilled workers or tending public hospitals, running laboratories, and hosting museums and observatories—and meeting the expectations of elite groups and the expanding middle sectors to acquire educational credentials required for entry into the professions. Scientific research, however, did not necessarily find an easy home within the university, at least in part because of its international orientation (Schwartzman 1984). Although the quality of professional training could be examined and evaluated internationally—for example, when graduates apply for advanced study abroad—domestic requirements and regulations were paramount. Today, these traditional sources of public legitimacy have eroded; expectations have increased; and governments, often with the reluctant collaboration of universities, have created a variety of mechanisms to ascertain the value of what institutions produce and to design funding schemes to achieve expected results. Program accreditation, performance indicators, budgeting and funding, entrance examinations and indirect funding through student choice, are some of the available instruments in the toolbox. Competitive pressures are also fostered through bilateral, regional, and global trade agreements regulating degrees and qualifications and promoting methods for quality assurance (Post et al. 2004).

Furthermore, governments in developing countries are now looking at higher education within the context of broader goals in education and research. Learning in primary and secondary schools is now assessed systematically through standardized testing of reading and mathematics in many nations—including *all* the countries discussed in this volume—with policymakers, stakeholders, and the media reading the results as indicators of national performance in the global knowledge society (Baker and LeTendre 2005). Higher education is increasingly pressed to show educational outcomes that can be measured against benchmarks.

New demands upon the university originate in government strategies to increase national competitiveness in the knowledge-based global economy, in rich countries as well as in those aspiring to achieve that status.[2] The international trade sector, as a portion of the gross national product

(GNP), is increasing in both Asia and Latin America. The share of high-technology exports has exploded in the Asian economies and to a lesser but still significant extent is growing in Latin America. The new export economies rely heavily on domestic services that incorporate new technologies and widespread use of a skilled labor force. National innovation systems include higher education as a key element with the capacity to produce and disseminate knowledge deemed strategically important for the nation, while assessing that capacity with international standards.

I consider in the next section the contrasting institutional legacies of research universities in the two continents, while the following one is devoted to differentiation policies in the contemporary context of mass higher education systems. Three key dimensions of current government policy vis-à-vis research universities are then compared across nations: funding for research and development, building capacity for doctoral training, and reforms in the academic profession. Insights gained from this comparative exercise are summarized in the concluding section.

Institutional Legacies and Policy Contexts

The research universities identified in this volume are almost without exception public institutions, created by governments with high expectations about their mission and functions.[3] States lent them a special legal status and many privileges within the public sphere. The universities' ability to fulfill these expectations largely reflected the political and economic power of the founding state. Weaker states envisioned institutions that largely failed in their assigned mission, requiring sooner or later to be reorganized on a different basis—as was the case with Peking University in 1902 and the Universidad Nacional Autónoma de México in 1910. Powerful colonial administrators granted a dependent status and gave restricted missions to the universities they created overseas, yet they often established a legacy for future independent governments. The three universities established by the British in India in the 1850s, modeled after the University of London, consisted largely of affiliating and examining bodies yet were highly influential in the initial expansion of the system under colonial rule and after independence (Jayaram 2004). In 1924, Keijo Imperial University was built by Japan in occupied Korea after the model of its centralized imperial universities but with narrowly limited goals (Lee 2004). Although Korea embraced the US higher education model since the 1950s, a centralized tradition, as well as the relatively fluid relationship with industry, might be considered Japanese legacies.

The older universities within this group are to be found in Latin America. They were envisioned as unique institutions, to play a distinctively important role for state and society. They did not have competitors when originally envisioned, although they were designed to supersede Church-related institutions and were inspired by contemporary European models and ideals. They represented the nation and were seen as instruments for its construction or reconstruction. Distinction was built into their genetic code, so to speak. The University of Chile, founded in 1842, retained its monopoly in higher education and is identified with the nation to this day. It was meant to preside over the building of a public education system, to train the functionaries the new state required, and to construct the knowledge needed to unify the new nation (Serrano 1993). Its continuity as a central public institution for over 160 years reflects the institutional strength of the Chilean state. Other national universities in Latin America went through major reorganizations, often following extended periods of inactivity caused by political troubles and/or the transfer from provincial to national authorities.

The younger universities were founded in the 1960s, when the respective countries faced enrollment growth and signs of mass access to higher education. They were assigned distinctive missions within the emerging national systems. These institutions were meant to become "public research universities," on the US model, but were not part of a systemic approach to institutional differentiation within the system. The focus of these new institutions was graduate education rather than undergraduate or professional training. Partnerships between international development agencies and domestic leaders in public institutions pushed to move research and advanced training into the core of higher education (Levy 2005).

Both older and younger public universities enjoyed a number of privileges derived from close interaction with the elites and unique status within the state—either as public monopolies with little or no competition or as uniquely designed institutions within a colonial, national, or regional strategy. They were to be part of a state, although with a special status as state institutions that others did not enjoy that delegated to them some important public functions. Research was not one of them until the 1960s, although it may have been conducted on the margins. In the Latin American tradition the most important function concerned awarding professional degrees that provided access to regulated professions such as medicine, law, engineering, and others. Professionals, in particular lawyers, were public servants even when privately employed (Steger 1974). The public universities often enjoyed a special status in contracting work for government (national, provincial, or municipal), a status often retained to this day. The political centrality of these institutions is often associated with their location in the capital city (Brazil is an exception), the participation of key political figures as faculty or administrators, and the recruitment of political leaders, including presidents and cabinet members.

These privileges involved the responsibility over the guidance or mentorship of new universities. Older universities were assigned as examiners of programs and graduates of new institutions became the organizational model to be followed by other national and provincial institutions and the prototypes for programs and curricula in the professions, and trained the faculty and administrators to lead the new institutions. These universities became "flagships" in the sense of providing guidance and orientation to others in the system. They tended to define what a university should be and thus were sources of institutional isomorphism within their respective countries. Competition for resources played largely within the national political system, not necessarily on the basis of distinctive functions or programs. Universities did not usually compete with each other for students, faculty, resources, or prestige. The creation of new public universities represented a limited domestic challenge to the privileged status of the older public universities.

The greatest challenge to the dominance of public universities in Latin America came from universities under the Catholic Church (historically a competing source of political power to the colonial state) that were authorized to offer the same types of degrees and adopted similar organizational forms, although with distinctive governance and mission (Levy 1986). In China and Korea, as in many other Asian countries, private providers associated with a variety of Christian missions had extended throughout the 19th century, establishing a presence that—even when interrupted as in China under the socialist regime—is deeply rooted in other traditions, such as the mentor-disciple relationship in the Confucian tradition (Keun 2002). India inherited much of the British organizational tradition of universities and affiliated colleges under their supervision but created new and highly prestigious non-university institutions in the areas of science, technology, and management. Difference in governance and funding is thus better established in Asia than in Latin America, although with significant variation within each region. Difference in function has been much more difficult to regulate, as most institutions aspire to the status and privileges associated with the idea of a "university."

Educational policy in China and Korea as in many other East Asian countries is centrally planned by the executive branch of government, with limited participation of other levels of government, institutions of higher education, and stakeholders in the implementation of national plans. The private sector, very large in Korea and small but rapidly growing in China, is closely regulated by government. In contrast, national governments in Latin America, as in India, share responsibilities with parliaments and provincial governments; while universities are granted greater autonomy to develop their own programs with government funding; organized students and faculty exert much influence within the public universities. Governments have ineffectively regulated the private sector, lacking instruments to steer it within the system, and are highly sensitive to cross-pressures from regional and sector interests. East Asian education relies more heavily on contributions by students and their families for bearing the costs of education than is the case in Latin America (with the exception of Chile), allowing for public funding to be more strategically focused on sectors, institutions, and programs according to national political goals established by central governments.[4]

Regulating Higher Education Differentiation

Governments have attempted to regulate higher education systems through legal frameworks, recognizing distinctive functions and governance for the various segments and establishing mechanisms for articulation and coordination. Although institutional diversity and differentiation might be seen as a "natural" consequence of system growth, it is hard to find examples of a smooth transition into a formally diversified set of publicly funded institutions of higher education because differentiation always entails recognition of privileged access to valuable and scarce resources through government's actions (Smelser 1974). No differentiation exists without some form of stratification, competition, and conflict. Conflict may be circumscribed to a few actors within the system or, when higher education is more central and visible within the nation, it may become a thorny part of the broader political agenda. Furthermore, conflict may flare in the competition for resources between institutions—over the privilege enjoyed by some, and not others, to offer specific degrees, to access specific lines of funding, or to perform legislated functions for the state or society—but it is chronic within institutions, between schools, programs, or other units that compete for the attention of central authorities or government for more resources or special privileges.

Legal classifications, as in the binary systems developed with mixed results in a number of European countries, were deemed essential to regulate competition and conflict and to focus government funding on specialized functions. Often these attempts failed to restrict mission drift, with institutions in the "lower" segment striving to broaden the original mandate or to limit the institutional size or share of students in the upper segment of the hierarchy, the main goals governments would have wished to achieve. Additional restrictive features to fine-tune the classification are now usually incorporated in the legal definition of a university, such as the demonstrated capacity to offer graduate degrees and a quantum of research production. Institutional classifications created by nongovernmental organizations (NGOs), modeled after that proposed by the Carnegie Commission in the early 1970s, analytically classify institutions on the basis of similarities and differences. Driven by higher education stakeholders, institutions depend on their strength and autonomy from government, which, critics fear, will find use for the classifications in orienting public funding (Vught et al. 2005).

Differentiation is designed to attend to the needs of a highly heterogeneous student body, to nurture capacity for specialized functions, but also to contain costs and to guide public spending in higher education. With these goals in mind, governments often attempt to reorganize, merge, or tinker in a variety of ways with preexisting institutions or to establish entirely new segments, assigning specific functions to each of them (i.e., in the kinds of degrees to be awarded or the housing of research infrastructure). The underlying assumption is that the costs of research, teaching, and service activities can and should be measured and managed at the institutional and system levels, whether they are carried out by the same or different workers and units. This assumption and its consequences for management usually meet with considerable resistance from institutions and the academic communities.

Under today's policy mantra, differentiation policy may or may not involve tools to promote a larger role for private providers, but most likely it promotes at the system level an increase in the share of costs borne by students, greater diversification of the resource base for public institutions, and closer attention to the demands from local government and business for skilled workers and specialized services. Government attempts to subsidize research or to strengthen research capacity in selected centers or institutions rather than spreading research support throughout the university system also pits governments against academia, in particular, organized faculty and students.

China's reform is probably the most daring experiment ever in reshuffling a large-scale higher education system. The reform of the educational system first launched in 1985 emphasized local responsibility, institutional diversity, multiplicity of funding sources, and decentralization of authority. It preserved and expanded the privileges of "key universities," a sector of nationally prominent and older institutions that did not receive much research support until then, since research in the natural and social sciences and in the humanities had been largely restricted to other government institutions, the academies. Following up on major economic reforms throughout the state-dominated economy, the 1985 reform, refined and extended in the 1990s, left the party-dominated central government as a macro-manager for the whole system, within a model of centralized goal setting with decentralized implementation. By the 1990s, the Chinese recognized three broad segments of university, nonuniversity, and adult postsecondary institutions, with provisions for expanding the operation of private providers (often in partnership with local government and industry) (Min 2004). Institutional mergers became common to achieve organizational scale and to absorb academically weaker institutions within larger units. This complex and differentiated system has as its pinnacle a set of public universities designated to become world-class institutions, distinctive in their capacity to carry out research. Ownership and management of large-scale industrial concerns is another unique feature of these universities since the 1980s, creating a base for independent income.

After the Korean War, the government developed a clear difference between colleges and universities offering four-year and graduate programs, on the one hand, and junior colleges, universities of education, and other schools, on the other—limiting the share of enrollments in the college and university sector through government policy and regulation. Until recently colleges and universities with large enrollments were uniformly structured as research universities (Lee 2004, 63). In the 1990s, institutional diversification and specialization within the college and university sector became tools toward promoting greater competitiveness in Korea. The core policy instrument to achieve this goal is competitive public funding for research and doctoral education programs aiming to strengthen capacity in world-class universities in close articulation with regional universities proving excellence in undergraduate education.

The Chilean military government introduced in 1980 a tripartite system with two new privately run and financed segments, that of two-year vocational postsecondary schools and four-year institutions for education and professional training. Universities, whose primary functions are to offer degrees in the regulated professions and to conduct research, was differentiated between then existing universities, enjoying a greater degree of autonomy and limited public funding, and new ones to be created by private initiative. It also mandated a process of radical decentralization of the main two public universities, granting autonomy to their regional branches. Although quite a radical reform, the Chilean plan left unchanged some of the privileges associated with the traditional universities (government block funding, authority to grant prestigious degrees, relatively greater autonomy in programs and curricula, and a research-oriented faculty) and established the basis for the ambition among some of them to become "research universities."

Chile and Korea have in common the high share of higher education costs borne by students and their families, leaving public policy flexibility regarding direct subsidies to specific institutions, programs, and functions. In the case of Korea, private investment is even higher considering that families also tend to pay high sums for tutoring outside of the institutions. Chile and Korea also have in common a heavy reliance on private institutions (and not only private funding). An important difference, however, is the larger proportion of students in long-cycle university professional programs in Chile when compared to Korea, where vocational and other short-cycle programs predominate. More relevant to our discussion here, Korea's investment in science and technology, much larger as a proportion of gross national product (GNP) than Chile's, has as a goal strengthening capacity within a small segment of research-intensive higher education institutions.

The Brazilian approach to differentiation is quite unique. The main instrument, developed through the higher education reform of 1968, has been the creation of research-oriented graduate programs following the US model, with the MA and PhD as central organizing principles, and with traditional professional education reshaped in four-year undergraduate programs. The Brazilian federal government has since promoted differentiation through research and graduate fellowship funding supported through systematic and periodic program evaluation and accreditation. Uniformity within the public university system, where all faculty and staff enjoy the same status as civil servants, remains a major stumbling block for any further distinction within the university system (Durham 1998). The limited expansion of public university enrollments and a loose regulatory framework for the private sector have stimulated the growth of a large-scale system of private postsecondary institutions. Universities are only a small segment within this system, with a few of them—mainly the older, Catholic universities—with a significant research capacity. Last, but not least, Brazil is unique in the role of state (provincial) governments, in particular São Paulo. The three public universities within the São Paulo state system, supported through a mandated quota of the state revenues with fixed shares for each of them, include the two most prestigious, research-intensive universities in Brazil.

Recently, Argentina and Mexico have also developed legal frameworks regulating differentiation, coordination, and articulation within the higher education systems. By and large, however, these efforts have left the sector of public universities, supported by the federal government but with great autonomy over academic matters, at the core of the respective systems. The heavy reliance on block funding, in spite of the recent development of more focused funding mechanisms, seriously limits the government capacity to focus public subsidy on research activities within the university (Fanelli 2005). Differentiation within these public systems was pursued by the creation of new public institutions, with mixed results. Attempts to steer the mega-universities that concentrate a significant proportion of the research and advanced training infrastructure have been blocked by student and faculty unions and highly contested university electoral politics. National governments have been unable, in the longer run, to achieve the power or consensus required to develop goals and long-lasting plans for the institutional system, which has tended to grow through a mixture of uncoordinated market demands and political decisions.

While formal differentiation within the university sector has met with limited success in many cases, examination systems have helped in its implementation. The 1980s reforms in Chile had a limited effect in reducing the lure of long-cycle university degree programs, and against the wishes of government, the proportion of the student body in the non-university sector remained too small. The national entrance examination, however, became an effective mechanism for differentiation within the university sector since students with higher scores may choose among universities and programs while an important segment of state funding is tied to student choice. Brazil is another example of heavy reliance on entrance examinations and high selectivity among public universities for institutional prestige (but not directly for funding). Brazil is unique in implementing a national examination of graduates from different professional (undergraduate) degree programs at public and private universities aiming at bringing greater transparency to their quality. The examination was strenuously opposed by faculty and student unions and eventually dismantled (Moura Castro 2004). These examination systems pale when compared to the highly competitive entrance examinations run at the national and provincial levels in China. On the other extreme, countries such as Argentina and Mexico have largely relied upon open-admission systems in the traditional undergraduate programs of public universities, widely known for the huge size of their entering classes and the low graduation rates. The difficulties in implementing entrance examination systems for selective admission in professional degree programs at public universities date back to the reform movement of the 1920s that early demanded an expansion in the intake of students, against what they saw as "quota systems" designed to limit admission on the basis of strict examinations (Ennis and Porto 2001).

The litmus test of differentiation, however, lies in the mechanisms governments use to fund institutions, functions, and programs, often guided by formal distinctions between institutional segments and their functions. The public funding of higher education has changed rapidly in many countries as part of the broader attempts to reform public finance within the new public-management fad. A review of this topic is clearly beyond the scope of this essay. However, it seems appropriate to discuss briefly research funding, supported through investments both in research and development and in higher education, as it is at the core of attempts to build research universities.

The Role of Research and Development Funding

Large-scale government projects and agencies for science and technology date from the 1950s and 1960s. The size of the total effort, the role of different sectors in funding and performance of R&D, and the government strategies in research funding within higher education and/or industry are key areas where the Latin American and the Asian experiences have diverged for several decades. The initial advantage in scientific and technological research of the Latin American university when compared with the Asian counterparts has been overshadowed by the recent effort in R&D among the latter. The R&D strategy has been a key factor in the rationale for building research universities in Korea and China, while it is much less articulated in India or Latin America.

The share of these nations in the world production of science has consistently grown for both regions over the past two decades. The jump has been most impressive in China, whose scientists now write over 2 percent of the world's scientific papers, but Korea, India, and Brazil are all around the one percent figure (OECD 2005). Three decades ago, only India among the developing countries had a significant share of the world scientific production (Frame et al. 1977). All these countries have invested more in R&D in recent years than in the past, but the total effort in gross terms and as a percentage of the gross domestic product (GDP) is considerably smaller in Latin America than in Asia. R&D expenditures in Latin America increased 15 percent between 1995 and 2002, reaching US$11 billion for the region, still US$1 billion less than Korea. Brazil is spending around one percent of its GNP on R&D, with Chile, Argentina, and Mexico trailing behind, while China spends 1.4 percent and Korea 2.5 percent.[5] While business contributes only around one-third of the total R&D funding in Latin America, in Korea it contributes over 70 percent. The dramatic growth in private international investments in Asia is partially responsible for this difference, since new industrial ventures in the region usually entail a strong R&D component.

Performance of R&D activities is also concentrated in the business sector in Korea and now also in China, where the large share carried out by government-owned and -managed research institutions has decreased, moving to business laboratories. In contrast, government agencies, higher education institutions, and the business sector are equally responsible for performing R&D activities in Latin America, although with variations between countries. In relative terms, higher education is more important within the total R&D sector in Latin America than in Korea or China. These two countries, however, are moving strongly toward establishing a dynamic presence of university-based research. In both cases there is a determined policy to concentrate research funding on a few universities, but they differ in significant ways. China has added special funding packages to build world-class universities to a longer policy of fostering university-based and -managed industrial concerns. The funding packages from the central government—with subsidiary municipal funds in some cases—are administered by the central university administration. Thus, it is a vertically organized, noncompetitive allocation mechanism that assumes a previous decision on which institutions have the capacity or vision to become research-intensive universities.

Government support for scientific research became institutionalized in Latin America through national agencies created in the 1960s that first established national competitive mechanisms to allocate some resources, those distributed through individual fellowships and awards, while programs and institutions were usually funded in a noncompetitive manner. Neither the unstable democratic governments nor the authoritarian military regimes had an easy relationship with the universities. Universities in Latin America posed many problems to governments' efforts to build scientific and technological prowess in specific areas, and funding agencies reflected this tension. Participatory decision-making processes were slow and politicized. Student political radicalization always posed a threat to those deciding longer-term investments in laboratories and equipment. Academics had an ingrained mistrust of industry, while agencies wanted to link research with technological development and eventually to production. Universities were unprepared to administer research or any other project funding. Bureaucratically uniform and centralized, they proved inflexible to deal with difference. Academically decentralized, they lacked a central vision and authority to establish clear new policies. Military governments, perhaps with the exception of Brazil, subordinated all academic policy to perceived security threats, seriously limiting university research and academic freedom within higher education.

The resumption of economic growth in recent years enabled governments to increase their R&D effort, including the portion that is implemented through the universities. Private investment in R&D, however, remains marginal in Latin America. The weak effort is spread around a large number of institutions and programs, with great difficulties in establishing priority themes in the absence of strong demands. Competitive awards, with peer review systems, are often compensated to achieve greater equity in the distribution of funds between areas, disciplines, institutions, and regions of the country. Governments generally lack the capacity to establish thematic priorities and follow them up without serious damage. The weak articulation with industry does not help in sorting out priorities within the agenda.

Governments created special funds in the 1990s in Latin America to expand research funding outside the regular university budgets (Fanelli 2005). These competitive funds for research infrastructure and doctoral fellowship support tended to favor universities, schools, and departments with a stronger research base but in most instances under pressure to achieve greater equity between institutions and regions. Supported through credits from international agencies, the special funds did not become politically or financially sustainable. Academic communities in the region remain deeply divided around these issues. The politically better-organized segments, such as faculty and student unions, find reason to mistrust innovations in university funding, in particular competitive schemes endorsed by international agencies, and are instead strong defenders of government block funding and fixed salary scales, linked rigidly to seniority and academic degrees rather than performance, for rewarding faculty and staff (Moura Castro and Levy 2000).

Korean policies before the Brain Korea 21 (BK 21) plan of 1998 had distributed resources more fairly among universities and programs. The plan changed the focus from equality of opportunity to efficiency of investment. The principle of "selection and concentration" underlying the plan should benefit the traditional top universities (Moon and Kim 2001). Many fear this may reinforce the traditional pecking order as well as narrow specialization in research areas, both identified as weaknesses of the Korean system. The plan calls for nurturing regional universities' links with industry as well as the quality of their undergraduate programs.

University research with R&D funding in China dates to the 1980s, when the Chinese National Science Foundation was established to administer funds targeted to key national research laboratories in leading universities. Some basic research institutes were transferred from the academies to the universities. Leading university presidents are nominated by the academies or belong to them. In 1998 the Chinese government declared the intention to build several "world-class" universities, focusing much of the project on a few universities. Chinese universities now compete for research funding from various national and provincial agencies, but key universities and laboratories enjoy competitive advantages. Another unique feature of the Chinese model for building research universities has been the policy of fostering university ownership and management of major industrial concerns as a means to link scientific and technological research with industry.

Research Universities as PhD-Granting Institutions

The doctorate has been the degree that university reformers all over the world have long identified as a symbol of the academic profession in the university and thus as a must for the highly qualified faculty they wished to train and recruit. The capacity to grant the research-oriented PhD has become the US trademark of the research university and its assigned function within complex higher education systems. There is a clear continuity between these ambitious goals: contemporary reformers envision the strengthening of PhD-granting institutions as a means to train the new professoriate demanded to raise the quality of the higher education system as well as to support the improvement and expansion of academic research. The close association between these goals, however, inflicts dilemmas and, quite often, institutional conflicts, as strategies involve sizable public and private investments over time and collaboration between various institutional actors.

The emergence of research-oriented doctoral programs in Latin America created a tension between the professional and academic perspectives in the university. A source of tension was the degree itself: the doctorate was not new, since it had been recognized as a largely honorary degree granted in the professions, such as law and medicine, on the basis of a written thesis that often entailed little or no research effort. Another problem was the desire to make the new doctorate a symbol and requirement for the renewal of the faculty, turning it into an academic profession—a career path demanding full-time employment in higher education, as contrasted with the traditional part-time faculty integrated by prestigious practitioners in the liberal professions. The relatively greater strength of the profession-based university in Latin America with part-time faculty, in comparison with the Asian experiences examined in this book, explains why these tensions were more acute and difficult to solve in the former region than in the latter.

A research-oriented doctorate emerged in Latin America within the continental European model—as an extension of formal long-cycle professional studies in the humanities and sciences. The degree was rooted in academic schools within the university, in "faculties" of philosophy and/or science. The inflow of faculty recruited in Europe introduced the academic traditions of their respective countries. The research doctorate, however, remained an academic oddity, much at the margins of university life, awarding only a few doctorates each year (Alcantara, Malo, and Fortes forthcoming). Reform-oriented groups in the 1960s initiated plans for a doctorate based on the US model—the integration of research and teaching, full-time faculty, and a graduate school for advanced training and research. Paradoxically, the innovators tended to be leftist groups that often became confronted by both conservative groups within the university entrenched in the professional schools and governments on national political issues (Levy 2005).

The most successful, longer-lasting effort to build research-oriented graduate programs, including the MA and the PhD, originated in the Brazilian higher education reform of 1968. Key to its success was the centralization of accreditation and funding of graduate programs in the same agency, with complementary funding from R&D agencies. Accreditation and funding relied on the participation of the academic community in the peer review procedures, which gained initial legitimacy among reform groups not necessarily enthusiastic about other government policies. Fellowship funding was made available only for study in graduate programs ranked within the top categories by the accreditation agency. Although public and private universities could compete, preexisting research groups were much stronger among the former than the latter. Generous support was also provided through the national research agency for individual fellowships to pursue doctoral studies overseas.

One of the goals of the Brazilian strategy was to renovate the professoriate. Graduate training, starting with the MA degree, became mandatory for all university faculties, while the PhD is the standard for faculty in graduate programs. Today the goal is to raise the percentage of faculty members with a doctorate from the current figure, slightly above 20 percent, to 40 percent in the next 10 years (Ribeiro forthcoming). The figure for the public universities is considerably higher than for the private sector. Legislation has now been introduced in Congress to restrict the use of the name *university* to institutions, whatever their current denomination, with some accredited MA programs and at least one doctoral program. However, as elsewhere, the pressure on the demand side often leads to a decline in academic standards, a problem that quality assurance agencies attempt to deal with. The Brazilian agency has done so by using a more detailed ranking of graduate programs whose results have direct effects on the availability of public funding for graduate fellowships. Rankings are made public and guide the behavior of institutions and students.

A comparison of the Brazilian strategy vis-à-vis graduate education and university research with the more recent BK 21 plan seems useful. BK 21 is a $1.2 billion, seven-year plan to bolster higher education, with 75 percent of the total effort focused on selectively strengthening graduate schools and programs in science and technology, social sciences, and the humanities. Graduate students are the direct beneficiaries of funding through stipends, overseas study, and research infrastructure for team projects in world-class universities. Additional funding is available for nurturing regional universities to meet the needs of industry and to encourage highly qualified regional high school graduates to go to leading regional undergraduate schools. Thus, the plan envisions systemic linkages and institutional specialization within higher education, building upon the large investments made in the past to improve the coverage and quality of secondary education (Moon and Kim 2001, 100).

Although in both cases graduate education (particularly doctoral studies) is the backbone of efforts to build research universities in articulation with undergraduate studies, the Korean plan ties together the complementary functions of key national universities and regional institutions more neatly. In Brazil the planning has been more broadly focused on the supply of graduate degrees and the demand for credentials in the expanding higher education system, since the Brazilian government does not have the centralized capacity to steer the institutional system that Korea enjoys. Another crucial difference is to be found in the linkages with industry. Although both countries have given priority to this goal, Korean research universities have a longer history of relationship with industry, including reforms in the industry-based doctoral programs following the Japanese model. Brazilian university governance systems pose serious limitations to incorporate business concerns in shaping research or teaching programs.

Korea relied more heavily than Brazil or any other country in the world, with the possible exceptions of Taiwan and China, upon doctoral training overseas as a strategy to build the faculty for its expanding higher education system. The flow of Korean students, in particular graduate students to the United States, has been the largest in proportion to the national population. Through the support of US development projects, already in the 1950s Koreans were the third largest contingent of foreign students in the United States, behind Canada and Taiwan. Even today, there are more Korean than Latin American doctoral students overseas, although the population of Korea is only less than half of that of Brazil alone. Koreans earn about 10 percent of all doctorates in science and engineering granted to foreign students in the United States, while Mexican students earn 1.7 percent and Brazilian nationals even less. The community of Korean scientists living in the United States is four times larger than the Brazilian one, in spite of the recent reversal from brain drain to brain gain. The number of Korean doctoral students in the United States has tended to decline in absolute terms but more clearly in relative terms to those pursuing a doctorate at home. The growth of domestic doctoral education has been amazing in the major sending countries—China, Korea, and India. Until the early 1990s there were as many doctoral degrees in science and engineering awarded to Chinese students in the United States as in China. Today there are four times as many receiving their doctorates in China. Given the size of the countries, the growth in the output of Chinese, Korean, and Indian doctoral programs is changing the dynamics of the global market for highly skilled workers.[6]

Faculty at the Research University

A defining element of the research university is the reliance on outstanding faculty recruited nationally or, whenever feasible and desirable, internationally. Faculty members are expected to be top scholars and scientists in their disciplines, devoted full-time to research and advanced teaching, and committed to their institutions. While at the center of higher education reforms throughout the world, faculty reforms are embedded in broader efforts to reform civil services since, more often than not, research universities are publicly supported and managed and thus have to follow overall rules for public-sector employment.

China, Korea, and India have developed national and institutional policies to recruit researchers overseas, scientists and scholars from those home countries trained in the United States and Europe. These plans appear to have met with considerable success. Rigidities in public-sector employment needed to be lifted to make competitive recruitment possible. Peking University chose the most audacious strategy to renew its faculty, an approach many others may follow in China. In 2005, Peking University issued, after one full year of deliberation throughout China, the Teachers' Engagement and Promotions Reform Plan, with the decision to recruit faculty actively from the United States, the United Kingdom, and other English-speaking countries. Ninety-five senior positions were open throughout the university.[7] Many fear this strategy might displace numerous qualified Chinese scholars who might otherwise have been hired. Other critics are more broadly concerned about the long-term plans to use English as the language of instruction in graduate schools and its possible impact on Chinese culture and national identity.

International faculty recruitment shows how much China has moved away from a centralized system of public employment with fixed scales tied to seniority and location to one where institutions are encouraged to develop their own resources and strategies and thus recruit, reward, and promote the best faculty they can afford. Rewards and sanctions are used to enhance research productivity and the capacity of institutions to promote their own reputation. Publication in peer-reviewed journals—international publications in particular—and research grants count for a system of steep financial rewards. More recently, this system has been replaced by "position allowances" that include formalized contractual expectations for research productivity and teaching workloads, with sanctions for noncompliance, bringing in the usual concerns about quantitative benchmarks for accountability.

Until the 1980s, the funding model for public universities in Latin America created a major obstacle to establishing academic rewards related to performance in teaching, research, and service. The model was based on inertia; budget increments were approved either to adjust to higher costs or to create something new (positions, courses, programs, equipment, buildings) without modifying anything old. No clear rationale was provided for an institution to ever attempt to close any courses or programs or to dismiss any faculty in order to replace them or to free the use of funds for other purposes—except under military regimes, prone to use arbitrary authority to eliminate politically undesirable faculty or programs.

The funding model in Latin America contains an ingrained bias against innovation and change, providing protection to faculty and staff but offering no incentive for them to perform or for administrators to lead. Public universities' faculty and staff are civil servants—hired, rewarded, and promoted according to rigid rules in all the federal system and defended by strong unions. The system sets the same basic salary for each defined position rank in the hierarchy, with rewards based on seniority and earned degrees but not on performance since the rewards follow a bureaucratic rationale. Real salaries vary considerably between full-time and part-time positions (in many institutions the large majority are part-time). Salaries also may include additional payments for administrative duties, often covering past administrators as well (i.e., early retirement and other benefits). Teaching loads are assigned according to employment status, but all full-time appointments are based on the assumption of both teaching and research responsibilities. However, in fact, the bulk of teaching until today relies on poorly paid part-time faculty and teaching assistants.

Brazil, Mexico, and Argentina have relied upon R&D funding through specialized agencies to support researchers and their activities within the university, creating a system for faculty rewards above and beyond faculty salaries, which tend to deteriorate. Although they vary from country to country, these agencies have built parallel careers, with their own rules for entrance, evaluation, and promotion, based on peer review. Research incentives are individualized reward systems seldom tailored to the needs of research teams, centers, or institutions. The implicit policy goal has been to protect a high-cost, research-oriented sector from the overall decline of academic salaries throughout the system. This policy is challenged by faculty unions and the student movement, which generally demand across-the-board salary increases from governments.

Critics of reward systems based on research productivity often indicate that quantitative benchmarks place incentives on unethical procedures by faculty to increase the number of publications, regardless of quality or originality. Supporters tend to see the systems as the only kind of reward that is subject to peer review. Most observers probably agree that these systems have tended to separate research from teaching and to isolate the research-based nuclei of excellence within the university from the rest of the institution. In the absence of other indicators, universities use the number of academic faculty members with membership in the national research systems and their productivity to highlight the institutions' research orientation, even in cases when researchers contribute little to the institutions' core educational mission. Chile is exceptional in having created conditions for greater autonomy among public universities, which may now develop institution-wide faculty policies, stimulating a more competitive academic marketplace and more flexible rules for hiring and firing faculty (Bernasconi and Rojas 2004).

CONCLUSION

I have briefly examined four policy dimensions of government plans to achieve greater competitiveness in higher education: differentiation of mission and functions, research support, doctoral training, and faculty rewards and incentives. Although the goals and instruments are often similar across nations, governments differ from one another in their priorities as well as in the consistency and sustainability of their policies. Research universities, as is often stated in this volume, demand heavy public investment and privileged conditions for academic work to function properly. Not all governments, even within middle- and upper-middle-income countries with considerable research and training capacities, have the fiscal and political resources or the political will to focus on this goal. It seems a luxury many countries cannot afford to have and to hold. Furthermore, it is clear that one size does not fit all: research universities may come in very different models within the broad definition as institutions specialized in research and advanced training (Brunner 1997).

In this chapter I have focused on the conditions that affect the ability of governments to engage in research universities as a goal, without considering whether this is the right thing to do. From this discussion, some tentative generalizations come to mind.

The goal of building research-oriented, world-class universities is pursued by some governments as part of a more radical higher education reform agenda oriented to increase both access and national economic competitiveness. These are top-down rather than bottom-up reforms, to achieve systemwide institutional change to better address different societal needs through more diversified and targeted funding. The foci on institutional diversity and targeted public subsidy are consistent with, and perhaps dependent upon, heavy reliance on family contributions to bear the costs of education and on business investments to support and perform research and development activities.

Coordination between the education and the R&D policy sectors within government is a crucial condition to foster the notion of research universities. Those sectors are often in different silos and in competition with each other. Policy alignment is more likely to take place when there is a broader consensus in government and the policy community about the role of education and science in national development. A dynamic R&D sector in industry, often promoted by government fiscal and tax policy, may promote synergies with university research and broaden the domestic research communities.

Most governments aim to enhance the national capacity for advanced training at the doctoral level as a means to enhance the quality of higher education, engaging in both fellowship programs for doctoral training abroad and in programs supporting doctoral programs at home. They differ, however, in the size of their investments as well as in the degree of coordination between strategies in higher education policy and in the R&D sector. The emphasis on building research universities serves as a focus to orient policies in these two sectors more effectively.

Building or strengthening research universities requires reforms in how academic work is conducted and rewarded in different institutions. In particular, academic research and scholarship require highly specialized training and full-time dedication. The major stumbling block for reform is the notion of academic homogeneity that builds upon institutional isomorphism. In practice, these reforms tend to differentiate and stratify the professoriate and the academic profession.

Last, but not least, internationalization is a key dimension of the research university. Training overseas at the doctoral level has been the major venue for internationalization that has also fostered research within the university. In spite of greater capacity for domestic PhD production, student and faculty mobility remain important to achieve excellence and increase competitiveness.

NOTES

1. The terms *differentiation* and *diversification* are used in the literature to refer to differences across institutions within a system. I take them as synonymous. See Levy (2005, 326, note 1).

2. Nowhere is this more evident than in Europe. See European Commission (2005). For the United States, see Douglass (2006).

3. In this and the following sections I make extensive use of information and analyses presented in the preceding chapters, without citing them, to avoid boring repetition. However, original authors should not be held responsible for my interpretation of their work.

4. The contrast between East Asia and Latin America has been made by many authors, often praising the former as a model to be followed. See, for instance, Birdsall

(1999); Ferranti et al. (2003); and Ratliff (2003).

5. All figures are taken from Inter-American Development Bank (2006).

6. National Science Board (2006). See also Wyckoff and Schaaper (2005).

7. Lixin and Jie (2005). I thank Laurie Behringer for calling my attention to this controversial issue.

REFERENCES

Alcantara, A., S. Malo, and M. Fortes. Forthcoming. Doctoral education in Mexico. In Nerad and Heggelund, forthcoming.

Altbach, P. G., and T. Umakoshi, eds. 2004. *Asian universities: Historical perspectives and contemporary challenges.* Baltimore: Johns Hopkins University Press.

Baker, D. P., and G. K. LeTendre. 2005. *National difference, global similarities: World culture and the future of schooling.* Stanford, CA: Stanford University Press.

Bernasconi, A., and F. Rojas. 2004. *Informe sobre la educación superior en Chile: 1980–2003.* Santiago: Editorial Universitaria.

Birdsall, N. 1999. *Education: The people's asset.* Working paper no. 5. Washington, DC: Carnegie Endowment for International Peace, Center on Social and Economic Dynamics.

Brunner, J. J. 1997. La economía política de la educación superior. In *Los temas criticos de la educación superior en América Latina,* ed. R. Kent. Mexico City: Fondo de Cultura Económica.

Douglass, J. A. 2006. *The waning of American higher education advantage: International competitors are no longer number two and have big plans in the global economy.* Occasional Paper Series. Berkeley: Center for Studies in Higher Education, University of California.

Durham, E. R. 1998. *As universidades publicas e a pesquisa no Brasil.* Working paper 9/98. São Paulo: NUPES, Universidade de São Paulo.

Ennis, H. M., and A. Porto. 2001. Igualdad de oportunidades e ingreso a la universidad pública en la Argentina. Documento de Trabajo no. 30. La Plata: Departamento de Economia, Universidad Nacional de La Plata.

European Commission. 2005. *Towards a European research area: Science, technology, and innovation, key figures, 2005.* Brussels: European Commission.

Fanelli, A. M. G. de. 2005. *Universidad, organización e incentivos.* Buenos Aires: Fundacion OSDE.

Ferranti, D. de, et al. 2003. *Closing the gap in education and technology.* Washington, DC: World Bank.

Frame, J. D., et al. 1977. The distribution of world science. *Social Studies of Science* 7:501–16.

Inter-American Development Bank. 2006. *Education, science, and technology in Latin America and the Caribbean: A statistical compendium of indicators.* Washington, DC: Inter-American Development Bank.

Jayaram, N. 2004. Higher education in India: Massification and change. In Altbach and Umakoshi 2004, 85–112.

Kehm, B. M. 2006. The German "Initiative for Excellence" and rankings. *International Higher Education,* no. 44:20–22.

Keun, S. H. 2002. Intellectuals and power: The changing portrait of university professors in South Korea. *Development and Society* 31 (1): 107–24.

Lee, S. H. 2004. Korean higher education: History and future challenges. In Altbach and Umakoshi 2004, 145–73.

Levy, D. C. 1986. *Higher education and the state in Latin America: Private challenges to public dominance.* Chicago: University of Chicago Press.

———. 2005. *To export progress: The golden age of university assistance in the Americas.* Bloomington: Indiana University Press.

Lixin, W., and Z. Jie. 2005. The whole story of the Beida personnel system reform and the controversy. *Chinese Education and Society* 38 (1): 18–37.

Min, W. 2004. Chinese higher education: The legacy of the past and the context of the future. In Altbach and Umakoshi 2004, 53–83.

Moon, M., and K. Kim. 2001. A case of Korean higher education reform: The Brain Korea 21 project. *Asia Pacific Education Review* 2 (2): 96–105.

Moura Castro, C. de. 2004. Success and perils in evaluating Brazilian undergraduate programs. *International Higher Education*, no. 35:16–18.

Moura Castro, C. de, and D. C. Levy. 2000. *Myth, reality, and reform: Higher education policy in Latin America.* Washington, DC: Inter-American Development Bank.

National Science Board. 2006. *Science and engineering indicators*, vol. 1. Washington, DC: National Science Foundation.

Nerad, M., and M. Heggelund, eds. Forthcoming. *Changes in doctoral education worldwide: Proceedings of the International Conference on Forces and Forms of Change in Doctoral Education Internationally.* Seattle: University of Washington Press.

OECD. *See* Organization for Economic Cooperation and Development.

Organization for Economic Cooperation and Development (OECD). 2005. *Science, technology, and industry scoreboard, 2005.* Paris: OECD.

Post, D., et al. 2004. World Bank okays public interest in higher education. *Higher Education* 48:213–29.

Ratliff, W. 2003. *Doing it wrong and doing it right: Education in Latin America and Asia.* Stanford, CA: Hoover Institution.

Ribeiro, R. J. Forthcoming. The evolution of the doctorate in Brazil. In Nerad and Heggelund, forthcoming.

Schwartzman, S. 1984. The focus on scientific activity. In *Perspectives on higher education: Eight disciplinary and comparative views*, ed. B. R. Clark, 199–232. Berkeley: University of California Press.

Serrano, S. 1993. *Universidad y nación: Chile en el siglo XIX.* Santiago: Editorial Universitaria.

Smelser, N. J. 1974. Growth, structural change, and conflict in California public higher education. In *Public higher education in California*, ed. N. J. Smelser and G. Almond, 9–141. Berkeley: University of California Press.

Steger, H.-A. 1974. *Las universidades en el desarrollo social de la América Latina.* Mexico City: Fondo de Cultura Económica.

Vught, F. A. van, et al. 2005. *Institutional profiles: Towards a typology of higher education institutions in Europe.* Working paper. Enschede, Netherlands: Center for Higher Education Policy Studies, University of Twente.

Wyckoff, A., and M. Schaaper. 2005. The changing dynamics of the global market for the highly skilled. Paper for the Conference on Advancing Knowledge and the Knowledge Economy. Washington, DC: National Academy of Science.

Contributors

Philip G. Altbach is J. Donald Monan SJ Professor of Higher Education and director of the Center for International Higher Education at Boston College. He is the 2005–2006 director of the Fulbright New Century Scholars program. He is author of *Comparative Higher Education* and *The Knowledge Context*, editor of *The Decline of the Guru*, and coeditor of *Asian Universities, American Higher Education in the 21st Century, International Handbook of Higher Education*, and other books. He was editor of the *Review of Higher Education*.

Jorge Balán is senior program officer for higher education at the Ford Foundation in New York, where he manages both domestic and international portfolios with a focus on higher education research and policy. He is also an adjunct professor at the School of Education, New York University. He has taught at the University of Buenos Aires, where he held a chair between 1986 and 1997, and has held visiting professorships at the University of Oxford, the University of Chicago, the University of Texas at Austin, and Dartmouth College. For 20 years he was a senior staff member and director of CEDES—a private nonprofit research organization in the social sciences in Buenos Aires, where he built a research team on higher education policy issues.

Andrés Bernasconi is a researcher at the Institute of Political Studies at Universidad Andrés Bello, Santiago, Chile. A lawyer by training and formerly a dean of the Law School of Universidad de Talca, also in Chile, he holds a master of public policy degree from Harvard University and a PhD in sociology of organizations from Boston University. His fields of study are sociology of organizations and comparative higher education.

Ana M. García de Fanelli has a PhD in economics from the University of Buenos Aires and is a senior researcher in the Higher Education Department, Center for the Study of State and Society and the National Council of Research in Science and Technology, in Argentina. She is a professor at the University of Buenos Aires and the University of San Andrés. She has published work on comparative policies in higher education, the management of public universities, and university financing.

P. V. Indiresan was educated at the Indian Institute of Science and at the University of Birmingham, United Kingdom. In his teaching career spanning 40 years, he taught at Roorkee University (now the Indian Institute of Technology, Roorkee) and at the Indian Institute of Technology, Delhi. He was also director of the Indian Institute of Technology, Madras. He has been the president of the Institution of Electronics and Telecommunication Engineers and of the Indian National Academy of Engineering. He has been honored by the Institute of Electrical Electronics Engineers, United States, and has been the recipient, from the president of India, of the Padma Bhushan award.

N. Jayaram is director of the Institute for Social and Economic Change, Bangalore, India. He was professor of research methodology at the Tata Institute of Social Sciences, Mumbai, India. He is on the steering committee of the International Network on the Role of Universities in Developing Areas and the Editorial Advisory Committee of the Indian Council of Social Science Research (ICSSR). He is the managing editor of *Sociological Bulletin* (Journal of the Indian Sociological Society) and the Editor of *ICSSR Journal of Reviews and Abstracts: Sociology and Social Anthropology*. He has published extensively on the sociology of higher education in India, and his books include *Higher Education and Status Retention*, *Sociology of Education in India*, *Social Conflict* (coedited with Satish Saberwal), and *The Indian Diaspora*.

Ki-Seok Kim is professor of education at Seoul National University, Korea, and distinguished visiting scholar of the Paulo Friere Institute at UCLA. He is vice chancellor for student affairs at Seoul National University. He holds a PhD from the University of Wisconsin–Madison.

Nian Cai Liu is the director of Institute of Higher Education, Shanghai Jiao Tong University, where he is also a professor. His current research interests include world-class universities, research universities, science policy, and strategic planning of universities. He studied chemistry at Lanzhou University of China and obtained his master's and doctoral degrees in polymer science and engineering from Queen's University in Kingston, Canada. He was a professor at the School of Chemistry and Chemical Engineering at Shanghai Jiao Tong University from 1993 to 1998. He moved to the field of higher education research in 1999. During the past six years, he has published more than 20 papers. His online publication, *The Academic Ranking of World Universities*, has attracted worldwide attention.

Wanhua Ma is professor of education at the Graduate School of Education, Peking University. She received her PhD at Cornell University in 1997, specializing in educational psychology and higher education administration. In November 1997, she joined the Faculty of Education at Peking University, and carried out research projects funded by the United Nations Development Program, UNESCO, and the Ford Foundation in the past few years, concerning issues on girls' education, vocational education in China, and the development of higher education in Asia and the Pacific Rim. She has taught at the School of Education, the University of California, Berkeley, and has been an affiliated faculty member at the Center for International & Development Education, University of California, Los Angeles. She is a 2005–2006 Fulbright New Century Scholar. Her most recent book is *From Berkeley to Beida and Tsinghua: The Development and Governance of Public Research Universities in the US and China.*

Salvador Malo is currently on the senior staff of IMCO, the Mexican Institute for Competitiveness. With a PhD in physics (Imperial College, London), he has had a long career in science, technology, and education. After many years at the Mexican Petroleum Institute as deputy director for research, he joined the Ministry of Education to promote graduate studies in public universities. For nine years he was vice president at Universidad Nacional Autónoma de México (UNAM—Mexico's national university) and for four years was CEO of the National Center for the Assessment of Higher Education. He has been president of the Board of the Consortium for North American Higher Education Collaboration, was founder and first director of the National System of Researchers, and at present coordinates an international project for higher education collaboration between Latin American and European universities. He is the author and editor of many books and papers relating to higher education in Mexico and Latin America.

Sunghee Nam is a research associate at the Paulo Freire Institute at the University of California, Los Angeles and a lecturer at the California State University at Channel Islands. She is currently involved in a research project on educational reform and globalization.

Imanol Ordorika holds a PhD in social sciences, policy, and educational practice from Stanford University. He is professor of social sciences and education at the Universidad Nacional Autónoma de México (UNAM). He has held fellowships from the Consejo Nacional de Ciencia y Tecnología, UNAM, and other agencies and was the recipient of the Frank Talbott Jr. University Chair at the University of Virginia in 2004. He is the author of *Power and Politics in Higher Education*, as well as other books, chapters, and articles in Mexico and abroad.

Brian Pusser is an assistant professor in the Center for the Study of Higher Education of the Curry School of Education at the University of Virginia. His research focuses on the politics of higher education, the organization and governance of postsecondary institutions, and the role of state and federal policies in shaping the postsecondary arena. He is the author of *Burning Down the House: Politics, Governance and Affirmative Action at the University of California* (2004) and is coeditor of *Earnings From Learning, the Rise of For-Profit Universities* (forthcoming).

Simon Schwartzman studied sociology and political science at the Federal University of Minas Gerais, Brazil, and at the Latin American School of Social Sciences in Santiago de Chile, and obtained his PhD in political science from the University of California, Berkeley. He has written extensively in the fields of science, technology, education, and social policy and is currently president of the Institute for Studies on Labor and Society, in Rio de Janeiro. Between 1994 and 1998 he was the president of Brazil's National Statistical Office (IBGE).

João E. Steiner is professor of astronomy at the University of São Paulo and director of the Institute of Advanced Studies at Universidade de São Paulo. He was undersecretary in the Brazilian Ministry of Science and Technology during 1999–2002.

Index